P9-CMW-937

Language and Literacy Series

Dorothy S. Strickland and Celia Genishi, SERIES EDITORS

Envisioning Literature: Literary Understanding and Literature Instruction
JUDITH A. LANGER

Teaching Writing as Reflective Practice
GEORGE HILLOCKS, JR.

Talking Their Way Into Science: Hearing Children's Questions and Theories, Responding with Curricula
KAREN GALLAS

Whole Language Across the Curriculum: Grades 1, 2, 3
SHIRLEY C. RAINES

The Administration and Supervision of Reading Programs, SECOND EDITION
SHELLEY B. WEPNER, JOAN T. FEELEY, and DOROTHY S. STRICKLAND, Editors

No Quick Fix: Rethinking Literacy Programs in America's Elementary Schools
RICHARD L. ALLINGTON and SEAN A. WALMSLEY, Editors

Unequal Opportunity: Learning to Read in the USA
JILL SUNDAY BARTOLI

Nonfiction for the Classroom: Milton Meltzer on Writing, History, and Social Responsibility
Edited and with an Introduction by E. WENDY SAUL

When Children Write: Critical Re-Visions of the Writing Workshop
TIMOTHY LENSMIRE

Dramatizing in Literature in Whole Language Classrooms, SECOND EDITION
JOHN WARREN STEWIG and CAROL BUEGE

The Languages of Learning: How Children Talk, Write, Dance, Draw, and Sing Their Understanding of the World
KAREN GALLAS

Partners in Learning: Teachers and Children in Reading Recovery
CAROL A. LYONS, GAY SU PINNELL, and DIANE E. DEFORD

The Social Worlds of Children Learning to Write in an Urban Primary School
ANNE HAAS DYSON

The Politics of Workplace Literacy: A Case Study
SHERYL GREENWOOD GOWEN

Inside/Outside: Teacher Research and Knowledge
MARILYN COCHRAN-SMITH and SUSAN L. LYTLE

Literacy Events in a Community of Young Writers
YETTA M. GOODMAN and SANDRA WILDE, Editors

Whole Language Plus: Essays on Literacy in the United States and New Zealand
COURTNEY B. CAZDEN

Process Reading and Writing: A Literature-Based Approach
JOAN T. FEELEY, DOROTHY S. STRICKLAND, and SHELLEY B. WEPNER, Editors

The Child as Critic: Teaching Literature in Elementary and Middle Schools, THIRD EDITION
GLENNA DAVIS SLOAN

(continued)

The Triumph of Literature/
The Fate of Literacy: English in the Secondary School Curriculum
JOHN WILLINSKY

The Child's Developing Sense of Theme: Responses to Literature
SUSAN S. LEHR

Literacy for a Diverse Society: Perspectives, Practices, and Policies
ELFRIEDA H. HIEBERT, Editor

The Complete Theory-to-Practice Handbook of Adult Literacy: Curriculum Design and Teaching Approaches
RENA SOIFER, MARTHA IRWIN, BARBARA CRUMRINE, EMO HONZAKI, BLAIR SIMMONS, and DEBORAH YOUNG

Teaching Writing as Reflective Practice

GEORGE HILLOCKS, JR.

Foreword by Michael W. Smith

Teachers College, Columbia University
New York and London

Published by Teachers College Press, 1234 Amsterdam Avenue, New York, NY 10027

Copyright © 1995 by Teachers College, Columbia University

All rights reserved. No part of this publication may be reproduced or transmitted in any form or by any means, electronic or mechanical, including photocopy, or any information storage and retrieval system, without permission from the publisher.

Library of Congress Cataloging-in-Publication Data

Hillocks, George.
Teaching writing as reflective practice / George Hillocks, Jr.
p. cm.—(Language and literacy series)
Includes bibliographical references and index.
ISBN 0-8077-3434-9 (cloth : acid-free paper).—ISBN 0-8077-3433-0 (paper : acid-free paper)
1. English language—Rhetoric—Study and teaching. I. Title.
II. Series: Language and literacy series (New York, N.Y.)
PE1404.H56 1995
808'.042'07—dc20 95-2103

ISBN 0-8077-3433-0 (paper)
ISBN 0-8077-3434-9 (cloth)

Printed on acid-free paper

Manufactured in the United States of America

07 10 9 8 7 6 5

In memory of

my father,

my best friend and teacher

Contents

Foreword

One question seems to me to account for much of the controversy in the literacy education community. P. David Pearson (1994) phrases it this way: "Must we teach what must be learned?" For over 20 years George Hillocks has been a provocative advocate for answering in the affirmative. But although George's work has been central to the scholarly debate on this issue, it hasn't had the influence on practice that George would have liked. *Teaching Writing as Reflective Practice* should change all that, for in this book George shares himself as a teacher in a way he hasn't in any of his other writing. As one of George's students, I know how powerful that sharing can be.

I'm afraid that George's previous work has been marginalized by the internecine warfare that has afflicted our field. George has used experimental and quasi-experimental designs. And in his *Research on Written Composition: New Directions for Teaching,* he used quantitative methods to help him make sense of the welter of composition studies that appeared in the two decades that followed the publication of Braddock, Lloyd-Jones, and Schoer's *Research in Written Composition,* the book that heralded composition as a field worthy of study.

Many teachers, it seems, are at least suspicious of the kind of research George has done. Donald Graves (1980) gives voice to these suspicions when he writes that teachers find experimental research of "limited value" (p. 914), in large measure because experimental research is "written in a language guaranteed for self-extinction" (p. 918). I'm afraid that Graves is right in his assessment of the influence of experimental research, but I believe the suspicions are rooted not in the language of the research but rather in the ethos communicated by the writer. In this book George argues that "every piece presents a set of cues that an astute audience will use to construct a picture of the writer. Writers ignore those cues at their peril." I'm afraid that George hasn't heeded his own advice. I'm afraid that the picture readers have constructed of George on the basis of his previous scholarly writing doesn't jibe with their image of an effective teacher. And I'm afraid that they may have dismissed his ideas as a consequence.

What is likely missing from their picture is the love George feels for his students, what Herbert Kohl (1984) calls "loving students as learners," a kind of love that he contends "is essential to good teaching" (cited in Gere, Fairbanks, Howes, Roop, & Schaafsma, 1992, p. 28). George displays that kind of love throughout this book. We see it in his concern for disaffected students, among them Richard, a student for whom reading was almost a physical battle. We see it in his joy at the progress of Verita, an inner-city seventh grader, during a unit on descriptive writing that George and his M.A.T.'s from the University of Chicago taught to her class. We see it in the pride he takes in the accomplishments of the teachers he has trained, teachers like Deborah Stern, who works in an alternative school in one of Chicago's toughest neighborhoods. We see it most clearly in his belief that all students can achieve given appropriate instruction, and in his discussion of how teachers can create environments for active learning—the concerns that dominate the book.

The stories that reveal George's passionate commitment to teaching and to his students are embedded in a theoretical framework that I believe will help the field evaluate current instruction as well as generate new approaches. George builds his theory through a careful consideration of both the nature of writing and the nature of the students who do the writing, considerations aided by a discussion of a remarkable variety of sources. For example, he uses Derrida's notions of polysemy and living discourse to call for teaching that features "continuing dialogue about meanings," the details of which he explains through a Vygotskian perspective. His discussion of the composing process features the work of composition researchers and theorists from a variety of perspectives, psychologists, and literary theorists as well as the testimonies of journalists, novelists, and poets.

The guiding metaphor for his effort, as he explains in Chapter Three, is one he borrows from Michel Serres, a professor of history and science at the Sorbonne: the journey. Serres sees knowledge as geography, the topography marked by identifiable cultural formations, but also by faults, folds, and fractures. Traversing this landscape requires building bridges, something George does with great care in this book. George has been criticized in the past for contributing to the professional disagreements that have distracted the field from what is truly important: increasing students' ability to use writing to make meaning. As this book makes clear, the stakes are simply too high to keep these disagreements in the foreground.

I began this Foreword by noting that *Teaching Writing as Reflective Practice* allows readers to see the George Hillocks that his students have always seen. But I think it does more than that. In George's discussion of the implications of the indeterminancy of language, he cites Gerald Graff's characterization of "a deconstructive view of writing" that centers on the belief that "to write well, you have to become a reader, to divide yourself from the text (from self), to generate a second, third, or fourth self to see what is written from the outside." George extends Graff's argument this way:

> The important generated self is not just the reading self, however, but the writing self. It is arguable that the writing self is even more important. This is the self that must pull together, in meaningful ways, bits and pieces of one's experience in ways they have never been conjoined before. To the extent that one's self is a combination of one's total collection of memories *and* the manner in which one has placed them in relationship to each other, writing that shifts or adds to those relationships, such writing remakes the self to that extent.

In this book, therefore, George remakes himself. And what seems to me to stand at the center of that remade self is George's identity as what Schön would call a reflective practitioner. Many have noted that the academy rewards scholarship in direct relationship to its distance from practice, so naming oneself as a practitioner carries some risk. George, however, takes this risk in the way that he places details in relationship to each other. We see how his teaching junior high school in Euclid, Ohio gave rise to the questions he has spent his life pursuing. He develops and tests "warranted assertions" (see his discussion of Dewey in Chapter Two) every autumn when he and his students work together to teach a class of inner-city seventh graders. (I wonder how many other full professors could make such a claim.) When he writes about planning, he shares a protocol of his planning rather than the data he has collected of other teachers' planning.

This is a scholarly book written by a devoted and innovative teacher. I am delighted that George uses it to share with his readers what he has always given so generously to his students, and I hope that the sharing he does in it will lead to more generous readings of his other work. I hope, too, that writing it will make George content to name himself first as Teacher.

Herbert Kohl contends that teachers must love their students as learners. But that love isn't a one-way street. Students know when a teacher is absolutely dedicated to doing all that he or she can to help them become all that they can be. *Teaching Writing as Reflective Practice* reveals why George's students, myself included, love him.

Michael W. Smith

References

Gere, A., Fairbanks, C., Howes, A., Roop, L., & Schaafsma, D. (1992). *Language and reflection: An integrated approach to teaching English*. New York: Macmillan.

Graves, D. (1980). Research update: Research doesn't have to be boring. *Language Arts, 56,* 913–919.

Pearson, P. D. (1994). The integrated language arts: Sources of controversy and seeds of consensus. In L. Morrow, J. Smith, & L. Wilkinson (Eds.), *The integrated language arts: Controversy to consensus*. Boston: Allyn & Bacon.

Acknowledgments

One can probably never know all the sources influential in the process of writing a book, let alone developing the knowledge that one uses in teaching. But because this book is about teaching writing, it is necessarily rooted in experiences throughout my career. In more than simply a comic or ironic sense, it owes its existence to what I regarded as a "demotion" early in my career from high school to junior high. It turned out to be the best demotion that anyone might have wished for. Perhaps I should begin by noting my thanks to that principal, whom I had had the audacity to challenge about a set of criteria for evaluating teachers. But the demotion by itself would have made no difference without so many good and helpful colleagues.

One of the most important among them was Robert L. Holloway, my Scoutmaster and friend for many years before I began teaching, and the principal who first hired me to teach. He will probably be very surprised to see himself mentioned in relation to theories of teaching writing. But under his direction, I learned more about engaging young people in activities for learning and more about patience and the need to understand a student's perspective than I could possibly have learned in any number of college courses.

The most important was Bernard J. McCabe, a junior high teacher when I met him and a supervising teacher when I returned to the same school and began planning materials and activities for teaching writing and literature with him. We worked together for three exciting years before he left Euclid (Ohio) to work on a doctorate under Priscilla Tyler at Harvard. That collaboration with Bernie was one of the most important of my life, forging for me the beginnings of many practices that I continue in my classes, teach to my students, and discuss in this book. Fortunately, Bernie's move to Harvard did not end our friendship or collegiality. We continued working together on a variety of projects for many years until his death in 1975. His mark is on this book, and I need to thank him for it and hope he would have been pleased with the result.

Over the years I have had many colleagues who have helped me think about the practical problems of teaching writing. Here I can thank many but name only a few: from the Euclid Public Schools, James F. McCampbell and Michael C. Flanigan, with both of whom I continue to discuss the fascinations, difficulties, and pleasures of teaching; from Bowling Green State University (Ohio), where I served as Director of Freshman English Programs before moving to Chicago, Richard Foys, Kathy Hart, David Hay, Emily Kilby, and Anita Skeen, with all of whom I enjoyed sometimes unreasonably extended discussions of ideas and strategies for teaching Freshman Comp. I cannot imagine more enthusiastic, interested, and thoughtful colleagues.

Many other colleagues at the college and secondary levels have contributed, directly or indirectly, to the thinking that has gone into this book. Two deserve special mention: Charlie AuBuchon, whose work appears in Chapter Nine, and Faye Kachur, who allowed me to teach her classes to try new ideas.

My greatest single resource in developing and testing informally the ideas for practice that underlie this book has been my years working with the Master of Arts in Teaching English program at the University of Chicago. After 1971, every year's program has included a composition "workshop" for middle school youngsters that my M.A.T. students and I plan, teach, and evaluate together. This workshop has afforded an unparalleled opportunity for observing and analyzing teaching strategies in great detail. More than that, the M.A.T. students themselves have brought and continue to bring, even as I write this, a rich store of experience, intelligence, and generosity to their teaching that one cannot help but learn from. I am fortunate in their willingness to continue the conversation about teaching long after they have graduated from the program. I thank them all for helping me think about the ideas underlying this book.

I owe special thanks to many of the M.A.T.'s for the insights they have provided me in and beyond the actual program: Dorothea Anagnostopoulos, David Anderson, Jane Curry-Berndson, Ann Goethals, Fred Hamel, Mike Segal, Jim Stahl (now the publisher of *Merlyn's Pen*), and Deborah Stern. Some I have had the pleasure of working with over many years on a variety of projects. My work with Steve Gevinson, Larry Johannessen, Elizabeth Kahn, Steve Littell, Michael W. Smith, Peter Smagorinsky, and Carolyn Calhoun Walter has enriched my thinking about the practical and theoretical problems of teaching writing enormously. I owe a similar debt to many students who did not begin their work at Chicago in the M.A.T. program. These include Ellen Anderson, Lisa Kirchhoff, Sherri Koeppen, Carol Lee, Tom McCann, and John Whitehurst.

The actual writing of the book would not have been possible without the support of two of my department chairs: Larry V. Hedges and Robert Dreeben. Larry, before he had been in office very long, saw to it that I learned to type, became computer literate, and had time to begin writing. Robert Dreeben has continued support that has allowed me to complete the manuscript. Grants from the Benton Center for Curriculum and Instruction and the Ford Foundation have provided resources for developing certain key ideas that appear. Without such support, this writing would have been far more difficult.

I have also received the full support and understanding of my family as I have undergone this process. My wife Jo has understood my need to indulge in occasional depression and to find some level of isolation to work on the manuscript and has helped with some of the research on which these ideas are based. My son Mac and his wife Sandi have both contributed to these pages. I am grateful to Mac for doing the graphs that appear in the Appendix. My daughter Marjorie has allowed me to use her work in Chapter Eight. Their support has been a source of pleasure.

In the preparation of the manuscript I have been fortunate in having the insights of a number of colleagues and students. Recent groups of my M.A.T.'s have read parts of the manuscript in one or another of its transformations and have not hesitated to make suggestions about language and ideas. Graduate students in a seminar on theories in the teaching of composition have provided helpful readings of parts or all of the manuscript. Several colleagues have also given me time and the benefit of their advice on various chapters. Lee Odell provided helpful commentary on early versions of two chapters. My colleague at the University of Chicago, Joseph Williams, has offered useful suggestions. Russell Durst provided wonderfully detailed commentary on the first four chapters. John R. Hayes has provided very helpful suggestions on six chapters. Michael W. Smith has been my chief support and most persistent reader in this endeavor, having read the entire manuscript in at least two quite different versions. He used an early version of the text with my permission in a graduate class at Rutgers, thereby providing me another set of perspectives on the manuscript. All of these readers have been insightful, generous, and thoughtful in their advice and encouraging in their delivery. The comments of each have pushed me to revisions that have greatly benefited the manuscript.

There is another group to whom I owe an immense debt, a group who never are named in this sort of introduction. There is no group from whom I have learned more about teaching and about simple basic humanity than my students. In a career as long as mine, it would be impossible to name all the students even if I could remember all their names. But I would like to thank the seventh graders of my first year of teaching who began my love affair with seventh graders when they brought me their vibrant energy and intelligence. I will always owe a special debt of gratitude to the ninth graders with whom I worked upon my return from the University of Edinburgh (Scotland) as I began to think about how to make my own teaching more effective. These include Karen Heckert, Mark Hobzek, Sonja Jerkic, Barbara Kramer, Carleen Mack (now Mack-Smith), Roger and Tom Murphy, Mike Orazen, Richard

Paige, Richard Seaman, Judy Tharp (now Murphy), Douglas and Jan Vukcevic, Tim Wolf, and many others. I owe a similar debt to the many freshmen with whom I worked at Bowling Green.

No matter the help one receives from students, colleagues, and family, the manuscript remains the responsibility of its author. Its flaws are mine alone. I have done the best I can to minimize those. My father would have said, "That's all anyone can expect." I hope my readers will be as generous.

Introduction

This book is about teaching writing at the secondary and college freshman levels. It is concerned with the question: What is involved in the effective teaching of writing? It is an attempt to provide a kind of metatheory in response to that question. To begin with, it assumes that writing is at the heart of education. If Derrida (1981) is right in suggesting that nothing is not a text, people educated in various fields construct representations of matters that concern them: Ptolemy of planetary motion; Lavoisier of the relationships of the element we know as oxygen to life; Aristotle of the nature of the virtues, their opposites, and their relationships to each other and to human conduct; Dickens of the causes and effects of revolutionary strife as they touch individual lives. All of us construct our representations of what our experience means, and we fabricate, at least in part, how it will be played out. And we construct our own representations of the meanings of others.

It is this construction of meaning that lies at the heart of education. However we have divided the world into subject matters, what counts for learning in any of the divisions or across them and outside them is the ability to develop new meanings through acts of composing that bring our unique experience and perspective into conjunction with what the world thinks it knows. Writing has been and remains the chief means, though not the only means, as Smagorinsky and Coppock (1994) remind us, of formatting and presenting those ideas.

Seen in this way, writing cannot be disconnected from its sources, the processes of observation, interpretation, imagination, and inquiry, without which writing must remain little more than a tool for copying what has already been thought. We know that these processes are integral to writing. They govern what is written. At the same time, however, the act of writing, in Langer and Applebee's phrase, "shapes thinking" (1987). Writing is a recursive process that requires the reconstruction of text already written, so that what we add connects appropriately with what has preceded. That process brings ideas not written into conjunction with what has been reconstructed, providing endless opportunities to reconsider ideas and reengage the processes that gave rise to them in the first place. This generation and reprocessing of conceptual content takes place in the context of purposes that involve the writer's knowledge of inquiry, discourse, and audience. All of this argues that writing is a very complex process.

Accordingly, any approach to teaching writing must recognize the complexity and attempt to bring together the various theories involved, not only in writing, but in a pedagogy of writing. This book endeavors to outline the theories involved, indicate the bridges among them, and provide a coherent basis for thinking about the teaching of writing. It begins, in Chapter One, with the assumption that as teachers of writing, we have two major concerns: the nature of writing and the students we teach. It examines Plato's complaint about writing, Derrida's analysis of that complaint, and what those ideas mean to our conception of teaching writing. Then it moves to a consideration of the assumptions we make about students and what our Platonic/Derridean thoughts about writing mean for our students and our teaching.

Chapter Two examines "Some Basics for Thinking about Teaching Writing." Its main argument is that effective teaching of writing is reflective, continually reexamining assumptions, theories, and their practical implications at every stage from developing knowledge for practice, to planning, interactive teaching, and evaluation.

Chapter Three focuses on the difficulties of integrating theories, knowledge gained through practice, and that gained through research. In particular, it examines the qualitative/quantitative split; the bridges that exist in the landscape of knowledge, to use Serres's idea; and argument as a major tool for integrating the diverse sources of knowledge that we work with as teachers of writing.

In an attempt to bring this range of knowledge and theory together, Chapter Four explicates a few minutes of classroom talk to illustrate the diverse theories and sets of knowledge involved. At the same time, this chapter presents an example of what I will argue through the remainder of the book is an effective learning environment. The chapter introduces Vygotsky's learning theory and the important idea of the "zone of proximal development," that zone being the difference between what a learner can do independently and what he or she can do with various kinds of support. This idea is crucial to the discussions of planning and teaching in Chapters Seven through Ten.

Chapter Five undertakes an examination of what we have come to call "the" composing process, as though this process never varied from one writing situation to another. People who view the writing process in a unitary way often reduce it to five or six "stages" (see Graves, 1983; Koch & Brazil, 1978): prewriting, drafting, revision, editing, publication, and sometimes receiving feedback. The recognition of these stages or simply the process character of writing has begun to make a difference in the way teachers use their class time for teaching writing. This chapter considers elements in the nature of writing and writing situations that suggest that while the general model of the composing process is useful, it cannot begin to account for variations in process that appear to be dependent on a variety of factors.

Chapter Six examines the writer's repertoire, the kinds of knowledge that writers must have or develop to function effectively in a variety of writing situations. The two major categories considered here are knowledge of discourse and inquiry. This chapter presents theories of inquiry and discourse as a means of thinking about writing curricula and the content of instruction.

Chapter Seven opens the sequence of chapters that deal specifically with planning for instruction. It examines the goals of planning and the necessity of analyzing writing tasks that appear in the curriculum. It proceeds with three examples: personal narrative, argument, and satire. Next the chapter considers the analysis of student performance, focusing on personal narrative as an illustration. Out of these two analyses (of tasks and performance), the chapter argues, must come the setting of goals for teaching.

Chapter Eight represents a crucial stage of planning. The invention of what I have called gateway activities is the key to moving students beyond their present levels. The gateway activity is intended to enable students to engage in tasks that are beyond their current level of performance. In doing that, it mediates their movement to a more sophisticated level of performance. I believe that many of my students in classes on the teaching of writing consider the invention of gateway activities one of the more difficult parts of planning and one of the most interesting and rewarding. They call that fun.

Even after tasks and students' writing have been analyzed, and crucial gateway activities have been designed, there remains the problem of sequencing sets of activities that will result in improved writing. Gateway activities must be conjoined with other kinds of activities that involve inquiry, processes of writing, learning about discourse, and practice. Chapter Nine examines some of the dimensions of sequencing such sets of activities with special attention to sequencing so that learning in one activity contributes to learning in the next.

Once sequences likely to be effective have been planned and put into operation in classrooms, they become subject to moment-to-moment revisions, sometimes minor, sometimes major, as students begin interacting with each other and the teacher as they respond to the materials and activities. The character of these moment to moment classroom processes determines the effectiveness of the planned learning experiences. To insure maximum effectiveness, the teacher must be alert to student interest and attention, to factors that might disrupt that, to progress toward the goals of the particular activity and the larger learning context, to difficulties students may have with concepts and materials, to relationships among students, and so forth. Chapter Ten examines the nature of such reflective practice with a discussion of an example of reconstructed "reflection in action" during one classroom process. Such reflection, of course, amounts to continuous evaluation, which can play an important role in more formal and traditional evaluation that may be undertaken during and after the interactive stage of teaching.

As a whole the book argues that the ideas of these ten chapters provide a kind of metatheory that pulls together the range of individual theories implicated in the teaching of writing, providing a framework for thinking about the specifics of teaching writing. The framework is necessarily temporary and certain to shift its dimensions as we make claims for new knowledge and values. Nevertheless, some framework for decision making is necessary if only because so many decisions must be made. Without a coherent rationale, the multitude of decisions have to be faced, each independently, with no means of reducing the complexity through integration. Without some coherent set of theories, teachers must simplify the overwhelming demands of teaching by focusing on some fragment of the whole, such as our textbooks have presented for centuries. Chapter Eleven pulls together the diverse parts of the metatheory.

Chapter One

A View of Writing and Students

When I decided to become a teacher some years ago, the state of Ohio required all prospective teachers to observe classes for two weeks prior to the senior year, what we at the College of Wooster referred to as our "September experience." The bureaucrats who had decreed our two weeks of observation apparently believed that two weeks would be enough for us to arrive at some understanding of how schools and classes operated. With the exception of two classes, I remember nothing of those two weeks, but those two I remember in surprising detail.

I observed both in the same school on the same day. Mr. Robert L. Holloway, who had been the leader of my Boy Scout troop and one of the three or four people whose actions and ethos had led me to consider teaching as a career choice, granted me permission to visit classes at the school where he served as principal. He welcomed me, set up a schedule for me to follow, and sent me on my way.

The first class I remember visiting was a ninth-grade English class taught by a striking woman in her late forties or early fifties. She greeted me pleasantly, welcomed me to the school, and, after asking me about my visit, indicated where I should sit. Then she went to the door and greeted students as they entered. When the bell rang, the students went immediately to their desks in neat rows. When she called them to order, they faced forward and became quiet instantly. "Open your books," she said and gave a page number. Without taking her eyes from her students, she walked toward me, a textbook in her outstretched hand. It was a grammar of recent vintage. (A year later I was using the text myself, but I have forgotten the title.) Although I did not know what was on the page she named, I guessed immediately the pattern of what was about to happen. My experience in hundreds of similar classes as a student, what my colleague Dan Lortie (1975) calls "the apprenticeship of observation," had prepared me well for this.

My guesses were on the money. The first 15 minutes or so were devoted to checking homework, with students marking written responses to two exercises that had required them to insert commas according to several different rules they had been studying. In the remaining time, the teacher directed students to turn to a new set of rules in the text; provided an explanation of them, using examples she had put on the board ahead of time; asked several students to respond to items; assigned two new exercises; and asked students to use the last three or four minutes to begin their homework.

The only thing that surprised me was how diligently the students worked, not at all like most classes I recalled in my own high school career. Clearly, here was a teacher who commanded the respect and attention of her students, and as she smiled and talked to them after the bell, she seemed to have their affection as well. After thanking the teacher, I left her room impressed, wondering if I could do half as well, if I could be as efficient and gain the cooperation of students. What worried me most was the prospect of keeping order. I had seen a lot of teachers fail at that in my high school.

The second visit I remember was to a seventh-grade combined English/social studies class. I arrived at Mr. McCabe's door just as the bell rang. When I told him my name and business, he pushed his glasses up, smiled almost mischievously, and ushered me through the door, pointing me to a seat. He walked to the other side of the room, seated himself in the rear corner behind his desk, and picked up what appeared to be a packet of three-by-five cards. I was puzzled. He seemed not to care about his students at all. As I was sitting down, a girl walked to a teacher's desk at the front of the room, struck a gavel on it, and called the class to order. She called on "the secretary" to read the assignment for the day. A boy stood up and read it, including pages to have been read, a brief report to have been written, and what appeared to me to be an outline of what the class was expected to know. I was astonished. Next, a different student took the floor and began asking questions about the geography, politics, and economy of Eastern Europe. Ten to 15 students had their hands up for each one. I looked furtively over to McCabe, who seemed to be paying no attention, just making notes on his little cards. The same students directed the class through several student activities, including a small-group session in which students shared folktales they had been collecting from relatives. During the final few minutes, as the class turned to the reading that a student had assigned for the following day, McCabe met with a small group of students at his desk, his first direct intervention in the double period. His time with the students went beyond the bell, so that he simply waved goodbye to me, and I hurried off to my next visit.

I think I paid little attention to the next classes I saw. I was too busy wondering what had been going on in McCabe's class. I had no conception of how students could be expected to lead the class. How could they know enough? I was impressed with the seriousness of the students, but I had questions. My apprenticeship of observation had simply not prepared me for anything like Mr. McCabe's classroom.

By the time I was ready to check out for the day at the principal's office, I remained flabbergasted by Mr. McCabe's class. Not wanting to appear totally ignorant, but determined to know something about what that man was doing, I finally managed a feeble question to the principal. "Tell me," I asked, "is Mr. McCabe a good teacher?" I remember his response precisely. "Well," he said with a little laugh, "I'm not sure." He looked through the top of the office window for a moment; then he looked me square in the eye. "But I'll tell you this. Whenever we have a sub for him, the sub never has to do anything." I remember wondering what that was supposed to mean and why Mr. Holloway, one of the people I trusted most in the world, had been so evasive.

THE QUESTION OF EFFECTIVE TEACHING

It took me two years to figure out what Mr. McCabe was doing and to begin to understand Mr. Holloway's evasiveness. In fact, I did not guess, until much later, why Mr. McCabe was "doing Eastern Europe" so early in September. When I began teaching in the same school the next year, I learned that 40% to 50% of the students were first- or second-generation descendants of immigrants from Eastern Europe. A street in the town was named for Ljubljana, the capital of Slovenia. Putting that together with one of the class's ongoing projects, collecting folktales from parents, grandparents, aunts, and uncles, and I began to have a better take on what was going on, at least as far as understanding why he had begun with Eastern Europe.

Holloway's implied question about what constitutes good teaching is far more involved than it seems, and it is applicable to any subject matter. If we apply it to writing, then we may read it as involving the questions of what we hope our students will become through our teaching of writing, both as people and as writers, how our means and methods of teaching influence that, and what must (or may) be taught (the matter of curricula, plural) to reach those goals.

Although some educationists do not seem to believe it, *teaching* is a transitive verb. It takes both direct and indirect objects. While they seem occasionally willing to admit to the indirect object, they are almost universally unwilling to announce a direct object. The educationist seems to believe that teaching is generic: Once one knows how to teach, one can teach anything.

Because this book focuses on teaching *writing* to students, thereby recognizing its direct object, it seems important to begin with that part of the syntax, the nature of what is to be taught. Those of us thinking about the teaching of any specific subject matter are becoming more and more aware that neither the character nor quality of teaching can be usefully separated from what is taught (e.g., Stodolsky, 1988). Since no one can teach anything without considering the learners, the chapter will move next to the indirect object, without whom this book would have no reason for existence.

THE NATURE OF WRITING

What is the special nature of writing after all? Plato condemned writing in the *Phaedrus* pretty roundly 2,000 years ago. Today, on the one hand, we hear from the writing establishment that writing is a special craft that requires a trained professorate. But college and school personnel administrators tell us, through their actions, that nearly anyone can teach it. In the field of writing studies, we focus attention on written texts, the processes related to their production, and their contexts. By written texts we generally mean those consisting of culturally recognizable symbols that represent the spoken language. However, from Derrida's point of view, in Barbara Johnson's words, "Nothing . . . can be said to be *not* a text" (Derrida, 1981, p. xiv). Among other things, he means that what we think we know about "real life," we know only through chains of shifting significations in the same way we know texts, at a level of remove and abstraction mediated by language made up exclusively of elusive signs. What are the implications of this idea for writing?

Leaders in the field tell us that when we write, we "make" meaning. The word *make* is such a solid term, carrying with it connotations of the perceptible, the final, the definite. What does it mean to make meaning in writing in light of Derrida's notions of linguistic indeterminacy or post-structuralism more generally? Or in light of the Socratic claim that writing is no more than an aid to recollection? Does engagement in any kind of writing automatically engage one in meaning making? Does filling in name and address for an application count as meaning making?

Other leaders make the claim that writing is a process of "discovery," another term heavy with connotations of palpable, independently existing phenomena. How is it that writing leads to discovery, if it does? Socrates would argue that writing is not a good tool for discovering anything; it can only aid in recollection. To use Derrida's words, "Whoever might think he has produced truth through a grapheme would give proof of the greatest foolishness. . . . Whereas the sage Socrates knows that he knows nothing, that nitwit would not know that he already knows what he thinks he is learning through writing, and which he is only recalling to mind" (1981, p. 135).

These questions are not trivial. Before we can begin to consider the teaching of writing, it seems necessary to examine their ramifications: what linguistic indeterminacy means for writing, what it means to make meaning, and what it means to discover *through* writing.

Plato and Derrida on Writing

Let us begin with Plato's condemnation of writing and Derrida's deconstruction of it. In the *Phaedrus,* in answer to his own questions about the propriety and impropriety of writing, Socrates tells the Egyptian myth of Theuth, who invented calculation, geometry, astronomy, draughts and dice, and writing. Theuth took these inventions to the king of the country, the principal god Thamus (the sun god Ra), explaining each one in turn and suggesting that they ought to be made known to all of the Egyptians, so great were their benefits. "But when it came to writing, Theuth declared: 'Here is an accomplishment, my lord the king, that will improve both the wisdom and the memory of the Egyptians. I have discovered a sure receipt for memory and wisdom'" (Plato, 1973, p. 96).

But the king pointed out that the "'discoverer of an art is not the best judge of the good or harm which will accrue to those who practice it.'" In fact the king stated that Theuth has attributed to writing "'quite the opposite of its real function.'"

> Those who acquire it will cease to exercise their memory and become forgetful; they will rely on writing to bring things to their remembrance by external signs instead of their own internal resources. What you have discovered is a receipt for recollection, not for memory. And as for wisdom, your pupils will have the reputation for it without the reality: they will receive a quantity of information without proper instruction, and in consequence be thought very knowledgeable when they are for the most part quite ignorant. And because they are filled with the conceit of wisdom instead of real wisdom they will be a burden to society. (Plato, 1973, pp. 96–97)

This passage is not all Socrates has to say about writing, but it will suffice as a beginning. Derrida's (1981) deconstruction of the dialogue focuses on Theuth's use of the term *pharmakon,* translated above as "receipt," meaning remedy, a term whose linguistic relatives appear in this dialogue in many different contexts and with many meanings. It appears at the beginning of the dialogue with a reference to the myth of Orithyia, who was carried off by Boreas but who, in Socrates' mock learned explanation, is blown to her death while playing with Pharmakeia. Derrida points out that *pharmakeia* is also a "common noun signifying the administration of the *pharmakon,* the drug: the medicine and/or poison" (p. 70). A bit later in the dialogue, Socrates compares the written documents that Phaedrus is carrying with him to a drug (*pharmakon*) capable of enticing one to stray from one's normal ways.

Derrida's discussion sets forth an array of such uses in order "to display . . . the regular, ordered polysemy that has, through skewing, indetermination, or overdetermination, but without mistranslation, permitted the rendering of the same word by 'remedy,' 'recipe,' 'poison,' 'drug,' 'philter,' etc." (p. 71). Thus, by the time Theuth introduces writing as *pharmakon,* the word's ambiguity has been clearly established.

Derrida continues to extend the chain of significances informing us of one more word in the set that has not been used in the dialogue, *pharmakos* ("wizard, magician, poisoner"). This term, however, has an additional use: scapegoat—a role that Socrates himself will play. Even the poison hemlock (*pharmakon*) that Socrates must drink becomes part of the chain. The hemlock "is presented to Socrates as a poison; yet it is transformed, through the effects of the Socratic *logos* . . . , into a means of deliverance, a way toward salvation, a cathartic power. The hemlock has an *ontological* effect: it initiates one into the contemplation of the *eidos* and the immortality of the soul. *That is how Socrates takes it*" (pp. 126–127).

Derrida argues that such polysemous chains of meaning are the norm in human language, not a phenomenon that appears only in Plato. Indeed, they might be said to be part of the condition of human language, a system that is built on contrast, as linguists have recognized, rather than independent units of meaning. We recognize words by their contrasts with other words, by what they are not. Sounds are only meaningful in a given language if they exhibit minimal contrast with other sounds. Thus, whenever there is meaning, there is automatically *not meaning.* Any assertion simultaneously means and does not mean. Derrida terms this hop or skip in signifying *differance.*

One might expect such *differance* to provoke a kind of double-take at the occurrence of these little hops or skips. But Western culture, Derrida believes, has long held an ideal of meaning as immediate and present that encourages the suppression of *differance* and that results in the illusion of meaning as present, immediate, and fixed. In the *Phaedrus,* Socrates' criticism of writing challenges that ideal for writing.

Derrida thinks Socrates is right, of course, but that he has not gone far enough. Spoken language is not exempt from the same charges. The polysemous condition of speech and writing is inherent in the nature of language that comes to us through a culture that allows significations to shift, disappear, accrete, and cares not a whit for the ideals of immediacy and presence. Where does this condition leave us? Must we give up hope of ever communicating anything? Is attaining meaning impossible? What are the implications of this condition for writing?

First, consider that Socrates does not quite give up on writing. After the initial condemnation, he asks Phaedrus, "Can we distinguish another kind of communication which is the legitimate brother of written speech?" A moment later when he names it, he uses the metaphor of writing to talk about it. "I mean the kind that is written on the soul of the hearer together with understanding; that knows how to defend itself" (Plato, 1973, p. 98). As Derrida (1981) notes, it is "remarkable here that the so-called living discourse should suddenly be described by a 'metaphor' borrowed from the very thing one is trying to exclude from it, the order of its simulacrum" (p. 149).

It appears that the dialogue has not been so much a condemnation of writing as it has been a show of preference for good writing over bad writing. It is important to note the qualifications that Socrates insists must attend upon "living speech": understanding, ability to defend itself, and knowledge of whom to address and not to address. It is in the dialectical process that all these come to bear, where understanding must interpret what is said on either side, where the speaker/writer explains and defends what is said and addresses those who are engaged in the issues. For Socrates, what is important is the "serious treatment" of words "which employs the art of dialectic" (Plato, 1973, p. 99, in Derrida, 1981, p. 155), the art of teasing out meaning, examining contradictions, peeling back metaphor, in short, coming to grips with meaning in a forum to which those present contribute. (I will use *argument* in this sense.)

Only under such conditions can the writing be living and vital, only in dialectical forums can the vast polysemy of language and the range of possibilities for its interpretation be brought under examination. Only there can the arguments underlying interpretations be examined with continuing energy and care. Such conditions help to avoid sterility in speech or in writing and the formulaic in thinking. But they have other important ramifications as well. I shall continue to return to this theme, the need for active discussion of ideas and language, for continuing dialogue about meanings, especially in classrooms.

A second important implication of polysemy is that every text is divided and fissured in such ways that it produces what Gerald Graff (1992b) calls a multiplication effect. He puts it this way: "Deconstruction is a theory that inside every text are several other texts waiting to get out. When we sit down to write, we find ourselves saying something we did not expect to say. Then we try to unify our text around this new idea. This multiplication effect is not an aberration; it is inevitable." Accordingly, "whether talking or writing, we have to be readers of our own language. We can misunderstand our own thoughts. Whatever we say can be contested." Therefore, "a deconstructive view of writing suggests that to write well, you have to become a reader, to divide yourself from the text (from self), to generate a second, third, or fourth self to see what is written from the outside."

The important generated self is not just the reading self, however, but the writing self. It is arguable that the writing self is even more important. This is the self that must pull together, in meaningful ways, bits and pieces of one's experience in ways that they may never have been conjoined before. To the extent that one's self is a combination of one's total collection of memories *and* the manner in which one has placed them in relationship to each other, writing that shifts or adds to those relationships remakes the self. I suggest that this generation of another self is not easily accomplished and may not even be recognized as a need outside the kind of active dialectical process that Socrates sees as so important to understanding and, therefore, to good writing.

Given such linguistic indeterminacy and the idea that "inside every text are several other texts waiting to get out," what are we to make of claims of writing as "meaning making" and as a "process of discovery"? Although these ideas are related, it will be useful to examine them independently.

Writing as Meaning Making

The word *make* connotes a resulting object that is substantial, palpable, something not to be ignored. The word does not indicate some trivial rearrangement or even interpretation. Rather it suggests something made from scratch, made of whole cloth, an original invention, not simply an improvement on an old one. When we talk about making meaning as though we were the sole makers, as though meaning were ours to make, we forget that the materials available for this task are the product of our whole cultural history. At the very least our meaning making is a partnership between each individual and all who have gone before, another reason our meanings cannot always be as fixed and immediate as the ideal of Western culture might wish. The process of making meaning must be an effort in conjunction with other times, other people, other texts. It is never individual. Although a writer might work alone, the dialectical process is not only unavoidable but, more significantly, indispensable.

Let us assume, then, that meaning making is possible, given the restrictions on that concept outlined above. What then constitutes minimal meaning making? The meaning of an object or activity must inhere in its relationships to its contexts, including participants, other objects or activities, and the language invested in them. An attempt to describe such relationships is an attempt to make meaning or interpret it. But what if the activity is repetitive and has been described many times before? To the extent the description reiterates what has been said before, it cannot be said to *make* meaning. As Derrida points out, one of Socrates' major complaints against writing is repetition: that "if you ask [written words] what they mean by anything they simply return the same answer over and over again" (Plato, 1973, p. 97). To make meaning, returning the same answer is insufficient.

A good friend of mine is a wonderful storyteller. He knows how to get attention and keep it through gesture, facial expressions, the use of dialogue, and the structure of a story, which nearly always sets up a problem or question. He keeps his audience engaged in a variety of ways, never letting them escape his story line. But after hearing a story once, one is likely to hear it again, told to another group in very much the same way, down to the gestures and words. When my friend develops the story the first time, he is certainly engaged in an act of meaning making. But when he tells it the second or third time in very nearly the same way, he is simply conveying a meaning that he has already made. Only if he enlarges on some detail or changes the point of the story or makes some other comparable change is he *making* meaning.

Much of the writing that children have to do in school does not involve meaning making by any stretch of the imagination. A 9-year-old living in the house we rent at this writing in Antigua, Guatemala, showed me her composition notebook. Her teacher had written a sentence at the top of each page, for example, "El color de leche es blanco." She was to fill the page with copies of the sentence, one to a line, for 15 copies. Manuelita strongly resisted making the requisite copies.

The practice of writing book reports is frequently another example of non–meaning making. We have it on the authority of syndicated columnist Bob Greene (1987) that he and other students in his high school commonly read Cliffs Notes and wrote a summary of a summary, appending a few sentences that might be regarded as original, if not meaningful, about how they liked the book they had not read.

Britton, Burgess, Martin, McLeod, and Rosen (1975) demonstrated that most writing in English schools required students to reiterate what they had found in some other source or had gleaned from classroom lectures. In Derrida's terms, it was writing that repeated itself.

What will count as meaning making? Does anything we say "make meaning"? From Derrida's point of view, remember, everything is a text. When we repeat an experience in writing using the general language that stores the experience in memory, we may simply be copying from one kind of text to another. In this case, the global, matter-of-fact account is tantamount to the schemata that hold memories of specific experiences together. It is usually a bare-bones structure, a kind of experiential summary, that neither demands nor allows inference on the part of the reader and provides little or no interpretation.

The following piece is by a student in one of the seventh-grade classes that my students and I teach each fall in the Chicago public schools. Before we arrived, the regular teacher, a math specialist, had asked the students, at my request, to write about an experience that was important to them for some reason and to write about it in such detail that anyone reading their compositions would be able to see what they saw and feel what they felt. Verita wrote the following:

> My birthday is coming up. I hope I get almost all the things I asked for, and maybe the rest of the things I didn't get for my birthday I

> can get for Christmas. I know I'm getting an electronic game. My brother is giving it to me. I don't know a single seventh grade girl who has a wild fire, but since my brother doesn't have his ten dollars anymore . . . I'm assuming he bought it with his own money, and I'd hurt his feelings if I didn't take it. So I'll take it, and thank him for it. I really try not to pick on my brother, or any seven year old, for that matter, but sometimes they get in your way. I guess my favorite holiday is my birthday, so I hope I get what I want.

Verita's response is interesting for a variety of reasons. It focuses on an experience that is about to occur rather than one that already has. It appears to be developed using what Bereiter and Scardamalia (1982) call the "what next" strategy in which the writer thinks of one thing to say, and having said that, generates another related in some way to the preceding sentence, but not necessarily related to all of the preceding sentences. Each chunk generated appears to be an abstract formula that implies a good deal of unstated information. No doubt Verita could say a great deal about her favorite holiday, or her 7-year-old brother, or the electronic game *Wildfire,* or how 7-year-olds get in your way, or why she must try not to pick on her brother. Instead, she presents a series of topic-like statements that represent the schemata holding many pieces of information together in memory. No doubt embedded in any one of these are several narratives that Verita might have explored.

The closest this piece comes to narrative are the references to a forthcoming birthday, a possible gift, how the writer guesses the possibility of the gift, and its probable acceptance. One can speculate on the ways a narrative with these elements might develop. However, since Verita's piece includes no event, the other parts of the minimal story are also missing, what story grammars call an initiating event, an attempt, a result, and so on (Stein & Glenn, 1979). It includes no concrete sensory detail and no dialogue.

However, Verita's piece does have many positive features. Her grouping of topic-like statements is tantalizing. She appears open about stating her own reactions to and opinions of things, a proclivity that many students do not share. She also has a sure touch with her syntax (not to say conventions). The ellipsis is unusual for the students who are enrolled in these classes, and the aside is effective.

This book will be concerned with writing that involves meaning making, writing that either (1) constructs a new relationship with an intended audience, as in an empathic piece that attempts to generate an emotional response of some sort; (2) constructs new relationships in the substance of the writing, as does Derrida in "Plato's Pharmacy"; or (3) both. As Verita's piece stands, it neither establishes a relationship with an audience nor explores relationships in the substance of the experience. Its level of abstraction, which is, unfortunately, not uncommon at all grade levels, appears to exist in memory as a text or bits and pieces of text that writers can transfer directly to paper. Students who produce such writing almost invariably believe they have written pretty well.

Such writing, I would argue, is at the lower end of any continuum of "meaning making." At the same time, there are certainly other texts buried in that language, waiting to get out. For example, the comments about not picking on any 7-year-old surely hide an interesting story. Perhaps writing is, among other things, a process of digging through superficial abstraction to get at the details that reveal the meaning of experience, not only to the reader but to the writer. Most students can generate details underlying each predicate. The problem is not so much one of having inadequate information (Scardamalia, Bereiter & Goelman, 1982). The problem appears to be some combination of inadequate knowledge of what effective writing requires, absence of the strategies for producing it, and an assumption that "people will know what I mean."

By way of contrast, turn for a moment to a piece by a boy in a seventh-grade class I taught some years ago, a piece written at the culmination of a unit on writing about personal experience. Arne Kildegaard has the knowledge of how to establish a relationship with an audience and provide the detail that prompts interpretation of the experience. His details allow us to imagine his scratching the Cadillac, his squirming in the principal's office, his building fears at home. Further, all of them direct the interpretation of the experience, an interpretation unusual in a 12-year-old.

Understanding

> "I'll pay for it!" I kept insisting as I was being towed to the principal's office by both ears.
>
> "You'll pay for it with your hide!"
>
> School had just let out when I was caught in front of the school "scratching profane language" on the hood of a decayed white convertible Cadillac with the edge of a penny. At the moment I was desperately trying to think of a way to avoid letting my parents know about it. It was a hot day, but the owner of the car was wearing a white fur around her neck. My stomach rose into my throat as I was seated in a large office chair. The elderly lady that was principal of the school sat and looked at me in utter amazement. I pretended to be very contented watching the walls as I avoided her staring eyes. My mother was called in, and she sat next to the principal, also star-

ing with amazement. I began to get squeamish and my mother, seeing this, asked to talk to me alone.

"It's not so bad that you scratched the car, but did you have to write something that offends people? Couldn't you just have written your name?"

"Well I wasn't . . . I mean if . . . I guess . . . er . . . well?"

I was made to apologize to this black lady about twice my height. I shivered as I told her I was sorry; she looked back very coldly.

In the car on the way home my mother told me about how she had once entirely torn up her English book, and how she never knew quite why she had done so. I continued to look at my feet. At home I picked up the newspaper and opened it so no one could see me. There I sat for two hours wondering why I'd done it. Dinner came and I sat and looked at my food. "Why?" I kept asking myself. I didn't eat that night, and the family was unusually quiet. After dinner I went up to my room, turned out the light and sat, wondering why. At 9:30, "click" the light went on and my father walked in. He pulled the covers up to my neck and said, "Arne, we still love you just as much as before. . . ."

"Dad?"

"Just as much, Arne." . . . click

The details that Arne includes not only help us understand his own response to the deed but his relationship to his parents, their expectations of him, and his own resulting expectations of himself. Every action contributes to and takes on meaning from the developing context. When Arne hides behind the newspaper, we know that he is ashamed. At the same time, the context of the story so far allows us insight into the values of a home that produces such a reaction without any overt scolding. Every sentence, down to the final word, *click,* contributes to the developing meaning. *Click* not only indicates that the light has been turned off, but, given the context, it indicates with some finality that the parents approve the actor, if not the action, and it is time to move on.

Verita's composition, written at the beginning of a comparable unit on personal experience writing, does not begin to compare. As you will see later, however, Verita learned to look into her experience and provide detail that would help establish a relationship with an audience and the basis for interpreting an experience. Without that knowledge, Plato's goal of writing on the soul "together with understanding" will remain unobtainable. And without it, in my opinion, we will not have writing deserving the name of "making meaning."

Writing as Discovery

One of the most common clichés about writing is that it is a process of discovery. Frequently the phrase is used, whether by accident or by intention I do not know, to suggest that the process of writing, of producing written text, is the process of discovery, that the two are virtually one and the same. One simply writes and, in the act of writing, discovers new ideas and new relationships. To say that is either to limit the conception of writing so that it excludes what I call inquiry, the primary processes of research (observation, interpreting, imagining, hypothesizing, testing, evaluating, and so forth), or to simplify the conception of those processes so that they can be assumed to take place as the writer produces text.

Anyone who has engaged in serious writing in the arts, humanities, social sciences, or natural sciences knows very well that writing a book or article is no simple matter of sitting down, engaging in a little brainstorming, throwing some ideas on paper, drafting and revising, and in the process discovering new ideas and concepts. On the contrary, sometimes years of research go into developing the ideas that go into a brief article, let alone a book. Not infrequently the serious writer's inquiry takes place over a lifetime.

A computer expert whose job it is to keep a *Fortune* 500 company up to date on software spends hours examining the extent to which new software packages meet her company's requirements. She will examine the capabilities and shortcomings of the new software, review the applications currently used in various departments, estimate the benefits and costs of switching to a new program, and write a recommendation that the new package be considered. Writing the recommendation may take only an hour or two, but the processes indispensable to the writing may involve many days (Anonymous, personal communication, 1992).

Feature writers for magazines and newspapers spend the bulk of their time researching their subjects. Brenda Shapiro, a feature writer whose work has appeared in *Mirabella, Chicago Magazine, Town and Country,* and *The New York Times,* has written features on fashion, snoring, chocolate, good guests and bad guests, prairies, and gardening. She regards research and writing as integrally related.

> Although you begin with snoring as a real world problem, the writers' task is to create a thesis and prove it. The material suggests what's going on. You've got to let the material develop your thesis and, as you work, the piece takes on a shape. Before you've even written a word, you begin to see the shape, the outline, in your head. The research suggests the form of the piece, what's important, what's not, what will give it wings, what will make it interesting to read. . . . Research and writing are absolutely integrated.

> You can't do anything without research. Writing is taking place all the time in your head. You're a sleuth. You say, "That's how it is!" with surprise. (personal interview, 1993)

Rising Sun, Michael Crichton's (1992) popular thriller about the conflicts between Japanese and American business, includes a bibliography of 43 items, most of them books, many published by university presses.

Upton Sinclair studied the conditions of the meat-packing industry in detail to write *The Jungle.* In his autobiography (Sinclair, 1962), he writes that having decided to depict the struggle over "wage slavery," he chose the Chicago stockyards as the scene for the novel he would write (partly because of a recent strike there) and set out for Chicago in 1904 and "for seven weeks lived among the wage slaves of the Beef Trust." He writes that he was horrified at what he saw, that he felt as though he were "confronting a veritable fortress of oppression. How to breach these walls, or to scale them, was a military problem." He continues,

> I sat at night in the homes of the workers, foreign-born and native, and they told me their stories, one after one, and I made notes of everything. In the daytime I would wander about the yards, and my friends would risk their jobs to show me what I wanted to see. I was not much better dressed than the workers, and found that by the simple device of carrying a dinner pail I could go anywhere. So long as I kept moving, no one would heed me. When I wanted to make careful observations, I would pass again and again through the same room. (p. 109)

But Sinclair did not simply collect data. As with other writers, his composing, at some level, began and continued throughout the inquiry. He writes that at the end of a month or so he had his "data" and knew the story he wanted to tell but had no characters. Then one day as he wandered about the Back-of-the-Yards district, he saw a wedding party going into the back room of a saloon. He writes:

> I stopped to watch, and as they seemed hospitable, I slipped into the room and stood against the wall. There the opening chapter of *The Jungle* began to take form. There were my characters—the bride, the groom, the old mother and father, the boisterous cousin, the children, the three musicians, everybody. I watched them one after another, fitted them into my story, and began to write the scene in my mind, going over it and over, as was my custom, fixing it fast. I went away to supper, and came back again, and stayed until late at night, sitting in a chair against the wall, not talking to anyone, just watching, imagining, and engraving the details on my mind. It was two months before I got settled at home and first put pen to paper; but the story stayed, and I wrote down whole paragraphs, whole pages, exactly as I had memorized them. (p. 110)

Clearly with Upton Sinclair, as with other writers, the process of inquiry is integral to the writing process. The "texts" from which he borrowed were the scenes he observed, the lives of the people he met and spoke to. Our inquiry results in a construction, an account of our observations and the transformations we impose upon them. When we write, that construction is very likely transformed again with the written product. But it may not be. Sinclair was able to compose on the spot, memorizing whole passages that he wrote down two months later. For him, everything might have been a text.

The point is that in practically no place other than school and college writing classes is writing treated as something that can be accomplished with little or no inquiry. To satisfy this requirement of no inquiry, students are asked to write about topics of such a general nature that they can be expected to fulfill the assignment off the top of their heads. Such topics hardly ever allow for real meaning making. They encourage students to rely on texts that float in the community mind, much as waste paper blows about the windy streets of Chicago.

This is not to say that writing need always be based on some sort of systematic inquiry undertaken with writing in mind. Often it is not. Sometimes it is based on the writer's remembered experience, particularly in the case of personal narrative and poetry. Even in those cases, though, various strategies of inquiry frequently come into play, consciously or not, as the writer pushes, prods, compares, interprets, and reinterprets the stuff of the experience as it exists in memory.

Writing is a process of discovery; without question, there are, in Donald Murray's words, "always surprises on the page. Sometimes . . . large, sometimes small, but . . . always something unexpected" (1987, p. 2). At the same time, writing clearly includes more than the discovery that the writer produces in writing. Derrida tells us that nothing is not a text. As writers do research, they formulate and reformulate meanings and relationships, engaging in a wide range of inquiry. Though these formulations may never be written, appearing only in the writer's mind, the inquiry comprising them becomes part of the written texts—part of the writer's perspective and, therefore, personality. If we are seriously concerned with the teaching of writing, we must ensure that inquiry is incorporated into our model of what writing involves. This book will return to the important issue of inquiry and writing.

STUDENTS: DISAFFECTED AND ENGAGED

When students come to class, they bring with them a wide range of experience and knowledge from home and community environments with which we as teachers may have little familiarity. Indeed, we are only beginning to realize the subtle ways in which home environments teach values and modes of thinking that are at variance with those of the school.

Shirley Brice Heath's (1983) ethnographic study of Trackton and Roadville, two neighborhoods in two small working-class towns, provides a wealth of examples. Heath and her colleagues studied the language processes of these two communities and the milieu in which they took place. She found that the children of these communities, both African American and white, learned patterns of behavior and language that were understood by neither the African American nor white teachers, who were from what Heath calls mainstream communities. Even the ways that children had learned to play at home did not fit the patterns that the teachers expected at school. The girls from Roadville, for instance, played house in their home kitchens or in outdoor playhouses that parents had made for them. In those places they were used to incorporating water and other real substances for "brewing tea" and "making cookies." But in school, though they were invited to play house, they could use only imaginary substances, and many ceased to play "in those areas of the room where they could not bring their home play habits" (p. 274).

Teachers set up centers in preschools and kindergartens for different activities, for block building, playing with puzzles, painting, and so on. Children from Roadville had no difficulty dealing with these place/activity restrictions, because "adults in their communities also demanded that certain activities take place only in certain areas" (p. 273). African American children from Trackton, on the other hand, had learned to play with toys outside the house and to use them in a variety of ways, mingling them and using them for purposes other than those originally intended. If a piece of a puzzle reminded them of a tool or kitchen utensil, they would incorporate it into their play away from the puzzle corner. "Teachers despaired when they found what they classified as *puzzles* in the sand box or doll corner." The result was that "the most well intentioned teachers found themselves making invidious comparisons between the Trackton children and those from Roadville 'who were so obedient and so neat with their toys'" (p. 274).

Similar problems arose with the schools' expectations about time. Roadville children had experience with regular patterns of family meals, nap times, bedtimes, playing games with time limits, becoming familiar with scheduled and timed activities in Sunday school and Bible classes, and even proverbs about time. Heath found that Trackton children, on the other hand, had had little experience with timed activities or schedules. "At home there had been few constraints on time; children had not been admonished to sleep, eat, or play within certain blocks of time. At home, there were no timed tasks or time-task links" (p. 275). The result was that Trackton children were frustrated by the school's time schedule. "In the preschool, they found it frustrating to have the clay or paints taken from them before they finished their preconceived project; they resisted having toys put away before they had been able to complete a play strategy in progress" (p. 275). Unfortunately, teachers often interpret such cultural differences as signs of lack of ability, lack of discipline, and other undesirable abstract traits.

Language differences are perhaps what most often prompt teachers and many others to unwarranted judgments about the ability and knowledge of their students. Those who grew up in working-class neighborhoods, as I did, will recall teachers' apparent animosities toward *how* we said things. What we said did not matter much, as long as we said it in a fashion that met that teacher's view of "correctness." For example, my seventh- and eighth-grade English teacher had clear rules about usage that she expected us to meet. When we did not, we were sure to meet some degree of public embarrassment, from simple correction to sarcastic humiliation. This teacher could not abide *seen* instead of *saw*, the pronunciation of *roof* to rhyme with *book* instead of *sooth*, and *I don't got anything* instead of *I don't have anything*. In my mind, the worst moments came in conjunction with requests to visit the *lavatory*, the word taught in the Cleveland public schools as the appropriate euphemism for *toilet*. When we could remember *lavatory*, we would miss the proper verb. The request, "Can I go to the lavatory," was always met with the response, "I don't know. *Can* you?" For my part, I recall letting such a response go until pressures had reached a certain level that I regarded as maximum. At that point, I would raise my hand and ask once again, "May I go to the lavatory?" To this, the teacher responded pointedly, "Yes, you *may*." Although I would like to think that this verbal dictatorship has had little effect on me over the years, it certainly had the effect, at the time, of shutting down student talk, except for the surreptitious, illegal kind.

Heath's examples of teachers' negative responses to student language suggest the possibility of a much more harmful impact. These involve teachers' failure to understand students' meanings and their corrections that suggest the students' inability to think. For example, Heath cites the case of a boy who tried to explain that a fellow student had not ridden the bus to school on a particular day but that she ordinarily did. Heath reports the following conversation:

TEACHER: Where is Susan? Isn't she here today?
LEM: She ain't ride the bus.
TEACHER: She *doesn't* ride the bus, Lem.
LEM: She *do* be ridin' the bus.

According to Heath, the teacher "frowned at Lem and turned away." In Lem's system of black English, *ain't* is equivalent to *didn't*, thus indicating that on this particular day, Susan did not ride the bus. The teacher assumes that Lem uses it mistakenly for *doesn't* and "corrects" him but derives the meaning that Susan does not ride the bus at all. Lem's response attempts to tell the teacher that Susan does ride the bus regularly. But the teacher frowns and turns away, apparently regarding Lem as incapable of meaningful statements.

My English teacher always knew what we meant, just did not like the way we said it. Lem's teacher, however, without meaning to, rejects both usage and meaning, a rejection that seems far more likely to have a deeper and more lasting impact. Mike Rose (1990), in *Lives on the Boundary*, presents portraits of many young people alienated from school and college. He is concerned with students from what he calls America's educational underclass, students who bring to classrooms not only their differences in language and experience but personal difficulties that lead teachers to mark them as mentally deficient and in need of special "remediation." In portrait after portrait in Rose's book, such students remove themselves, sometimes at an agonizingly early age, from any connection with the processes of schools. They know that the classroom is not for them, particularly the English classroom. The way they sit at desks, their facial expressions, their gestures, all are calculated to convey the indifference of self-protection. They say, in the words of one of Rose's students, "I just wanna be average" (p. 28). Too often this carefully developed public identity, one developed to protect against the possibilities of more failure, becomes, in Rose's words, "too powerful an identity to avoid" (p. 114).

I became familiar with this studied indifference in my first year of teaching, but I had no real insight into what might lie beneath it until my first encounter with what we called remedial reading. Because our belief was that successful reading would beget confidence and more successful reading, one of the most important tasks was to estimate the level at which each student could read independently with comprehension but with some challenge. In part, this involved the students reading aloud passages, prepared beforehand, that we estimated, on the basis of test results, were at their independent reading levels.

Bernie McCabe had carefully explained all of this in considerable detail and how to make notes on the readers' progress. But nothing prepared me for seeing and hearing these students struggle to read. In particular, I remember Richard, black T-shirt with the sleeves rolled up, heavily muscled, a wrestler later in the year, quietly hostile and nonchalant in order to indicate how little he cared about school and particularly my class. He clutched the volume from which I had asked him to read so tightly that his knuckles showed white. His arms and body were taut with the strain. As he tried slowly to mouth the words, his jaw appeared rigid, and he seemed to struggle to move it. He began to move the book in little circles, as though trying to maneuver it into submission. Every syllable was a battle. He struggled with *their, such,* and *orange.* He blocked on *isn't* entirely and looked to me for help. When I told him that he did not have to read anymore, he said through clenched teeth, "I can finish."

I heard three more readers that period, two of them very much like Richard. By the end of the hour almost all I could do was stare, incredulous at what I had witnessed. Never before had I seen such violent physical struggling to do schoolwork. I had believed that nonchalance was a cover for school problems, but I had never realized the depth of the humiliation at not being able to read that it covered. These 14-year-olds knew that they could not read very well, were deeply humiliated by that knowledge, and would have liked things to be different. But since reading seemed out of reach to them, as were the grapes of Aesop's fox, the best defense was often a pose that said they did not care and, therefore, had no reason to try. And for these young people, the grapes had been sour for most of their short lives.

But it is not just the "educational underclass" who are alienated by schools. It appears to be most students in even the best schools, most of the time. Csikszentmihalyi and Larson (1984) have studied the affective states of adolescents extensively and intensively as they go about their daily routines. In this and other studies, they have used stratified random samples of high school students who volunteered to carry pagers and to respond to a questionnaire when the pagers beeped at random times during the day. The questionnaire asked them to record what they were thinking about, what they were doing, and how they came to be doing it and to indicate their mood by responding to a series of scales and questions. Based on the analysis of several thousand of these reports, the authors conclude that "the average student is usually bored, apathetic, and unfriendly" (p. 205) in school situations. In fact, Csikszentmihalyi and Larson state that "schools are essentially machines for providing negative feedback. They are supposed to reduce deviance, to constrain the behavior and the minds of adolescents within straight and narrow channels" (pp. 198–199). The authors argue that schools do not provide what they call "flow" experience, the kind of experience that results in high levels of pleasure, confidence, and absorption by the tasks at hand.

They argue that intrinsic motivation is "relatively high in informal activities like group work and discussions. This is also when students are most happy and active. Passive activities like listening to the teacher or to other students [as in listening to a report] are much less pleasant" (pp. 206–207). Consider this idea in light of Goodlad's (1984) estimates, from his study of over 1,000 elementary and secondary classrooms, that about 70% of all instructional time consists of talk, with teachers on average doing 75% of the talking, and that at the senior high level discussion of any kind takes place only 5.2% of the time. It is little wonder that students are disaffected.

Can Disaffected Students Learn to Write?

If we assume that writing is a gift that we either have or do not have, as many people appear to do (Palmquist & Young, 1992), then we will not be surprised when not many of our students show much improvement. What can we believe about students' potential to improve as writers? More precisely, for our purposes here, can most writers we encounter in schools and colleges, even those who are perceived to be severely deficient in skills, become better writers. For my part, the answer is *yes, absolutely.* We cannot have research that will provide definitive answers to such questions, but research surely provides some strong indications that improvement is possible.

Research on Engagement. Some of the most encouraging research for anyone teaching anything is the research that shows the possibilities for engaging students in activities where what students already know is valued in various ways and they become active doers and planners. Several studies in Heath and McLaughlin's (1993) volume *Identity and Inner City Youth* indicate that young people whose lives might appear to be headed for disaster connect with groups in which their ideas are respected and in which they take an active role in planning and preparing as a group for various projects. Ball and Heath, for example, study the appeal of three dance groups to young people in urban areas. They find that frequent positive reinforcement, active participation at various levels, and high mutual expectations result in high levels of engagement over periods of years.

Csikszentmihalyi and Larson (1984) and Csikszentmihalyi, Rathunde, and Whalen (1993) present many examples of students who are highly engaged in what are often difficult and challenging activities in athletics, art, and academics. At one time or another most of us have experiences that absorb us so completely that we lose track of time. We may be working at the office late at night so deeply engaged that we forget to check the time, fail to hear others approach, forget about hunger, and display other seemingly absent-minded tendencies. Activities that can so capture and absorb attention are those for which there is high intrinsic motivation. That is, the top three reasons students list for their engagement in activities have little to do with recognition or making money. Rather, the top reasons given are (1) "I enjoy it," (2) "I get satisfaction from getting better or from learning," and (3) "It is interesting to me" (Csikszentmihalyi et al., 1993, p. 138).

Csikszentmihalyi and his co-authors (1984, 1993; see also Csikszentmihalyi, 1990) call these "flow" experiences. Csikszentmihalyi, Rathunde, and Whalen (1993) cite several conditions as making the "optimal experience of flow possible." First, they say, "a deeply involving flow experience happens when there are clear goals and when the person receives immediate and unambiguous feedback on the activity." The researchers point out that most games and artistic performances provide these. Note the allure of video and computer games for many young people and adults. By way of contrast, they point out that "in classrooms, individuals don't really know what the purpose of their activities is, and it takes a long to find out how well they are doing" (p. 14).

A second condition is "the balance between the opportunities for action in a given situation and the person's ability to act" (Csikszentmihalyi et al., 1993, p. 14). That is, in order for a person to attain flow, that person must have both the ability to act and the opportunity to act. In classroom situations, students frequently have neither. They are not sure what to do, even in listening to the teacher talk, and they are constrained to remain passive. They have few opportunities to respond. When the conditions of flow are present and individuals engage in the activities, their skill increases and they seek out more and more complex versions of the activities. A musician moves to more complex music, an athlete to more skilled opponents, a scholar to more complex or less familiar problems, and so forth. Without the increasing complexity, there would be no absorption in the task, for what was once challenging becomes easy and routine.

In short, there is adequate evidence that engagement is possible for most students. Given the right conditions, nearly all students can become engaged. Which is to say they can learn.

Research on Potential. Research on potential has been around for a long time. For me, some of the most convincing appears in Benjamin S. Bloom's books *Stability and Change in Human Characteristics* (1964) and *Human Characteristics and School Learning* (1976). Bloom produces arguments to the effect that the variability (technically, variance) in school learning is far greater than for other human characteristics. The variability in physical characteristics is much less, for example. He argues that the variability in school learning is far greater because of educational practice, factors such as failure to take into account what students know and what their attitudes are, and teaching them in relatively large groups as though they were alike. According to Bloom, large gaps between top-achieving students and those at the bottom begin to appear in third grade and increase at succeeding levels of schooling.

As students get further behind, they have less and less opportunity to catch up on more and more. The school curriculum has never been organized to adapt to students, to accept what they know and can do and build from there. Perhaps writing teachers, more than teachers of any other subject, have attempted to begin with what students know. Even there, for students working at a deficit, writing in school becomes more and more complex and frustrating, less and less rewarding, and more and more socially stigmatizing.

Bloom (1976) argues that "what any person in the world can learn, almost all persons can learn *if* provided with appropriate prior and current conditions of learning" (p. 7) He makes the case that "generalized characteristics of the learner—such as intelligence and aptitudes—are highly resistant to modification, while characteristics such as the specific prerequisites and motivation for a particular learning task are modifiable to a greater degree at most stages in the individual's history" (1976, p. 15). That means that we need to forget about generalized notions of intelligence and aptitude and concern ourselves instead with working out where students are in relation to specific learning tasks in the curriculum (e.g., writing an effective narrative about personal experience), what students have to know to accomplish that, and how they can enjoy learning those things.

Bloom's prescription for promoting higher levels of learning with less variability includes analyzing the learning "tasks" carefully, sequencing them so that learning one or some promotes learning others, preparing learners for the task, and providing high-quality instruction that includes appropriate learning "cues," involving students actively in the tasks, and reinforcing what they learn. Several of these are comparable to the conditions requisite to flow experience.

Perhaps Bloom's view of what most or nearly all students can learn is over-optimistic, but it does not seem entirely unreasonable. The main problem with the contention is that we do not know what all the "appropriate learning cues" are. But as I will argue later, we do know what some are, and we should be able to begin decreasing the learning gap, even as we raise standards across the whole range of students.

IMPLICATIONS FOR TEACHING

Holding strong to a belief that students would like to and can succeed is necessary but is *not in itself sufficient* for effecting change in learning. Consider Verita's writing: at the low end of the scale we use to judge what we receive from seventh graders, flat content, no detail, little emotion, and no concern for focus. Imagine subjecting Verita and her classmates to the kind of teaching Goodlad (1984) and Csikszentmihalyi and Larson (1984) found in schools. There would be lectures, exercises in workbooks, simple paragraphs to use as models, and formulas of various kinds.

Our deconstructive view of writing, in itself, suggests that such teaching will be inadequate. To write well, one must become a reader, to divide oneself from the text (from the self), "to generate a second, third, and fourth self to see what is written from the outside" (Graff, 1992b). True enough. But more than reading is involved. Making a statement in the first place requires the invention of self. We define ourselves by what we say, and our construction of self governs what we say. When we write or speak, we posit ourselves as persons with beliefs, memories, motives, and aspirations, none of which exist independently of the others. The person is the integration of all these and more, and our writing derives from the product of that integration. Since those beliefs, memories, aspirations, and motives change from moment to moment, we find ourselves in a constant state of reintegration, of reinventing ourselves, as it were. Add to that the polysemous webs of meaning in which any culture casts a writer, and the complexity of the problem of expression is magnified many times, for the objects of integration are only dimly perceived through the dark glass of shifting meanings.

If writing demands such invention and reinvention of self, then the kind of teaching that Verita would receive from Goodlad's teachers would surely fail her. The abstract rules and formulas of such teaching exclude the self. Rather, they demand mechanistic thinking about parts treated interchangeably with little or no attention to content or to the whole that reflects the self. It will be a major argument of this book that students can learn to write more effectively—particularly with teaching that considers what students know, uses that to engage them in more complex procedures, provides support of various kinds, and allows them to become active learners, the kind of learners I watched in Bernie McCabe's class that long-ago September.

Chapter Two

Some Basics for Thinking about Teaching Writing

In various projects that my students and I have been conducting to discover how teachers think about their teaching, one distinct profile has emerged so far that hinges on a common set of attitudes toward students, teaching, and learning. While our sample is drawn from teachers in a large urban community college system, experience indicates that the same profile appears at other levels. I present this profile as representative of beliefs shared by several teachers in the sample, but certainly not all.

This representative professor holds a Ph.D. in English from a prestigious university. He believes that the primary task of his freshman composition class is to teach the "modes of writing." Of his students, he says, "I'm always surprised at how little the students do know about a given subject or a given approach to writing about something." He believes that, after mechanics and editing, "Perhaps their second weakest area . . . is what I would loosely call reading between the lines, thinking for oneself, thinking, using analogy, being creative."

Classes observed begin with the professor making an assignment followed by a presentation of information about the mode of writing represented in the assignment. This complete, he turns to the previous assignment and asks several students to read their papers aloud. After each reading the professor comments. This goes on until class ends. In one class he presents the mode of writing he calls "extended example." He explains at some length that it will not be the same as classification or narrative.

> The essay that I am about to put on the board, where we use example as a way of developing a paper, will be somewhat closer to the classification one, but not the same. There will never be a paper that is exactly like the last one. Don't you see? Don't think that just because you did that last time, that somehow you've got to do it this

> way this time and if you can't fit it, there is a problem. Don't *try* to fit it. It's a different assignment. It has an entirely different set of problems that you have to work on solving. When you tell your story, it's just like if I turn on the television and I had missed the commercial. I am seeing characters developing some conflict. I'm seeing them change as a result of the pressures they are under. It's a *story.* I'm trying to say that over and over again, it is a story. It is not a classification of anything. You are telling a story. So there's no first, second, and finally. There is a plot which may have a beginning, a middle, and an end. That is not first, second, and finally. There is no conclusion; there is an ending.

He continues for 30 lines of transcript, talking more about narrative, which students have already written and will read aloud later, and contrasting it with news commentaries on TV. He says he wants to "take a minute and throw some things on the board so you have a sense of where we're going." He says, "Do not hesitate to ask questions if the assignment is still not clear to you. I'm not trying to rush you. I thought it was fairly well understood, but if it's not, I can only know unless, you know, you ask me questions and indicate what's not been made clear. OK. Just copy what's on the board, but don't copy anything yet. Some of this is just a reminder which you probably already know." Perhaps not surprisingly, no one asks questions. He writes several assignments in abbreviated form, including one for "theme three," the next composition that students will write.

> Theme 3 (extended example)
>
> Choose only one:
>
> (1) What are three dangerous drugs?
> (2) What are three situations where we should not drink and drive?
> (3) What are three jobs for the future?
> (4) Who are three well-known illiterates?

After 39 lines of transcript and a period for role taking, he turns to theme three:

> Now the expository mode, we call an example. Really example is not an expository mode, but I'll make it one anyway. Secondly, example is used in all the various modes to get the point across. And we are concentrating on using example very explicitly this time, so I think we will just say the expository mode is example. You have to decide who the audience is and who you are as a speaker, what your attitude

> is, and if you're having some difficulty with that we can discuss it on Thursday. Give it some thought before Thursday. For number six I have given you four questions which will force you to write a paper in which you have: an introductory paragraph, three developmental paragraphs, each of which will have one example in the second form, and then you will have a fifth paragraph which is a conclusion. Now this time you are *not* telling a story. You are explaining something. You must use one of the four, only one. If you choose number one I'll see your topic is drugs.

The professor continues for 65 lines of transcript, which include a lecture on famous illiterate athletes, before asking volunteers to read their narratives.

THE BASICS OF PRACTICE

Any teacher of writing is faced with a wide variety of possibilities for teaching that range from the imposition of little or no structure to very tight constraints on students, from teacher lecture to free-flowing class discussion with no limits on topics students may wish to mention, from daily free writing to daily drill on usage, from the use of computers to the use of chalkboards, from curricula based on the writing types of current traditional rhetoric to those that seem to admit to no important differences among writing tasks and sometimes no curricula at all. In this welter of possibilities how can we know how to proceed in making decisions about both curriculum and specific classroom practice? What prevents classrooms from becoming a hodge-podge of activities: 10 minutes of free writing, 5 of sentence combining, 15 of lecture about "description," 12 on vocabulary, and, assuming a 50-minute class, 8 minutes of small-group discussion on a topic of the students' choice?

What is it that renders the classroom process coherent? What can be the basis of future practice with particular students? I think the answer to both these questions is *theory*. Every teacher of writing has a set of theories that provide a coherent view of the field and means of approaching the task of teaching. Leon Lederman (1991), the physicist and Nobel laureate, says simply that theory is "the best explanation of the data," taken to include their nature and relationships. Theories may be based on a combination of assumptions, constructions derived from empirical research, and argument. They vary in quality with the care exercised in establishing each component. One such "explanation" for writing teachers has to do with written discourse, some explanation of the features of writing, their occurrence, and relationships.

The profile with which this chapter opens illustrates several theories. Let us look at four. The most obvious is the explanation of discourse that leads to the teacher's opening discussion about how "extended example" differs from "classification" and narrative. In this teacher's theory, written discourse includes many such "types." He will teach ten of them in the course of the semester. Each is characterized by a structure that he endeavors to explain to his students, contrasting it with others that may be similar in certain ways. Thus, he says, of narrative: "There is a plot which may have a beginning, a middle, and an end. That is not first, second, and finally. There is no conclusion; there is an ending." Further, he believes that the central features of each type are adequately represented in his chalkboard outline of the assignment. He believes that if students understand these features, they will be able to generate an example of the type.

The second theory underlying this profile is pedagogical and quite straightforward. Simply stated, it holds that teaching is tantamount to telling. It is based on the assumption, which Lindley Murray (1849) states in the 1795 preface to his venerable grammar, that people can, using appropriate language, "transfuse . . . sentiments into the minds of one another" (p. 5). In the classes of these teachers, observations reveal that their talk dominates the available time by wide margins, not infrequently 100 to 1. In the class transcript excerpted above, the teacher has 229 lines while one student speaks for two lines up to the point that students read their essays aloud.

A third theory, one of epistemology or knowing, appears to underlie both of the above. It appears to be what post-modern critics would call a "positivist" epistemology, one that holds reality and knowledge to be directly apprehensible by the senses without interpretation, almost without ambiguity. Such a theory endorses teaching as telling. The professor simply needs to "infuse" his ideas of "extended example" into the minds of students. Further, those ideas can be adequately represented simply by means of the outline on the chalkboard. The same epistemology is implicated in the theory of representational discourse the professor holds. He seems to believe that the substance of at least some kinds of discourse may be directly apprehended without the filters of persuasion on the part of the writer or interpretation on the part of the reader. Thus, he says, "example is used in all the various modes to get the point across." For him, the import of an example is self-evident.

These three theories are closely tied together so as to support one another. Their interlocking results in the smooth functioning of the class, which rolls along under the professor's direction without any apparent difficulty.

The fourth theory is based on the assumption that students have weak backgrounds that render them unlikely to learn. This assumption is taken as fact, as the epistemology might lead us to expect, and statements about student weakness tend to the absolute; for example, "No matter what I do, there is very little improvement." Because they perceive students as very weak, they adopt the corollary that whatever is taught must be simplified and "highly structured." That simplification and structure should enable them to "transfuse" the necessary information directly into the minds of students who cannot think for themselves and "want to be force fed." They say, "The more structure they have, the more comfortable they are with an assignment." Note the simple structure of the five paragraph theme assignment above.

The basic assumption about students and the theory of teaching in this profile, taken together, form a very tight syllogistic system for thinking about teaching. If teaching is telling, then proper teaching has taken place when the proper basic formulas about writing have been presented. If students do not learn much even when proper teaching has taken place, it is not surprising because they are weak and cannot be expected to learn. The teaching has not failed; the students have. Therefore there is no reason to change the method of teaching. Teaching writing becomes a protected activity. There is no need to call assumptions about methods into question, no need to try something new, no reason to doubt oneself as a teacher. Of course, not all teachers in our sample conform to this profile. Many believe that students can learn, and this belief appears to influence what they do. The point is that *the assumptions we make and the theories we hold have a powerful effect on what and how we teach.*

I believe that teachers of written composition must work from at least four major, interconnected sets of theories: (1) composing processes, (2) written discourse, (3) invention or inquiry, and (4) learning and teaching. These theories will necessarily be the basis for the content and organization of students' experiences in any program intended for helping people learn to write.

This is not to say that theory is the only source of what we do as teachers. Two other sources are equally important: what has been called reflective practice, and the teacher's general fund of life experience.

THE NATURE OF REFLECTIVE PRACTICE

Many people believe that research and theory govern practice. The relationships, however, seem far more complex than that, particularly if we think of "practice" in more than the simplest sense of the word as, according to the *Oxford English Dictionary (OED),* "the action of doing something." What I intend here is more akin to the third and fifth definitions offered by the *OED:* (3) "the doing of something repeatedly or continuously by way of study; exercise in any art, handicraft, etc. for the purpose or with the result of attaining proficiency" and (5) "the carrying on or exercise of a profession or occupation. . . ." Taken together, these suggest a kind of practice that is reflective, that permits the practitioner to learn through practice, not simply through *trial and error,* an expression that suggests a kind of randomness that does not allow for the building of knowledge. Others suggest that practice is essentially routine.

Practice as Routine

Stephen North (1987) writes of the knowledge of practitioners as a body of lore that he characterizes as "the accumulated body of traditions, practices, and beliefs in terms of which practitioners understand how writing is done, learned, and taught" (p. 22). He argues that "practice is largely a matter of routine. . . . Practitioners operate within the bounds of lore's known: they approach the matter of what to do by reducing the infinite number of new situations into familiar terms, then handling them with familiar strategies" (p. 33).

North allows, however, that under three conditions "practice becomes inquiry" but only

> (a) when the situation cannot be framed in familiar terms, so that any familiar strategies will have to be adapted for use;
> (b) when, although the situation is perceived as familiar, standard approaches are no longer satisfactory, and so new approaches are created for it; or
> (c) when both situation and approach are non-standard. (p. 33)

North speculates that, judged by these standards, with the normal freshman composition teaching load, "practice qualifies as inquiry less than ten percent of the time" (p. 34).

These guidelines for thinking about what constitutes inquiry in practice are useful. To use them for the analysis of inquiry in the practice of teaching writing would require definitions of the key terms, of course. What constitutes standard and nonstandard situations? What constitutes "an approach" in the teaching of writing? When is an approach standard or nonstandard? North's examples suggest that a nonstandard situation represents a shift in circumstances comparable to the advent of the open admissions policy that brought underprepared students into Mina Shaughnessy's (1977) classroom, prompting the inquiry that resulted in *Errors and Expectations.* In the same way, a nonstandard approach is one that leaves behind most, if not all, of the teaching tactics previously used.

Reflective Practice as Inquiry

It seems to me, however, that inquiry occurs in practice on a far less grand scale. Assume that a teacher who has been using a story from the classroom anthology to exemplify specificity in writing has decided to dump it because she feels her students are unenthusiastic about it and do not seem to care about its specific imagery. Instead she selects a passage by a ninth grader from the student magazine, *Merlyn's Pen,* as a model of effective, specific writing, asks a ninth-grade class to read and respond to it, and examines students' responses to it in some way to determine its impact on students' understanding of what specific prose is. Does that sequence constitute inquiry? The sequence will not allow the teacher to explain the kind of cause-and-effect relationship that North talks about. She will not know if there is a more or less effective passage. And if she uses other activities to promote specific imagery in the writing of her ninth graders, she will not be able to judge how important her prose model was in that effort.

Her evaluation of the impact of the passage is likely to sound something like this: "I think the kids liked the passage a lot. They were very attentive while I read it aloud, they had lots to say about it when I asked what they liked about it, and they were able to find many examples of specific details. I think it has given them a better idea of what it means to be specific in their own writing." Clearly, the teacher has engaged in a kind of practical inquiry that includes the identification of a problem (an ineffective model), the hypothesis of a reasoned solution (that a piece written by a student might have greater appeal), the informal testing of the hypothesis, and an arrival at some resolution of the problem. In Dewey's (1938) terms, this process that originates in doubt and moves in a rational way to resolution constitutes inquiry.

If the teacher uses the same model with many ninth-grade classes over a period of several years, does the practice become what North calls routine? The *OED* defines *routine* as "of a mechanical or unvaried character; performed by rule." To say that teaching is routine is to suggest its comparability to operating a punch press, without having to set the press up. If our teacher is aware that no two groups of students are the same and uses the selection in an interactive way, monitoring responses, responding to students as individuals, and evaluating the effectiveness of the selection, then the teaching cannot be mechanical, unvaried, or performed by rule. (By the same definition, the kind of teaching represented in the profile that opens this chapter is routine.)

If the teacher remains open to the possibility that the piece of writing may not have the desired effect for one reason or another, if she monitors student response to determine how it is or is not working, then the teacher maintains the basic posture of inquiry in teaching, regarding actions as hypotheses to be assessed. If, on the other hand, the teacher presents material without regard to any student response and makes no attempt to assess student understanding as teaching proceeds prior to grading assignments at the end of teaching sequences, then the teaching must be regarded as routine: mechanical and unvarying. We may call the former by Donald A. Schön's (1987) term: reflective practice. And such reflective practice is the basis for inquiry in teaching. Indeed, reflective practice becomes inquiry, in North's sense, as it becomes more formal and systematic.

The Priority of Reflective Practice

Quite clearly, in the case of teaching writing (and perhaps in other cases as well), research and theory would not exist if practice were entirely unreflective. More than creating a need, however, reflective practice can provide the foundation for research. A number of research projects, for example, seem to have been instigated by classroom practice. Teachers have noticed something interesting, curious, or unexpected in the process of interacting with students and have developed and examined those possibilities with great care, using a variety of research strategies from case studies to quasi-experiments designed to examine hypotheses (e.g., Atwell, 1987; Cochran-Smith & Lytle, 1993; Hillocks, 1979, 1982; Olson, 1992; Sager, 1973; Troyka, 1973).

At the same time, practice appears to generate important ideas for theory. For example, some teachers were using small student-led group discussions long before Vygotsky was translated into English. The success of small-group collaborative learning has a potential for adding to Vygotskian theory. The success of the practice drives a need to develop an explanatory theory.

Further, practice may give us cause to question theory. For example, I recently witnessed a teacher attempting to capture the interest of what had been designated by the school as one of its lowest-level ninth-grade groups. She had asked them to write journal entries about their own personal experiences or whatever concerned them, to share entries they liked with others, to revise them, and so forth. So far as I could see, she was doing everything she could to follow Donald Graves's (1983) recommendations. Nonetheless, these African American inner-city youngsters were not buying it. They saw no value, at the time, in writing about their own personal experience. Several students had even asked the teacher if they could go back to doing fill-in-the-blank exercises. This they regarded as "real" English. What does one do if the theoretical stance recommends an open approach to topics and structures but the students view such an approach as silly? Such situations wrestle us into rethinking theory.

If practice can lead us to reexamine theory, it must be the case that practice may take a theoretical stance. Reflective teachers develop a stance based on sets of ideas about their students and their subject, ideas that may be more or less systematically developed but that are able to provide tentative hypotheses about how students will react and what they are likely to learn under certain conditions. As the initial profile of this chapter indicates, even the least reflective teachers operate on the basis of some theories of learning and subject matter.

Frame Experiments

When teachers move beyond the automatic and begin to consider the effects of their actions on students and to devise alternatives, they find that, as Schön (1987) points out, they "deal often with uncertainty, uniqueness, and conflict. The non-routine situations of practice are at least partly indeterminate and must somehow be made coherent" (p. 157). To do that, Schön argues, they "frame" the "messy" problem by attending selectively to certain features, organizing them, and setting "a direction for action" (p. 4), which becomes a "frame experiment."

Between the body of knowledge and theory available in a field and its skillful application in a concrete situation, there is always a "gap of knowledge." Bridging that gap requires "a thoughtful invention of new trials based on appreciation of the results of earlier moves. The application of such a rule to a concrete case must be mediated by an art of reflection-in-action" (p. 158). "Skillful practitioners learn to conduct frame experiments in which they impose a kind of coherence on messy situations and thereby discover consequences and implications of their chosen frames" (p. 157). For Schön, the "frame experiment" is the essence of reflective practice. I argue that it is also the basis of inquiry in teaching.

What would such a frame experiment look like in the teaching of composition? Over 30 years ago, well before the current popularity of "process instruction," my friend and colleague, James F. McCampbell, was teaching a class of ninth graders, mostly boys, whose reading in a remedial reading class had improved enough to move into a regular English class. Because other students making this shift had experienced so much difficulty in expressing themselves in writing, we had decided to keep them together as a group to try to help them become more fluent as writers. At the time, no one was doing much of anything about the teaching of writing, let alone with students who were particularly weak as writers. The automatic response to weak writing for most teachers at the time was to go for the grammar book, reasoning that if only students knew their parts of speech, their syntax, and usage, they would be able to write adequately. Making this assumption required ignoring the fact that these means did not bring about the desired end, not even with students who did not experience inordinate difficulty with writing (Braddock, Lloyd-Jones, & Schoer, 1963; Hillocks, 1986a).

Jim McCampbell noted that the papers attempted by these students were characterized not so much by poor spelling and lack of proper punctuation as by brevity. Most students in this group would not write much more than three or four lines for any assignment, no matter how much time had been involved in what we would call "prewriting" today. Jim was using our normal literature program, one that had been developed by the faculty over a period of several years (Hillocks & McCampbell, 1964). Generally writing activities grew out of unit activities. For example, in a unit on the "Outcast," students wrote about their own feelings of being ostracized, their responses to and interpretations of events and situations in stories and poems, and a story in newspaper format about a case of ostracism.

Normally, our instructional emphasis was on the development of content as students wrote, shared drafts, provided feedback in small groups, and revised. Because these students normally wrote so little, McCampbell decided to jettison the usual emphasis and adopt one that concentrated on encouraging students to write more. After a classroom discussion that began with student reaction to a recent news story about a child who had been locked away in a trunk for many months and ended with students telling about how at one time or another they had felt left out, if not ostracized, he asked his students to write whatever they wished as long as it related somehow to the topic they had been discussing. As he circulated among the class as they wrote, he complimented students on what they had written and asked them to write more. He reported that students did produce more. In fact, after a few weeks, they were producing 10 to 15 times the amount they had prior to his beginning this "frame experiment." At the time, we all thought this appeared to be a remarkable result, one that we could attribute to Jim's having simplified the task and reinforced students as they wrote more.

Six Dimensions of Frame Experiments

What Jim did in this instance exemplifies at least six basic dimensions of the "frame experiment" essential to reflective teaching: (1) analyzing current student progress in relation to general course goals; (2) positing some change or range of possible changes sought in the writing of students; (3) selecting or devising a teaching strategy or set of strategies to implement the desired change; (4) devising a plan for implementing the teaching strategies; (5) assessing the impact of the teaching strategy in order to "discover consequences and implications of [the] chosen frames"; and, perhaps most important, (6) confirmation or change of the strategies used. For it is easy to imagine a teacher who, while noting the failure of students to learn what was taught, simply proceeds with more of the same, assuming that the "consequences and implications" of the "chosen frame" are the students' problems, not the teacher's. Let us examine each of these six in somewhat more detail.

The first dimension of reflective teaching appears to be an ongoing analysis of student progress in terms of the course goals. By *ongoing* I mean the daily consideration of student progress as indicated in responses during teacher-led discussions, participation in small groups, and the full variety of writing that is part of an active composition class. Most of these judgments will be informal, concerned with the quantity and character of individual responses in classroom talk and signs of understanding and change in pieces of writing at various stages of development; fewer will be formal, based on fully developed, final pieces of writing.

In reflective practice, assessment asks the extent to which the teaching and goals have been appropriate and effective for the students. Such assessments will be generated from the teacher's store of relevant theory and ideas garnered from practice and life experience. For assessment to be reflective, it must grow out of theory related to the particular teaching problem and students. In that sense, testing programs mandated by states and school districts or college English departments have nothing to do with reflective practice; nor do teacher-made tests that are administered without regard to specific teaching or learning problems.

In the example above, Jim McCampbell assessed the character of student writing in a way not foreseen by the existing course and unit structures. Those structures had assumed that students would have the ability or disposition to develop more extended pieces of writing. When Jim realized that his students did not, rather than simply bewailing the luck of the draw as others might well have done, he assumed that his students could move beyond their present stage and asked himself what he might do to help them. He also assumed that the problem was not one of intelligence or knowledge, but one of disposition. These students, he knew, had met with anything but success in the English classroom. Therefore he concluded that the ordinary goal of the unit (elaboration of ideas in different writing tasks) was inappropriate for his students. He adopted a modified goal. Students would still elaborate ideas, but developing a disposition to write would take priority.

The second dimension of reflective teaching is the envisionment of some desired change in light of the teacher's available theory. It requires deciding *in advance* what will be taken as evidence of success and generally means that the teacher can let the students know the purpose of instruction so that they can work toward the goal thoughtfully. To begin a personal narrative in the middle of an event (*in medias res*) might be such a goal, one that is based on a reasoned conception of personal-experience writing, an understanding of what students can already do, and some idea of how to help students reach that goal.

In the teaching of writing it is not possible, nor would it be desirable, to specify in advance precisely what success entails for any given piece of writing, certainly not with the precision engineers expect in specifying the characteristics and tolerances, let us say, for the construction of a bridge. Such standardization is antithetical to what most of us regard as good writing. At the same time, that we have and use criteria for judging writing is evident in a variety of settings. In Jim McCampbell's case above, the problem was rather a simple one, to write more words in connected discourse, at least loosely connected. Because the problem of goals is important and complex, I will return to it often throughout this volume, but particularly in Chapter Seven.

The third feature of reflective teaching is selecting or inventing particular strategies for particular purposes and particular students. Jim McCampbell's strategy above, though simple, is a good example of reflection-in-action. Jim assessed the students' writing, brought to bear his knowledge of what life in classrooms is like for students who have difficulty, recalled a study or two reported at National Council of Teachers of English meetings that indicated focusing on "correctness" resulted in shorter and simpler sentences, and decided that what he really wanted was to encourage students to write more. He decided to allow students to write what they wanted following class discussions and to encourage them, however he could, to write more.

Many strategies that teachers adopt are quite complex. Often, they seem simply to work from a good idea, an insight into what students might enjoy and could do with some support in the form of a model, a special activity, perhaps simply clear directions and support from the teacher during the process. When teachers have the support of theory, they can invent many "good ideas." Processes of inventing, sequencing, and validating activities will be examined in later chapters.

Because Jim's strategy was so simple, the plan for implementing it (the fourth dimension) was also simple: (1) Circulate among students while they worked in class and make such statements as, "That's great! You've written a lot. Try to write some more." (2) Write comments on papers in the same vein: "Terrific! You have written more than you usually do. Keep it up!" Unfortunately most plans for implementation are not so simple.

The fifth and sixth dimensions involve assessing the impact of the strategies and deciding whether the plan might be worth using again. As with the first dimension, judging the impact of the teaching strategies on students' learning will be based on the goals and the theory underlying them. But to focus only on the goals and nothing more is to ignore too much that may occur incidentally. For example, research suggests that a focus on "correctness" may result in a general degradation of writing including fewer words and simpler sentences as students strive to avoid error (Adams, 1971; Hillocks, 1986a). Teachers who focus on "correctness" tend to ignore decreases in complexity of thought and syntax in favor of their selected goal.

On the other hand, unexpected benefits can be ignored as a result of the excessive myopia that a mechanical adherence to goals might foster. My students and I discovered that about 21 of the 29 African American seventh graders assigned to what is called in Chicago a "low-level" language arts class began to produce interesting and lively figurative language when they were involved in writing descriptions of sea shells so that one of their classmates could pick out the shell described from the whole batch of 29 shells. Serendipity at its best. All we had hoped for was concrete detail.

In McCampbell's case, assessment was relatively simple. There was certainly no need for elaborate counting. A glance at earlier and later papers told the story clearly. Volume had increased enormously. Several students were producing between 200 and 300 words at each writing. The strategy was confirmed. Quality would be another question.

Frame Experiments and Theory

At the time of this success, we attributed the change in student production to Jim's having simplified the task and provided positive reinforcement on a regular schedule. These moves made good pedagogical sense, simply on the basis of our experience with students who had difficulty with reading. At the time, we thought of this as an essentially Skinnerian interpretation, one that is out of fashion now, rejected as mechanistic and shallow. But it is interesting that other, more recent theories also make use of the idea of positive reinforcement, for example, Csikszentmihalyi's (1990) *Flow: The Psychology of Optimal Experience.*

In retrospect, we can add a layer of interpretation. Bereiter and Scardamalia's studies of young children writing reveal that they knew a great deal more about given topics than they use in writing. In one study, students wrote about as many words as they would say in a conversational turn (Bereiter & Scardamalia, 1982). In a second study, the researchers urged the youngsters to write as much as they could, and they wrote about three times more than the students in the first study. When a researcher asked them simply to write more, they wrote about as much again as they had after the initial prompt. Additional requests to "write some more" yielded more (Scardamalia et al., 1982). These researchers reason that children have learned a schema for conversation but not one for writing. In their responses to assignments, they are fulfilling what they see as a conversational turn. It is possible that Jim's promptings to write more were serving the same function as that of the researcher in Bereiter and Scardamalia's studies.

Whatever the case, the point is that the act of considering such reasons in relation to experimental frames provides the theoretical base for reflective teaching. When teachers reason about choices, plan in light of those reasons, implement those plans, examine their impact on students, and revise and reformulate reasons and plans in light of all that experience, that conjunction constitutes theory-driven teaching. Such teachers are engaged in reflective practice and inquiry.

By definition, then, teachers who try new ideas, whether their own or those of others, without considering them in light of some organized body of assumptions and knowledge (including their own experience) that acts as a kind of preliminary testing ground for those ideas, cannot be considered reflective. A reflective practitioner will analyze a new idea in light of its appropriateness to the students and their present knowledge; its fit with available theory, experience, and the goals of teaching; and its probability for success as judged from the teacher's experience and knowledge. All parts of these theories may not be explicit, and those that are may not be fully tested or examined critically. But for reflective practitioners, the working or action theories they hold continue to grow as they conduct new "frame experiments."

LIFE EXPERIENCE AND TEACHING

Our ideas and beliefs about teaching come not only from theory, practice, and research, but from a variety of perhaps disparate sources. Ideas for some of my activities that have been most popular with students came from watching my own children at play. Many have come from news stories of various kinds. Some I have been able to tie to theory; others have seemed atheoretical in their early uses but aided in the development of theories that I have worked with over the years. My students report similar experiences. Some have said that they seem always on the lookout for materials that will be irresistible to their students. That kind of search appears to become part of the life pattern of teachers who invent materials and activities. It is habit forming.

Other influences on teaching come from sources that we can no longer identify: values, attitudes, beliefs. Sometimes it seems important to take stock of these, to say "What is it I believe and why?" These personal beliefs are difficult to explain and even more difficult to pass on to another. One of the most important beliefs for my teaching comes, at least in part, from my father's firm faith in the value of struggling to succeed even in the face of defeat. It is embodied in his favorite story of Robert the Bruce. Legend says that after suffering six defeats at the hands of the English, the Bruce lay in a cave one night, discouraged, even considering giving up the struggle against the English. He watched a spider as it painstakingly climbed a fine thread to its web, only to fall back and start over again. Six times the spider made its way slowly up the thread. Six times it fell back. But on the seventh try, the spider succeeded. The Bruce took this lesson to heart, gathered his forces, and began a successful campaign against King Edward crowned by the Battle of Bannockburn, where Bruce succeeded in crushing the English even though he was outnumbered three to one.

No doubt the story of the spider is apocryphal. The Bruce did not keep a journal, after all. But there is truth in it. Though someone has failed any number of times, there is no evidence that the next try will not succeed. For with every trial we reinvent ourselves. Only the failure to try assures failure.

Chapter Three

Integrating Theories for Teaching Writing

Those concerned with the nature and learning of writing come from a wide variety of fields that serve, willy-nilly, to separate us simply by the tools used in approaching our common subject: rhetoric, discourse analysis, critical theory, literature, linguistics, testing and measurement, elementary and secondary education, anthropology, sociology, psychology, and various amalgams of the above. Unfortunately, the fields have become camps, frequently armed and on guard against the commotion from other camps, for fear those other camps will steal a march and somehow gain a position of power over them. Rhetoricians ignore the findings of cognitive psychologists and even protest their presence and their methods in the field. Empirical researchers reject critical theory as little more than egotistical contentiousness. Some theorists who see themselves as associated with the process movement reject the insights of rhetoricians. And on and on.

One major goal of this book is to provide a basis for integrating these diverse theories so that both the theories and their integration have generative power, that is, so that they will promote the growth of the theories themselves and the invention of new ideas and approaches for practice. But the alienations are obstructive and destructive.

At the heart of the alienations is what one writer has dubbed "the paradigm wars," the rancorous controversy over what constitutes research. It has been construed as between quantitative and qualitative researchers, or positivists and constructivists, or realists and idealists, or empiricists and postmoderns. However we name it, the distinction divides us over what kinds of claims we can make, what counts as evidence, and what the principles are by which we connect evidence to our claims. Underlying all these questions are assumptions about the nature of reality and how we perceive and interpret it. These differences are, I suspect, exacerbated by the political needs of researchers in newer fields, such as the study of writing, to legitimize both their objects of study and their methodologies.

Whatever their cause, these perceived differences present at least two problems that must be addressed. First, can the paradigm split be overcome? If so, on what grounds? Second, even if it can be overcome, given the divisions between paradigms that must remain and the diversity of fields from which composition draws, is it possible to develop a basis for integrating the theories from which the teaching of writing must draw? Let us take up first the question of disjunction.

THE PARADIGM SPLIT

In educational research the most widespread version of the controversy, simply stated, has pitted research that uses statistical methods to test hypotheses against research that uses observational methods to reach an interpretive understanding of educational phenomena. The former has been called the positivist paradigm, while the latter has been called qualitative (because of its methods) or constructivist (because of its epistemology). The most extreme voices in the dialogue claim not only that the one has nothing to say to the other, but that one must be eliminated. Egon Guba (1990), for example, calling himself a constructivist, claims that the "positivist (and postpositivist) paradigms are badly flawed and must be entirely replaced" (p. 25). Guba's colleague Yvonna Lincoln makes the same point: "Accommodation between paradigms is impossible" (1990, p. 81). On the other hand, I have personal knowledge of professors who have attacked the work of qualitative researchers because it is qualitative and does not test hypotheses in the same way they might have. I should admit at the outset that I may be sensitive to these controversies because my best known work has been attacked and dismissed by some as positivist in nature. However, I have been on the other end too, when, as a teacher using what amounted to qualitative data, I had to defend a junior high school English curriculum against various attacks. It seems to me from this double perspective that the extreme positions advocated by some diminish all our efforts.

Are these two paradigms as irreconcilable as these researchers say? John K. Smith, in 1983, outlined polarities in the debate over paradigm assumptions and methods that we still find in Lincoln and Guba. His first polarity is based on "the relationship of the investigator to what is investigated" (p. 6). Those who have been called positivists are assumed to posit a reality outside themselves that can be examined in an unbiased fashion through the use of appropriate methods. Researchers in this tradition attempt to eliminate their own values, biases, preconceptions, and emotional involvements. Those who stand at the other pole believe that because everything must be examined through the human mind, separation of the investigator from the object of investigation is impossible. Therefore, they argue, there is no independently existing reality.

Smith's second set of polarities has to do with the nature of truth. Here the fight is over what can count as truth. Positivists are thought to be those who take a statement to be true only if it can be demonstrated to correspond to some independently existing reality. Guba's constructivists reject this standard. They believe that because any one observer's understanding exists only in that observer's mind, there is no outside referent against which to test a statement of reality. For them, truth becomes a matter of agreement, reached through and justified by interpretation.

These ideas of truth imply different ideas of objectivity, a third set of polarities. For the hard scientist or positivist, objectivity may be achieved through the use of methods that permit an unbiased examination of phenomena. These methods provide knowledge that can be tested by others, assuming they have similar levels of skill and use comparable methods on comparable problems. On the other hand, constructivists believe that, because any concept of reality is dependent upon the mind of the observer, objectivity of the kind sought by positivists is not possible. For Guba's constructivists, objectivity is social agreement. According to Guba the process of coming to that agreement has two parts: hermeneutics ("depicting individual constructions as accurately as possible") and dialectic ("comparing and contrasting these existing individual [including the inquirer's] constructions") (p. 26).

A fourth set of polarities has to do with the nature of the goals of the two research traditions. According to Lincoln and Guba, positivists seek "immutable natural laws." Guba says that the "ultimate aim of science is to *predict* and *control* natural phenomena" (p. 19; emphasis in original). Smith cites, as an example of such scientific law, the statement that if a metal bar is heated, it will expand. What constructivists seek is not a set of overarching laws, but rather what Smith calls "interpretive understanding." The hermeneutic process that gives rise to such understanding demands that the investigator examine relationships among parts and the whole of the phenomenon under investigation, including the investigator's own values and interests.

Do these polarities render the paradigms mutually exclusive? Any attempt I make to develop theory for teaching composition will almost certainly draw upon knowledge from a variety of sources. If the research traditions and separate fields are as incompatible as so many seem to claim, such attempts will be defeated at the start. They will be one more victim of the fragmentation of knowledge.

BRIDGES IN THE LANDSCAPE OF KNOWLEDGE

Michel Serres, professor of the history of science at the Sorbonne, offers what is for me a compelling metaphor that provides an alternative model of knowledge. Serres (1982) sees science as one among many cultural formations. Because there is no natural hierarchy among cultural formations, one may pass from science to any other formation or from any other to science. Thus appropriate metaphors for knowledge are the encyclopedia and the journey. Knowledge as encyclopedia permits not only access to all fields of knowledge but access to the world. The metaphor of the voyage permits us to view knowledge as geography, accessible without the impediments of disciplinary classifications and methods. In Serres's vision the topography would be complete and accessible but would contain "pits, faults, folds, plains, valleys, wells, and chimneys, fluids like the sea and solids like the earth. . . . Here and there, locally, I identify fractures or discontinuities, elsewhere, on the contrary, relations and bridges" (1982, p. xxii). Thus, for Serres to know is to move about this differentiated landscape, rejecting the walls that come with the ordinary classifications of epistemologies and seeking instead for relations and bridges.

To reject one research paradigm in favor of some other is to contribute to the dogmatism that Serres wishes to avoid. Far more important is to seek for relations and bridges, particularly for a theory of teaching in a field that we know in advance will be comparable to the landscape described by Serres. Ultimately, our theory will need to encompass far more diverse territory than the paradigms of immediate concern. The goal will be to integrate, but not to unify, vastly disparate fields of knowledge. That is, we will recognize them as separate but find bridges and passages that serve to integrate them.

Bridging Apparent Polarities

To build bridges, we need to consider whether the paradigms are as diametrically opposed as Guba and Lincoln claim. Let us return to the polarities cited by Smith to determine whether bridges and passages between the paradigms are possible.

Reality, Truth, and Argument. The first two polarities have to do with the nature of reality and the nature of truth. Guba and Lincoln, and many others who set up these classifications, say that quantitative researchers believe in a reality that exists outside themselves, while they, the constructivists, believe that there are multiple realities, all of which exist only in the heads of the believers.

A cartoon that first appeared in an issue of *Puck* in 1915 was originally entitled "My Wife and My Mother-in-Law." If you were to look at it, you would see the picture of a young woman, wearing a broad brimmed hat and a feather boa, her left shoulder bare above her gown, her face turned away so that we can see only the line of her cheek. She very likely would have appeared a fashion plate in 1915. Or perhaps you would see a crabby-looking woman, her hair piled up, her chin tucked down, her eyes glowering. No matter how you try, you will see only one of the figures at a time. As they appear to flip back and forth, you may remember one as you view the other, but you will not see both at once. Psychologists explain the apparent flipping from one image to the other as the effect of two competing learned schemata (Attneave, 1974).

This picture teaches what Gestalt psychologists taught us several decades ago: that we perceive whatever we look at as an undifferentiated panoply of lines, colors, and spaces. Then our brain goes to work and differentiates a figure or figures from the ground. In other words, our brains interpret our physiological perceptions to make some kind of sense of them (Kohler, 1959). And in the case of this particular mass of lines and spaces, with two visions that seem to hop back and forth before our very eyes, we simply interpret and reinterpret every few seconds. The experience seems to support Guba's contention that reality exists only in our minds.

At the same time, the experience does not clearly demonstrate that there is not a reality outside our minds. What would it take to demonstrate that reality exists only in people's heads? Our minds can make an old hag appear to be a fashionable young woman and vice versa. We can examine a picture by Picasso, Miro, or Chagall and imagine any number of images in it. However, if reality existed only in my mind, I should be able to make "real" whatever I wished. I should be able to see a rhinoceros instead of only some female figure. We appear to be constrained by the lines before us.

Other evidence as well supports the existence of a reality outside our minds. About 20 years ago my best friend lifted a .38 caliber pistol to his head and ended his life. My mind cannot reverse that event. If I could, I would have done it long ago. I am willing to accept this as incontrovertible evidence that there is an independently existing reality: *We cannot reverse events that have occurred.* The problem lies in attempting to interpret, to understand that reality.

At the same time, by virtue of the way our minds work, it is impossible to understand any reality in or outside ourselves without being influenced to some degree by the assumptions, predispositions, and knowledge that result from our previous experiences. Given our circumstances, the strongest "truth" we hope for is an approximation of reality tempered by the necessity for a healthy skepticism about what we think we know.

It is apparent, however, that most empiricists have never pretended to have a corner on reality in the sense that Guba and others claim they do. The philosophical movement that called itself logical positivism, upon which

Guba's portrait of positivists seems to have been based, was dead by the middle of this century (cf. Hayes, 1993; Phillips, 1990). Bruce Gregory's (1988) book, *Inventing Reality*, shows in example after example that physicists have, for centuries, invented models and languages (means of interpretation) for talking about reality and tested them for their ability to predict events at some level of approximation. If scientists do, on occasion, state generalizations as though they conveyed the "absolute truth," they are no different from avowed constructivists in that. Take, for example, Lincoln's (1990) generalization about what models of knowledge are available: "We simply do not have the metaphors we need yet for conceiving of knowledge in any other way but hierarchic, pyramidal, or taxonomic" (p. 84). This sounds fairly absolute to me, as though Lincoln has suddenly decided that there is an objective reality "out there" after all, and she knows what it is, even though she did not know about Serres.

None of us can escape an assumption that we know reality in some way. We think we know when it is safe to cross a busy highway. We do not convene a conference to obtain other opinions. We act on the basis of our perceptions and our existing knowledge, as though we had a grip on reality, even though we have only an interpretation of it. In effect, we develop an argument that it is safe to cross the highway: I see no cars coming; I know I can walk fast enough to cross the highway before any do come; therefore, it is (probably) safe to cross. Perhaps cars will appear traveling at 500 miles an hour and mow us down before we even hear them. There is no way to be absolutely certain of that. But the probabilities of safety are with us, and we act upon them.

Empirical researchers, whether qualitative or quantitative, develop comparable arguments in regard to teaching. They argue that what they describe occurred and, in the case of the quantitative, that the results occurred with some level of confidence. Further, qualitative and quantitative researchers argue that comparable conditions and methods used elsewhere have a chance of affecting some outcome. None is foolish enough to stipulate certainty. The key word here is *argument*. It is *argument* that makes the bridge possible.

The first of the "bridges" between positivists and constructivists, or between the qualitative and quantitative, then, is the view that reality exists independent of observers, that it is knowable in the sense of argued approximation, and that approximation must be attended by skepticism that entails continued testing of the generalizations or claims involved, their grounds, and the warrants that tie grounds to the claims. The differences among arguments emanating from various fields lie chiefly in the differences among the warrants perceived to be acceptable (Toulmin, 1958; Toulmin, Rieke, & Janik, 1984).

Objectivity. The third and fourth of Smith's polarities concern three matters of epistemology: objectivity, the uses of interpretation, and goals. Guba and Lincoln argue that positivists adopt a detached stance in order to be objective. This detached stance, according to Guba and Lincoln, minimizes interpretation in a vain attempt to establish "laws" or cause-and-effect generalizations. It is useful to examine each of these claims about objectivity, interpretation, and the goals of research in turn.

Guba claims that neither a detached stance nor objectivity is possible. Positivists, he says, believe that it is "both possible and essential for the inquirer to adopt a distant, noninteractive stance. Values and other biasing and confounding factors are thereby automatically excluded from influencing the outcomes" (Guba, 1990, p. 20). He claims that constructivists cannot accept such a division between the inquirer and the subject. "Findings are literally the creation of the process of interaction between the two" (p. 27). One of the problems of this position is that it treats bias as though it were of a single source. The phrase "values and other biasing and confounding factors" suggests that bias derives only from implicit sources such as values that have an unintentional effect on results. Clearly, bias can also result from the design of the study, or it can be intentional, as when scientists deliberately alter the results of research, "cook" their data for their own personal reasons.

Scientists, however, have realized for much longer than Guba thinks the difficulty of excluding bias from implicit sources. Phillips (1990), for example, cites the work of Hanson in 1958 as explaining that "observation is theory laden" (p. 34), not the neutral activity that some had thought. Earlier, others had commented on the need to "invent" categories and systems to describe the world, a move that clearly implies an understanding of the subjective nature of observation (cf. Newton and calculus). Nothing in the stance one takes, no matter how detached and distant, can eliminate the bias that comes with the culture and language of the observer. Neither qualitative nor quantitative researchers can eliminate cultural bias. But they can seek it out and analyze its influence, as does critical theory.

Quantitative researchers have developed methods to minimize bias from other sources, such as the sample examined, coder or observer variability, context, and various random sources. Qualitative researchers, because of the depth of their examination, find it impossible to institute comparable controls. Still, they recognize the danger of bias and minimize it by presenting possible distorting factors in meticulous detail. This localization in detail provides, at once, information necessary to understanding the case and to preventing inappropriate generalization.

In addition, both qualitative and quantitative researchers recognize the need to explain procedures, to verify observations, and to cross-check sources. All of these attempts to eliminate bias provide a second bridge.

Interpretation. Constructivists such as Guba and Lincoln seem to think that they have a corner on interpretation. In fact, they claim that hermeneutic interpretation lies at the very heart of constructivism while disallowing it from positivism. Such a view simply does not approximate existing reality very well. *Any use of categories, in research or in day-to-day thinking, necessarily involves interpretation* to decide which features determine membership in a particular category. That some low-inference categories may be used almost algorithmically does not change the fact of interpretation; it simply makes it easier. Such interpretation is involved in any discourse. Both quantitative and qualitative researchers use categories that are formally defined. The definition of the categories requires interpretation, a series of decisions about which characteristics are salient, which belong together, which should be separate, and for what reasons. The use of the categories requires argumentative reasoning about what constitutes an item for inclusion and what criteria are present to warrant it. These are often quite complex interpretations, as they are in the systematic analysis of the features of classroom discourse or of written composition.

Even the seemingly concrete categories used by survey researchers, such as age or salary brackets, involve an array of interpretive decisions. The limits of such categories are chosen because the researchers believe that they are likely to have particular meanings. They are based on a variety of data interpreted in such a way as to yield the categories as symbols. Thus, a salary bracket may be associated with consumer buying habits, educational level, political affiliation, and so forth. In many respects, the invention of the categories used is often the most interesting part of quantitative research. Unfortunately, it is usually hidden from view.

Here then is a third bridge between the positivist and constructivist: the use of interpretation to develop and use categories informatively and consistently. When the level of interpretation in either is shallow, or when categories are used inconsistently, the resulting research is likely to be of little interest. When the interpretation is rich and the categories are used consistently, the findings are likely to be provocative.

Goals and Experimentation. The third polar extreme alluded to above is that of goals. The goals of research are clearly related to both the use of detail and interpretation, as well as to the first polar issue of reality and truth. Guba (1990) claims that positivists seek to "predict and control natural phenomena" (p. 19). Guba and Lincoln both refer to "immutable" laws as the major goal of positivists, suggesting that "immutable laws" are "nature's secrets," that positivists "wrest" from nature in the course of working with "empirical experimentalism" (Guba, 1990, p. 19). However, neither Guba nor Lincoln provides a single example of an "immutable law" discovered through experiment.

Newton was one of the great thinkers who posited laws, but he did not arrive at them experimentally. Newton's first law, from his *Principia Mathematica*, is as follows: "Every body continues in its state of rest or of uniform motion in a right line [i.e., straight forward] unless it is compelled to change that state by forces impressed upon it" (1729/1934, p. 13). Even constructivists will have to admit that fairly heavy-duty experimentalism would be required to derive that "immutable law." Newton simply makes assumptions that permit him to construct a model that allows for accurate predictions about the movement of bodies on earth and in the heavens. The resulting "law" is not the product of "empirical experimentalism," but of careful interpretation of phenomena and an imaginative leap of incredible magnitude. To represent such thinking as experimentalism is not simply reductive, it is irresponsibly harmful in distorting the nature of inquiry.

Nowadays, not even the so-called hard scientists talk about seeking "immutable laws." They have learned to live with ambiguity (e.g., the Heisenberg principle in quantum mechanics). Often in fields such as particle physics, quantum mechanics, and the measurement of chemical and thermodynamic constants, different experiments frequently yield results that are statistically inconsistent. It is not unusual for reviewers of studies attempting to establish physical properties to eliminate 40% of the available studies to establish more reliable measurements (Hedges, 1987). In such cases, interpretation becomes essential for positing possible explanations for the differences and involves examining data in new ways, projecting alternative structures, and making imaginative leaps that may change the topography of science. Such thinking is far different from seeking certainty through "empirical experimentation."

Further, the work of careful quantitative researchers is always reported in terms of probabilities—not certainties. Statisticians report significant differences, differences that are probably not due to chance. They do not talk about "certain" differences. Rhetoricians examining such things report that important features of scientific texts are the presence of "hedges" (Crismore & Farnsworth, 1990) and "modal qualifiers" (Butler, 1990), both means of avoiding statements of certainty and implying the necessity of interpreting results.

If quantitative researchers do not seek immutable laws, and if they must contend with ambiguity, even in their quest for generalizations, what do they seek? For the most part, they attempt to construct a model that explains some set of data, some portion of reality, a model that has gaps of knowledge and degrees of ambiguity but that allows a better understanding of the phenomenon in question. Even Ptolemy, according to Bruce Gregory (1988), "made quite clear in his great work, *The Almagest,* that he was presenting a *model* to allow the positions of the planets to be calculated, not a description reflecting the way planets actually move" (p. 9). In other words, scientists have recognized for a very long time the imaginative and subjective dimensions of their work.

Although the model that Ptolemy developed is, in one sense, nothing like the thick description that an ethnographer might develop, both are nonetheless models. Both make use of symbol systems to represent some chunk of the world. The qualitative research of Clifford Geertz (1960) on *The Religion of Java* provides an example. Early in the text Geertz sets out to describe religious ceremonies of one "subvariant within the general Javanese religious system" (p. 5). As he begins to describe the marriage ceremony, he comments on his method:

> I shall describe the marriage ceremony in the fullest form in which it appears, but I shall include no practice not carried out on the occasion of at least one wedding I saw during the time I was in Modjokuto. It must be remembered not only that ceremonies for middle daughters are usually somewhat less elaborate, but also that various people omit various parts of the ceremony pretty much at will. (p. 54)

Geertz makes clear that he will describe no particular wedding ceremony, but rather his description will include all the elements observed at least once. He will present a kind of ideal model, not of one wedding but all that he has seen.

Here, then, is a fourth bridge between qualitative and quantitative research, the penchant for models that provide an argued approximation of reality in some way, to some degree.

Guba claims that positivists wish to control reality, to transform the world, while constructivists wish for no more than transformations of the mind. Certainly, Geertz, in his work on Javanese religion, does not see social change as a goal of his research. He has no reason to. But an ethnographer studying the operation of kindergarten and first-grade classes in Chicago's inner city could not help but consider the implications of her research for policy. Indeed, if educational researchers were to ignore the possibilities for positive change, their work would be irresponsible. As critical theorists point out, all actions in the world of academe have political ramifications (cf. Graff, 1987). The danger is not so much in having them, as in keeping them hidden. Here, then, is a fifth bridge.

Integrating Diverse Theory and Research

In what way may the findings of different research paradigms and diverse fields of inquiry and theory be brought together in an integrated, articulated set of theories for the teaching of writing? I have tried to suggest "bridges" between the paradigms. Those bridges apply to the various fields as well.

1. All fields and paradigms concerned present arguments in explanation of some portions of the problems and data relevant to the teaching of writing.

In doing so they suggest an independently existing reality that we can approximate well enough to provide a rational basis for action. They recognize, in their qualifications and in the practice within fields, that empirical findings must be subjected to skeptical review.
2. All are concerned with maintaining objectivity in research and use a variety of methods to do so. (It seems to me that an interchange of certain methods could be valuable.)
3. All use interpretation extensively. Each could probably benefit from examining, if not using, methods from other areas.
4. All build models that represent and interpret large sets of data, models intended to approximate reality and be subjected to skeptical analysis.

Although these bridges suggest greater compatibility than many may be willing to accept, it seems to me that they do not provide anything like a unified theory of knowledge of the sort that Heap (1992) discusses, a "metaperspective" for the evaluation of knowledge. As Heap states, "there can be no single metaperspective which would allow us to judge and articulate the claims of all the disciplines which study literacy. There can be no such metaperspective because there is no single conception of science which each relevant discipline shares" (p. 35).

Undoubtedly, Heap is right. At the same time, however, no single conception of science is necessary for differing research methodologies to be used successfully in a complementary fashion. There is no question that the diverse fields must be used to deal with the broad range of problems involved. For example, quantitative methods cannot deal with the historical problem of how the school writing curriculum came to be what it is. On the other hand, qualitative researchers would find it difficult, if not impossible, to provide a survey of writing programs in American schools. Further, different methods are also complementary in the sense of enabling researchers to bring different methodologies and insights to bear on the same problem—and this complementarity is possible without Heap's metaperspective.

The Role of Argument. We commonly synthesize different methodologies through argument, not arguments of the syllogistic type, but of the kind that Toulmin (1958) finds underlying our everyday discussions and the discourse of nearly every field of inquiry and practice. A complex argument involves a series of claims, used in a variety of ways to support a major proposition, which is the point of the argument. The minor claims may be of different types by virtue of being based on different evidence tied to the claims by different kinds of warrants. Those supported claims are not themselves in conflict because of that.

For example, the proposition that Mr. Zee is guilty of speeding at 55 mph in a 35 mph zone is based on three different claims, each based on a different set of evidence tied to the claim by a different kind of warrant. The claim that Mr. Zee's car was traveling at 55 mph is based on the evidence of a radar reading. The radar reading in itself, however, does not provide absolutely that Mr. Zee was actually traveling at 55 mph. In addition, the argument requires information about the reliability of the radar reading, its margin of error. The information about the radar instrument itself serves as a warrant that ties the evidence (the reading of 55 mph) to the claim that Mr. Zee was traveling at that rate of speed.

A second claim is that Mr. Zee was in a 35 mph zone at the time the reading was made. The evidence underlying this claim will have to do with the actual boundaries of the 35 mph zone and the police officer's interpretation of the position of the car in relation to the zone. The warrant that ties the evidence to the claim that Mr. Zee was in the 35 mph zone has to do with the veracity of the officer.

Finally, the claim that the speed limit was 35 mph is based on statutory evidence. The warrant tying the statutory evidence to the claim about the speed limit in a particular zone involves interpretations of the statutes, precedents, or both. Although each of these minor claims rests upon its own evidence and warrant, each different from the other, each claim plays a necessary but complementary part in the larger argument that results in a fine for Mr. Zee. (Of course, if Mr. Zee can beat any one of those arguments, he can avoid the fine.) Similarly, we must use claims derived from quite different research fields and methods in a complementary way to argue (that is, to confirm or disconfirm) theories about the teaching of writing.

Caveat. Nevertheless, a strong caveat is necessary here. Argument is primarily useful in verification or validation. An argument establishes Jim McCampbell's teaching moves as worth another try with comparable students in similar circumstances. Arguments will connect teaching strategies to each other, validate and integrate theories, and provide the basis for trying previously tested strategies.

Arguments may provide the groundwork for thinking about necessary innovations, about what is needed with a certain group of students. However, as we shall see, innovation cannot derive from argument. An innovation comes about through an imaginative process that no one understands very well. Once we have thought of a possible innovation, we use argument to examine it even before proceeding with it. But argument does not devise it.

Thus, when McCampbell decided to encourage his students to write more, he had no evidence that it would have any effect whatever. He could use arguments to eliminate some strategies that were popular at the time, for example, grammar drills. Once he had thought of encouraging students to write whatever they wanted in response to topics and praising greater length of response, he could support the possibility that it might work using evidence from our experience with encouraging reluctant readers to read, from what we knew about reinforcement theory, and perhaps from general experience with reluctant students.

But fixing on the strategy to use cannot be the direct result of argument. It is a matter of what I like to call an imaginative leap. Such leaps are not easy, nor can I, at least, explain how to make them. Perhaps others can. What I will attempt to do later in this book is suggest what the conditions are for making such leaps in the invention of materials and activities for teaching writing. In part the conditions involve a rich store of integrated theoretical knowledge.

EXAMINING THEORY FOR TEACHING COMPOSITION

The term *theory* has both positive and pejorative senses. In its most pejorative sense, it sometimes suggests an attempt to provide publicly acceptable reasons as a cover for ulterior motives. Even when used in its most positive sense it may still be seen as a smokescreen, an attempt to cover ignorance in high-sounding language that brooks no penetration by simple common sense. This is especially true when theory appears to contradict common sense. Common sense tells us that the earth does not move. We cannot feel it move. Yet highly respected theory tells us that it does.

Some theories, of course, have been quite wrong. The Ptolemaic theory of the universe, for example, turned out to be dead wrong about certain things. At the same time, we need to remember that that theory remained useful as a guide for about 1,400 years. We have a tendency to think of theories as being "discarded" and new ones as "replacing" them. A more useful metaphor may be to think of theories as evolving. People tend to think of Newton's theory of gravity and planetary motion as having been discarded, replaced by Einstein's theory of relativity. It is instructive to recall, however, that Newtonian mechanics and mathematics provide the basis for calculations requisite to launching rockets in our space exploration programs. So much for theories of the past.

The problem at hand is what we can and should expect of a theory purporting to deal with the teaching of composition. Recently, at a seminar on literacy at The University of Chicago, I asked Leon Lederman, a Nobel laureate in physics, what he meant by theory. Without hesitation, he said, "The best explanation of a set of data." Lederman's statement is deceptively simple. What the "best explanation" entails, as one might expect, is the kicker. At a minimum, it seems to me, the "best explanation" ought to provide the following:

1. A systematic account of the phenomena under consideration, including multiple levels of analysis as appropriate
2. Explanations of important relationships among the phenomena
3. Revelation of assumptions underlying the analysis.

Further, a useful theory ought to pass the following tests:

- Does the explanation account for or predict all instances of the phenomena in question? That is, is it inclusive? One serious problem with theories of discourse underlying textbooks on composition is that they fail to account for many types of writing.
- Does the theory have predictive power? Does the theory allow for instances of the phenomena yet to occur or be discovered? Einstein's theory of relativity predicted the occurrence of black holes, though none had been discovered when he first propounded it. Bakhtin's (1981) theory of the novel predicts the journalistic novel, for example, Truman Capote's *In Cold Blood.* Sandra M. Gilbert and Susan Gubar's (1979) theory of the nineteenth-century woman writer's imagination, based on the analysis of a finite number of texts, provides the basis for predicting the possibility of comparable interpretations in regard to other texts as well as the possibility of variations on their central concepts.
- Can it account for apparent contradictions in the data and their relationships? Any theory of planetary motion must account for apparent changes in the directions traveled by planets. Gilbert and Gubar's (1979) work must account for apparent contradictions to their theory.

In addition to these assumptions about what a theory ought to be, because we are concerned with the learning, welfare, and happiness of human beings, our theories need to fulfill other requirements as well. Back in my junior high school teaching days, I would have said that education, particularly in my classes, was altogether apolitical. By that I meant that I did not want to influence students for or against any particular political issue. I claimed that I only wanted my students to become thoughtful and insightful readers and writers, not simply tolerant of human differences, but understanding and appreciative of them. I believed that both the curriculum and classroom practices should reflect that point of view. I see now that even such a goal has clear political implications.

Our moral goal and our political intentions ought to be revealed and available for review, not so that we can eliminate them, but so that we can examine and strengthen them. The sum-total of what the proposed theories contribute to that moral goal needs to be constantly evaluated.

All of these questions and issues and those yet to come in ensuing chapters are really a development of the question that Mr. Holloway's comments on Bernie McCabe's classroom raised. What is it that constitutes good teaching? I am still trying to answer Holloway's essential questions: What makes good teaching and how can we know? To limit the question to writing hardly simplifies it at all.

Chapter Four

Environments for Active Learning: A Vygotskian Perspective

During my first summer of graduate school, I took four semester-long courses, each condensed into five or six weeks, each based on a set of pedagogical assumptions that I now reject. One, a course on Milton, met for two hours of lecture per day, five days a week, for five weeks. We "did," or perhaps more accurately, were scheduled to do, all the English poetry, much of the English prose including the divorce tracts, midterm and final papers, four five-page reviews of four book-length studies of Milton, a midterm exam, and a final take-home exam. (During the same semester I took Shakespeare—fifteen plays, et cetera, et cetera.) From eight to ten each morning, we listened to the professor drone on and on about texts most of us had not finished trying to read.

I remember dutifully forcing myself to eyeball and vocalize the words of *Paradise Lost,* struggling to wrest some kind of sense from what seemed to me to be labyrinthine syntax. By the time I finished a few lines, I realized, even when I understood them, that I had no idea of what that bramble had to do with what I had read earlier on the same page. I believed that death for me as a graduate student in English was imminent. I was terrified.

Then one day our professor did not appear in class; out of town hunting for a house to take a position at a prestigious university, we learned. We had a substitute for three days, a well-known Milton scholar, John S. Diekhoff. Instead of telling us what we *should* make of Milton's work, he asked what we *did* make of it. And he seemed to mean it. Why, he asked, did we think Adam had failed to obey the command of God. Why indeed, I wondered. If Adam were truly naive,

---

This chapter appeared in a slightly different form in Lee Odell, Ed., *Theory and practice in the teaching of writing: Rethinking the discipline,* (1993). Carbondale: Southern Illinois University Press. Copyright © 1993 by the Board of Trustees, Southern Illinois University. Used by permission.

as Milton claimed, why should he believe God's warning? If he were truly naive, how could he possibly understand what might await him outside the Garden?

These, it turned out, were not the questions Diekhoff had in mind. But he allowed them, encouraged them. We turned to some of the relevant passages concerning the warnings to Adam and Eve. I still remember how excited I was that Milton's syntax had *cleared up.* I could read it with only minimal difficulty. It was as though scales had fallen from my eyes. Later I reread the poem with interest and greater awareness of what was going on and of how the pieces fit together.

Even at the time, I recognized that this effect was more than serendipitous. In the more than 30 years since, I have had ample opportunity to think about it. The conceptual framework through which I examine it now allows me to see that in the first hour of class, Diekhoff had changed the learning environment radically. He refused the despot's throne and took instead the role of learned and empathetic counselor. He allowed our ideas, no matter how poorly conceived, to become a legitimate part of the conversation about *Paradise Lost.* In doing that, he allowed us an important degree of control over classroom events as our ideas became the focus of discussion. At the same time, this counselor retained control. We were still dealing with the themes and structures of Milton's work.

ENVIRONMENTAL AND OTHER MODES OF TEACHING

What Diekhoff did is basic to what I have called elsewhere environmental teaching (Hillocks, 1984, 1986a), by which I mean teaching that creates environments to induce and support active learning of complex strategies that students are not capable of using on their own. It is based on the assumption that teaching need not await development of students for learning to occur, but that, in Vygotsky's (1978) terms, "learning precedes development." In addition, it assumes that learning must take place in the "zone of proximal development," defined by Vygotsky as "the distance between the actual developmental level as determined by independent problem-solving and the level of potential development as determined through problem-solving under adult guidance or in collaboration with more capable peers" (p. 86). Finally, it assumes that teachers can create environments that support students as they engage in these complex tasks.

Such teaching stands in sharp contrast to at least two other instructional modes: the traditional mode that I have called "presentational" and what I have called the "natural process" mode. The first assumes that knowledge can be imparted by teacher or text directly to students prior to engagement in writing and that mastery can be achieved without the support of special teaching structures, such as peer-group collaboration, even when the knowledge imparted involves learning the use of complex strategies. The composite professor at the beginning of Chapter Two illustrates this mode of instruction. It is important to note that not all presentational teachers hold negative attitudes about their students.

Those advocating the second mode, what I have called "natural process," reject the use of models, the assignment of topics for writing, and learning the "types" or structures of writing such as the "paragraph" or compare/contrast essay. Some supporters of this mode believe that students should find their own topics and structures, that they should engage in the process of writing, receiving comments from peers as they work through multiple drafts toward a final version that will have developed its own organic structure (Graves, 1983). They believe that students learn best when left to develop naturally. As Schön (1987) points out, however, "picking up a practice on one's own has the advantage of freedom. . . . But it also has the disadvantage of requiring each student to reinvent the wheel, gaining little or nothing from the accumulated experience of others" (p. 37).

This natural process group has made three important breaks with the traditional "presentational" mode of instruction. First, it rejects the possibility of imparting knowledge about writing directly through lectures and textbooks without engaging the students in writing. Second, it focuses attention on the need for knowing and using general writing processes and provides general procedures for prewriting, revising, giving and receiving feedback, and so forth. Third, and perhaps most important, the natural process mode insists on the need to develop positive dispositions toward writing.

The environmental mode shares certain features with the first two but stands in sharp contrast to both. As Applebee (1986) has pointed out, it shares process with natural process. While it recognizes the importance of making general writing process an integral part of instruction, it moves well beyond general processes to focus on what Smagorinsky and Smith (1992) call "task-specific knowledge," the processes entailed in particular writing tasks. Nor does it take a laissez-faire approach to process. On the contrary, it places great responsibility on the teacher to develop materials and activities that will engage students in processes requisite to particular writing tasks.

In this, it shares with "presentational" approaches the recognition that success in various writing tasks requires specific knowledge. However, it contrasts sharply with the presentational in both the kinds of knowledge presented and the way that knowledge is presented. Presentational approaches focus almost exclusively on what Berlin (1984) calls "arrangement" in current-traditional rhetoric (the arrangement of elements in forms of discourse and in the paragraph and through the principles of unity, coherence, and emphasis). This knowledge is presented in lecture form, generally as a body of rules to be followed and examples to be emulated. Environmental approaches, in contrast, provide environments that support students in learning strategies for developing both the content and form of discourse. Rather than lecture on the procedures to follow, this approach engages students in the necessary processes, for example, generating criteria for formal definitions, examining data to develop interpretive generalizations.

Further, the environmental mode assumes with Vygotsky (1978) that students may operate in tutorials, in teacher-led discussions (provided they are true discussions), or in peer groups well above their normal levels when provided with support appropriate to their current understanding. At the same time, the environmental mode shares with natural process the insistence on engagement, recognizing that without it no amount of support will enable reluctant students to work beyond their current independent levels.

Although the environmental mode shares certain features with the other modes, the differences among them appear to result in sharp differences in the quality of student writing. My synthesis of research on these three modes of teaching, summarized in the Appendix, indicates that the presentational mode of instruction had the least impact on changing students' writing, with posttest scores only slightly better than pretest scores. The natural process groups made considerably more progress but remained well below the average gain for all studies included in the analysis. The environmental groups proved to have 2.3 times the effect of the natural process.

When John Diekhoff entered our Milton class that hot August day, his questions energized us. He knew that questions concerning Adam's motivation would be accessible to us, would engender some level of controversy, and would lead to more complex questions about Milton's theology and the structure of the poem. He transformed the class. At the same time, Diekhoff's seeds of transformation fell on fertile ground. We were, after all, an eager group of graduate students, hoping to become professionals in English. We had selected the course on Milton, had already struggled with the text, and were committed to the project of interpreting it. A group of students with such a rich combination of positive dispositions toward the subject is a luxury that most teachers of writing do not have.

For most teachers of writing, at whatever level, creating environments for active learning is nowhere near the relatively easy task it was for John Diekhoff. Sometimes such environments seem to occur in classrooms serendipitously. However, my experience and that of my students indicates that maintaining them regularly requires careful, creative planning and reflective practice. Before moving to an examination of a classroom discussion, let us look at what such teaching entails.

FEATURES OF ENVIRONMENTS FOR ACTIVE LEARNING

In 1986, I described the environmental mode in operational terms as "characterized by (1) clear and specific objectives, e.g., to increase the use of specific detail and figurative language; (2) materials and problems selected to engage students with each other in specifiable processes important to some particular aspect of writing; and (3) activities, such as small-group problem-centered discussions, conducive to high levels of peer interaction concerning specific tasks" (Hillocks, 1986a, p. 122). These three dimensions or characteristics of instruction identified the studies included in the category of environmental teaching. Although this operational definition was useful to the small community of researchers who were familiar with the implications of the terms of the definition, it was not very useful to anyone who wished to put it into action.

Indeed, there are at least four important dimensions of this mode of teaching that lie buried in my description. First, not only are the task objectives clear to teachers, but they are operationally clear to students. Second, the materials and problems engage students because they have been selected in view of (1) what students are able to do, (2) the likelihood of their interest to students, and (3) their power to engage students as real-world problems. Third, students engage in complex tasks with support from materials, teachers, and/or peers before they proceed to independent work with such tasks. Fourth, students develop a stake or sense of ownership in the classroom proceedings because their ideas and opinions become the focus of classroom activity. Let me examine each of these in greater detail.

Goals and Objectives

The approaches to teaching that seemed to have the most powerful effects on student writing, as revealed in the synthesis mentioned earlier (Hillocks, 1986a), always had clear, specific objectives. Further, instructors appear to have made objectives operationally clear to the students by modeling the procedures, coaching students through them in the early stages, or using specially designed activities to facilitate learning the new procedures.

For example, in a series of studies (Hillocks, Kahn, & Johannessen, 1983; Hillocks, 1989, in progress b) I have been focusing on a variety of approaches to teaching students to write extended, analytic definitions. The extended definitions involve comparing and contrasting cases to develop a series of criteria that delimit some particular, relatively abstract concept.

Such definitions, I believe, are important because they lie at the heart of analysis, argument, and the dialectical processes that drive inquiry in every field. They are ubiquitous, appearing in the work of philosophers (e.g., Aristotle, *Nichomachean Ethics* [1947]); literary critics (e.g., Northrop Frye, *Anatomy of Criticism* [1957]; M. M. Bakhtin, *The Dialogic Imagination* [1981]; Robert Scholes, *Textual Power* [1985]); psychologists seeking to understand various cognitive phenomena (e.g., Stein and Trabasso, "What's in a Story: An Approach to Comprehension and Instruction" [1982]); composition researchers (e.g.,

Hayes and Flower, "Identifying the Organization of Writing Processes" [1980]); and so forth. They are of utmost importance in jurisprudence (e.g., the Karen Quinlan case turns on a definition of the right to privacy) and any legislation that stipulates the conditions under which a law may be invoked (e.g., what constitutes first-degree murder).

One sequence of activities intended to help students learn strategies necessary for defining complex concepts provides students with a series of scenarios involving courageous and seemingly courageous actions. They were developed on the basis of Aristotle's ideas of courage in the *Nichomachean Ethics*. In this activity, groups of three or four students were to examine each scenario, make a decision about whether the actor was or was not courageous, and write a rule or criterion for guiding decisions in other cases.

Although students are quite able to make decisions about whether or not the actors in the scenarios are courageous, they do not use explicit criteria in presenting definitions (McGhee-Bidlack, 1991) and have considerable difficulty in devising them. This situation suggests that the proposed activity will be in the students' "zone of proximal development." The objective of the activity is to help students formulate specific criteria for determining whether or not an action is courageous. (The ultimate goal of this activity and others in the sequence is that students learn the process of formulating such criteria and apply it when they need to define abstract concepts.)

To make this objective operationally clear, teachers led discussions of one scenario and helped students develop a criterion by which they might be guided in future decision making. The scenario for this teacher-led discussion, originally developed by Elizabeth Kahn, puts Lois Lane dangling by her fingers from the edge of a 30-story building, while Superman flies to her rescue. He grabs her just in time and carries her safely to the ground. The question for students is whether or not Superman or Lois Lane might be considered courageous.

In the ensuing discussion, some students argue that Superman is courageous because he rescues Lois Lane. Others recognize that although Superman rescues Lois Lane, his act may not be courageous while Lois's might be. As the discussion develops, students usually decide that Superman is not courageous because the task involves no real risk or danger for him because of his supernatural powers. Lois Lane, on the other hand, who has no supernatural powers, refuses to panic and may be courageous because she overcomes her fear and remains clinging to the building. Occasionally, students argue that she had no choice and, therefore, is not courageous.

Student analysis, as it stands at this point, applies to only the particular incident. Additional discussion is usually necessary to reformulate student ideas as a rule or criterion. The question becomes whether or not the idea applies to everyone, or only to Superman. If it applies across the board, then how should the criterion be stated? Teachers lead the discussion until some rule emerges, perhaps one such as the following: "An action cannot be considered courageous unless it involves serious danger or risk to the person performing it." The purpose of such a discussion is to make the goal of the students' small-group discussions operationally clear, to give them a more precise idea of what their task is in small groups.

Once students begin working on additional problems in their small groups, the teachers circulate to various groups to determine from student talk whether they seem to understand the goal and, when necessary, to make suggestions and ask questions that will enhance understanding of the goal. At the same time, the group activity is itself an aid to understanding the goal of the larger sequence of instruction, in this case, the writing of an extended definition.

Selection of Materials and Problems

To promote successful peer-group and independent work, the problems and materials selected must be appropriate for the students, challenging yet within the realm of possibility when appropriate support is available, within the "zone of proximal development." If students can already do the tasks independently, ordinarily there is little point in having them do the tasks in groups. On the other hand, the tasks should not be so difficult that students cannot handle them at all.

In a study by Carol Sager (1973), sixth-grade students learned scales that they subsequently used to rate compositions. Working in groups, they then developed ideas for revising compositions that they had rated as poor. Sager believed that for this activity to be successful, the materials used had to be within the reach of sixth graders. For example, working with a scale for judging elaboration in writing, the students were asked to read a story entitled "The Green Martian Monster." The story was comparable to pieces that might have been written by one of the sixth graders in the class, although it was not written by any of them. They were told that it had received a zero on elaboration.

The Green Martian Monster

> The Green Martian Monster descended on the USA. He didn't have a mouth. "Who goes?" they said. There was no answer. So they shot him and he died.

Clearly, this is a simple story. However, the task related to it is relatively challenging. Students were to list as many reasons as they could think of why a "mouthless, green Martian monster might land in the USA," list possible places the Martian might have landed, list possibilities for who "they" might have been, list all the thoughts "they" might have had, and so forth. This is a task that these inner-city sixth graders could do well and enthusiastically, with support coming in the form of earlier teacher modeling, the prompts listed above, peer group discussion, and teacher coaching.

There is no algorithm that I know of for arriving at the appropriate level of complexity in developing such tasks. Teachers who listen to their students and observe what they can and cannot do in classroom discussions, in dealing with texts, in writing, and so forth, will have innumerable clues as to what may or may not be appropriate. However, making the initial judgment about appropriateness remains an art, but an art the results of which are subject to careful scrutiny. Anyone who tries new materials, including new textbooks, must introduce that new material with a fair degree of trepidation, eagerness to see "how it works," and a willingness to scrap the new material and try something else.

Any trial of new materials is a "frame experiment." The courage scenarios alluded to above were piloted by a variety of teachers in a variety of settings over a period of years as well as in informal studies before they were ever incorporated into a formal research design. It is important to judge new materials in terms not only of their level of challenge to students, but in terms of their interest for students. Sager reports that her students would discuss compositions at their recess breaks, continuing arguments about how a piece should have been rated or how it might have been improved. Similarly, students responding to the courage scenarios often engaged in heated debates about whether one character might be considered courageous or not. Groups would occasionally split on their decisions and write different criteria, with different factions supporting each.

Finally, the materials and activities are selected for their power to engage students in dealing with problems of the kind we encounter outside textbooks, problems that are fuzzy, not so clear that only one solution is possible. Whenever a problem has a single solution, discussion, and probably learning, ends when someone finds the solution. When problems are real, they are amenable to a wide variety of solutions, as are a definition of courage or a revision of "The Green Martian Monster." With such problems, discussion and learning can continue indefinitely. Undoubtedly, there is a place in education for algorithmic problem solving. But small-group discussion of the kind intended here is pretty clearly not it.

Providing Support for Learning

Key to the success of this mode of instruction is that it engages students in the use of the complex processes to be learned. That engagement is made possible by providing a variety of supports at the outset and gradually withdrawing the supports as students appear to become more fluent in the use of the strategies. Historically, teachers and textbooks have recognized the need to provide for the learning of complex tasks in writing. To do that, however, they have focused on the surface features and have developed methods for teaching the "basic skills": sounding out words, spelling, parsing sentences, punctuating, writing simple sentences, constructing paragraphs according to certain formulas, and so forth. In all such isolated skill practice, attention is fragmented, directed to bits and pieces of information that require little or no integration.

Underlying this basic skills approach to simplifying writing and reading tasks is a building-block conception of reading and writing. The idea is that if once you learn the lower-level blocks of which larger compositions are made, it is possible to string together the blocks and produce more elaborate compositions. Sometimes whole curricula are based on this notion. Many years ago I heard a gentleman present a new composition curriculum that was in use at a high school near the school where I taught. He announced with considerable pride that the ninth-grade composition curriculum would be based on the sentence. The tenth-grade curriculum would be based on the paragraph, the eleventh-grade on the 500-word theme, and the twelfth-grade on the 1,000-word theme. The idea is that once students learn to write sentences, they can add them up to write paragraphs, and so on.

Unfortunately, things are not that simple. When we spell a word in a piece of writing, we write a word that is, at once, part of a sentence, part of a paragraph, and part of a larger piece of writing intended to have some effect on an audience, if only the writer. Teaching focused on the so-called building blocks of writing tends to ignore such complexity. Comparable teaching of piano might require the would-be pianist to practice all possible scales, all manner of chords, various kinds of techniques such as *staccato* and *legato*, without ever asking the hopeful performer to put some of those things together in a meaningful piece of music.

What I have called environmental teaching engages students in integrated, "whole-language" tasks that involve complex processes. Because the tasks undertaken are more complex than students can be expected to manage on their own, this kind of instruction uses two important kinds of supports to secure student engagement: what I will call structural support and small-peer-group support.

Structural Support. By structural support I mean the provision of aid or the restructuring of the task so as to reduce its complexity while retaining its essential features. For example, writing an extended definition of an abstract concept entails finding or inventing examples, comparing and contrasting them, devising criteria, and so forth. One of the most difficult parts of that task is devising the criteria. One way of simplifying that task without changing its essential features is to provide examples from which the criteria are to be developed. Providing the examples allows students to concentrate on devising criteria and implies the kinds of criteria to develop.

Although some part of the task is taken over by the instructional environment, students must still use key strategies demanded by the task. As students become more adept at the task, the teacher withdraws part of the structure. That is, in later stages of teaching, students must undertake all phases of the task. In the case of definitions, for example, students must eventually invent their own examples as well as generate criteria and put all of that together into some sort of writing.

Another example is Lynn Troyka's (1973; Troyka & Nudelman, 1975) work, which provides materials on argument designed for college freshmen in basic writing classes. Troyka's materials focus on a series of issues that can be seen from a variety of perspectives: pollution of waterways by a chemical plant in a community where employment is a problem, purchase of a fleet of taxicabs for service in a particular community, a prison uprising. Each set of material presents the situation. For example, there is to be a meeting including officials from the chemical plant thought to pollute local waterways, officials of the tourist industry that has been harmed by the pollution, community members who need work, and so forth. The purpose of the meeting is to resolve the difficulty of pollution from the chemical plant. Additional materials present sets of data relative to the issues involved and roles to be played by students in the proposed meeting (each role representing a different set of interests involved in the issue).

The structure of the learning environment established by the teacher and the materials simplifies the task of developing an appropriate argument by taking over certain parts of the task, while engaging students in others. The learning environment presents the situation, the points of view involved, and the data to be used. Students need not find and sift through data about some issue that they do not understand. Rather, they may devote their attention to the more limited task of developing a solid argument using appropriate grounds to support a claim that comes out of a particular point of view. As they present arguments to one another, students will see how those coming at the same issue from a different perspective will respond to their arguments. In the process, they learn more about developing a complex argument.

Eventually, students will have to move to finding their own problems, points of view, and evidence. Having done the simpler activities first appears to provide frameworks and schemata for developing new arguments. Troyka's research at the college level, Hamel's (1990; E. M. Anderson & Hamel, 1991) work at the high school level, and McCann's (1995) work at three grade levels strongly suggest that this is the case for argument. The results of research related to a variety of other writing tasks strongly indicate the efficacy of this approach to structuring learning environments to make complex tasks more accessible to more students (Hillocks, 1986a).

Small-Peer-Group Support. Peer-group discussion or collaborative talk, usually in small groups, is the second essential feature, perhaps the *sine qua non,* of what I have called environmental teaching. Results of the synthesis of research on teaching writing (Hillocks, 1984, 1986a), summarized in the Appendix, strongly indicate that problem-centered peer-group interaction, the major feature differentiating these collaborative small groups from others in the study, is chiefly responsible for the gains made by the environmental groups.

Any teacher who has ever used small groups as a standard part of classroom activity knows that the rate of active participation in small groups far exceeds that in teacher-led discussions. Students who never contribute at all in teacher-led discussions may become very active participants in small groups. The rate of on-task response in some small groups has been as high as 10 to 15 responses per minute in some studies (e.g., Hillocks et al., 1983). In small problem-centered group discussions, students feel free to discuss actively and to build upon each other's ideas. Further, their interaction appears to generate more response and the careful examination of ideas.

Teacher-led discussion (TLD) in most classrooms, by way of contrast, frequently, but not necessarily, inhibits interaction. The desks are often in rows, so the students must speak to the backs of other students' heads. Nearly all student comments are funneled through the teacher and are seldom relayed back to other students. The number of turns available for individuals to respond is severely limited by the much larger size of the group in whole-class TLD. The willingness of many students to venture an idea aloud in front of a group of 20 to 30 peers and the teacher is often far less than it might be in a group of 3 to 5 peers. This is not an argument for eliminating TLD. The introduction and follow-up to small group work may very profitably be TLD.

Coaching Small Groups. Since I first used small-group discussion with ninth graders in 1960, such discussions have been an integral part of every class I have taught from seventh grade to graduate level. My own experience over those years and that of other teachers indicate that teachers must continue to support and coach if the small-group interaction is to have the kind of effect we hope it will. Certainly small-group discussions can flounder. The problem may be too difficult. Students may be distracted by an imminent holiday or school event. They may be frustrated by some relatively minor point in the problem. To insure that small-group discussions go smoothly, the teacher may circulate from group to group, listening in for a moment or two, perhaps asking a question to redirect attention, perhaps suggesting an example, coaching students as their discussions are in progress but without taking over the central tasks of the discussions. Because the task is slightly beyond what students can do independently, in the "zone of proximal development," coaching must be readily available.

Student Ownership

The activities that drive environmental teaching are ordinarily planned or invented by teachers. But not all activities invented by teachers result in what I have called environmental teaching. Only activities that result in high levels of interaction among students in regard to the materials and problems qualify. When the levels of interaction are high, and the interaction is *among* students rather than between the teacher and students in recitation fashion, student ideas and opinions become the focus of attention and substantially control the direction of classroom talk. This interaction gives students the necessary stake in what is happening. They become the authorities through their ideas.

The teacher's role is to coach and prompt, to ask questions that push at the edges of student ideas, and to sustain the interchange among students. If the teacher provides authoritative answers to the problems under discussion, the interaction among students ceases and learning is curtailed. For some teachers this appears to be a very difficult role. In one study, for example, observers noted one teacher who, when a disagreement arose among students in small-group discussions, would provide an authoritative answer. As the teacher moved from one group to another, he effectively ended real discussion. Students saw no point in pursuing the problem when they could see that the teacher would eventually provide "the right" answer. For one reason or another, this teacher could see no value in allowing students to work through the problem on their own (Hillocks, 1989).

Observations of hundreds of instances of group work indicate that for this kind of learning environment to have greatest impact, student ideas must remain the focus of attention. The goal of this work is always learning the strategies involved in the processes. The goal is not to find some "correct" solution to the problems at hand, a correct definition of courage, for example, if there were one. The problems are fuzzy and admit to a variety of solutions. The best days of group work that I have observed occur when groups derive conflicting solutions, report to the class as a whole, and begin to explore the reasons underlying the conflicts. The disagreements are the stuff of learning. That is what Graff (1992a) has in mind when he talks about teaching the conflicts in theoretical perspectives. When students are encouraged to disagree and to defend their ideas reasonably, they develop a very meaningful stake in classroom proceedings.

Students can develop a stake in what is happening in many other ways. They can make choices about topics they will study, texts they will read, data they will examine, as did McCabe's seventh graders. For example, Deborah Stern, whose English program at Prologue Learning Center in Chicago was recognized by the National Council of Teachers of English as one of five outstanding programs for at-risk students in the United States and Canada, typically gives her students many different choices about what they will study. Her students are young adults who have dropped out of public schools. Nearly all the women in her classes are mothers. In one class, all had seen a friend or family member zipped by police into a body bag. Their young lives have encompassed drugs, prostitution, gangs, crime of various kinds, and poverty.

Not surprisingly, when given choices of what to study, Deborah reports that they usually choose to study issues that concern them, "sex and violence" for example. With Deborah's guidance, they choose texts that they will read as a group and texts that they will read individually. They copy the lyrics of rap songs and bring them to class for study. When they write extended definitions of violence, they discuss examples from their own lives, from the rap songs they admire, and from the newspaper stories they have collected. The fact that students have choices does not mean that Deborah has relinquished control. On the contrary, students make choices within a carefully thought-out rationale that begins with what she wants for her students: "to have some tools to think about the chaos of their lives. Sex and violence sometimes seems beyond their control. If we look at it here deeply, at least they may have something to help them understand what's going on and what choices they have" (personal interview, 1992).

Making choices of topics and texts, however, is not essential to students' having a stake in their own learning, as some theorists would have us believe. What is essential is structuring the learning environment so that students can gain entry to the ideas and materials and can contribute to the group's and their own understanding of whatever is at issue.

THE POWER OF ENVIRONMENTAL TEACHING

The presence of all these supports, however, does not explain why problem-centered small-group discussion has such a powerful effect on learning. Let us turn next to an excerpt from a transcript of a small-group discussion that involves four juniors in a small-town high school. Their teacher had volunteered to conduct a pilot study of the materials to be used later in a more formal study. What follows is the discussion of one of twelve scenarios, each describing an action that the students might or might not consider courageous. The scenarios are based on Aristotle's *Nichomachean Ethics,* each prompted by a different distinction Aristotle makes in defining courage. The instructional goal for students is to learn strategies for developing criteria, strategies they will be able to use in developing their own definitions of other concepts. The important goal of this activity is for them to develop criteria, not to agree with Aristotle. (In fact, many of the students in a variety of studies undertaken using these scenarios do not agree with Aristotle. Many, for example, take considerations of steadfastness in the face of great danger to be of greater importance than considerations of moral rectitude. For many, breaking into a bank to steal a fortune in the face of imminent danger is the epitome of courage. I am pleased to report that not all students agree and very heated discussions often occur.)

The class, of which the following discussion is a small part, begins with the teacher leading students in a discussion of the scenario about Superman described earlier. After a brief discussion comparable to the one earlier in this chapter, the teacher divides the class into their groups for discussion of the scenarios. In the following excerpt, four students are engaged in discussing scenario #6. From the beginning of their talk, they refer to the second scenario.

> Scenario #6: On Monday the fire had started on the oil derrick far out at sea. By Wednesday the men working on the derrick had been rescued, but the fire was out of control. "Red" Granger and his men were called in to fight the dangerous fire. "Red" and his men had fought many oil fires. They had the training and experience to put out the fire. Are "Red" and his men courageous when they fight the fire?

> Scenario #2: Out of the corner of his eye the Secret Service agent spotted a gun aimed at the President. Instantly, he threw himself in the line of fire, taking the bullet meant for the President. Was the agent's act of jumping in front of the bullet courageous?

Scenario #6 is based on the Aristotelian idea that the high levels of experience and the superior equipment of mercenary soldiers make their actions only seemingly courageous. Their experience and equipment provide them with such a high level of confidence that they need not overcome fear. In Aristotle's view, courage has to do with the balance between feelings of fear and confidence. If the mercenary has less to fear, there is less reason to consider him courageous. The students come close to a comparable analysis.

Scenario #2 comes within the limits of the Aristotelian idea of courage, although it is possible that the agent's act is not deliberative, given the information available, and comes close to the foolhardy. Few high school students made this argument, however. Interestingly, though the scenario generates little discussion of its own, it generates far more when it is considered in contrast to some other scenario, as it is below.

When I began my ongoing study of environmental teaching and small-group discussion, I believed that the changes in student writing came about because of the process of inquiry in which students engaged. They make comparisons and contrasts. They report what they see, make interpretations, ask questions, bring prior knowledge to bear, develop analogies, test their ideas, and all the while move in the direction of a solution to a fuzzy problem. One might argue that they use all the basic strategies of inquiry and that practice in using those strategies carries over into writing about other concepts.

As I began examining the transcripts from several pilot studies, I began to see that, at their best, the student discussions were extended arguments. Indeed, we can examine the entire discussion below in terms of Toulmin's (1958) analysis of argumentative structures. Toulmin lays out the basic structure of argument as including claims, grounds, warrants, backing, and qualifications. In the discussion below, the students are working toward a statement of backing for a warrant: "A person is not courageous when they're trained and familiar with a situation that is usual for them." The basic argument developed by this group, in abbreviated form, goes as follows:

CLAIM:	"Red" and his men are not courageous.
GROUNDS:	They "had fought many oil fires. They had the training and experience to put out the fire . . . because they're experienced . . . they're not actually putting themselves at risk." (Keith)
WARRANT:	"A person is not courageous when they're trained and familiar with a situation that is usual for them."
BACKING:	Courage requires steadfastness in the face of great personal risk (an idea developed earlier in the discussion). However, training and experience lessen the risk. The idea that experience and training reduce risk in some instances (but not that of the Secret Service agent) remains implicit in the discussion.

The following discussion moves in the direction of the criterion that serves as the warrant in the argument that "Red" and his men are not courageous. In the course of its development, many other claims enter, each of which appears to clarify group ideas about the major argument. In the early part of the discussion, students engage in an argument that helps them consider a number of issues that, on their own, they would likely not consider. (A study of individual responses to the set of scenarios indicates that students consider a far narrower range of responses when working alone.) The argument they conduct serves to refine their ideas throughout.

The argument comes to a head when Amy restates Keith's ideas, making the point a bit more forcefully and in basic form: "So this one is not courageous," she says. "They had the experience, so they're not doing anything out of the ordinary." In turn 16, Keith appears to build on the preceding turns in clarifying the distinction between the two scenarios. He points out the near certainty of harm in the Secret Service agent's action and the relative safety of the firefighter's. Let us turn, then, to the discussion itself.

1. SCOTT: God, all these contradict the other ones.
2. KEITH: Yeah.
3. SCOTT: Six contradicts the one with the agent, the security agent.
4. KEITH: I don't think they're courageous because they're experienced, but they're not actually putting themselves at risk. They're just doing another job. It's not actual . . .
5. SCOTT: What did we have for number 2?
6. KEITH: Yes.
7. SCOTT: Yes. Then this one has to be yes. It's a job.
8. KEITH: No, not necessarily.

At the outset, Scott recognizes the connection of this scenario to what preceded, making the continuity of context explicit and setting up the pattern of contrast for the discussion. He makes the contrast specific in turn 3. Keith makes a claim about the action in turn 4, provides grounds for his claim, and provides a statement implying the warrant that ties the claim to the grounds, the major parts of an argument in Toulmin's terms. In turn 5, Scott indicates that he will treat this analogically, asking what the group decision was for scenario #2. He states the analogy briefly but fails to see that he has made doing a job the criterion. But Amy objects:

9. AMY: No, it's different. You're not putting yourself in front of a bullet.
10. KEITH: Yeah. Chances are that some people are going to die in car wrecks every day. Just because you get in a car doesn't mean you're courageous.

In the above turn, Amy disagrees with Scott and presents grounds that pinpoint a major difference between the "jobs." Then Keith develops a different analogy based on Amy's point, taken to an extreme, to emphasize the difference in the likelihood of hazard.

11. SCOTT: But really, it's their job to do something like that. And you have to be courageous to take a job like that in the first place.
12. SUE: He has fought many oil fires, it says.
13. AMY: (ironically) Yeah, that guy was going in front of many bullets.

Here, Scott seems to maintain his original point but switches from the action in question to the action of taking the job with no experience "in the first place." Sue refers to the printed text for grounds to reinforce the point about experience. Amy's ironic comment indicates the impossibility of the agent's gaining experience by "going in front of many bullets." Next, Sue goes on to point out differences in the relevant conditions of the two scenarios.

14. SUE: This emphasizes their training and their fighting many of them. The other one was just like I saw them out of the corner of my eye.
15. AMY: So this one is not courageous. They had the experience, so they're not doing anything out of the ordinary.
16. KEITH: Yeah, even if the bullet doesn't kill him, he's pretty sure he's going to get hurt.

In her turn above, Amy attempts to analyze the difference that Sue has focused on. Amy provides a claim based on the preceding discussion, indicates the grounds, and provides a different statement implying a warrant. The students continue to disagree for a few more turns, testing each other's claims by relating them to other scenarios or to their prior knowledge.

17. AMY: Right. (agreeing with Keith)
18. SCOTT: Yeah, but in number five, when a person goes to Vietnam or something like that and after he stays there a course of time, he's well trained in that too. Does that make him not courageous anymore?
19. AMY: No, he's not courageous to begin with because of the reason we gave.
20. SCOTT: No, I mean if a person was in Vietnam for a year . . .
21. AMY: No, we're still saying that he could still do something that would be courageous. We're talking about [unclear]
22. SCOTT: I was getting into death. I don't want to get into death. When I get into death, I don't know what I'm talking about, man. I'll be rattling off stuff.

In turn 18, Scott calls on prior knowledge for a contrasting example supporting his idea that at some point in their careers experienced people do not have experience. This point and the problems surrounding it eventually are lost. In turn 19, Amy refers to an earlier scenario about a person who volunteered to fight because he thought it was expected of him.

Below, in turn 23, Keith indicates some level of agreement with Scott. (His tone of voice appears to be one of mollification.) Sue brings the focus back to the task, and in turn 27 she begins to formulate a criterion, referring to a criterion the group had developed for scenario #4. The interesting change in what follows is that, having worked through their disagreements, they abandon their argument mode and switch to a collaborative one.

23. KEITH: I think anybody goes over there and they're well trained and stuff like that.
24. SCOTT: Yeah, like for a course of time.
25. SUE: OK, this one is . . .
26. SCOTT: They've mostly seen everything that has to be seen.
27. SUE: A courageous person will . . . Same as number 4?
28. AMY: No.
29. SCOTT: Let's read the book when it comes out.
30. AMY: He's not really in that much danger because of his training.
31. KEITH: I think they're a little bit courageous, but they're not . . .
32. AMY: But it's their job and they're being trained for it, so they're being trained for it. And they put out similar fires, too.
33. KEITH: They're not facing certain death or certain harm or whatever.
34. SUE: Something they are trained and familiar with? [asking about criterion phrasing]
35. KEITH: Yeah.
36. SUE: What would you say, "A person is not courageous when they are trained and familiar with . . ."?
37. AMY: A situation.
38. SUE: Usually a fatal situation?
39. AMY: No, they're trained.
40. KEITH: So it's not going to be a fatal situation to them.
41. AMY: Yeah, they're going to know how to take steps to make it . . .
42. SUE: OK, what if you say, "A person is not courageous when they're trained and familiar with a situation"?
43. KEITH: Well, it's usual for them. I think that's the big thing.
44. AMY: It's something they're used to.
45. SUE: So should I write that?
46. KEITH: Yeah.

Throughout this section, the students collaborate, building the shared criterion. In turn 30, Amy nearly makes explicit the idea that training reduces risk. A bit later, in turn 33, Keith makes clear the distinction the group has worked on in turns 8 to 16, 30, and 32. In the next turn, Sue asks about phrasing the criterion. From this point, the group collaborates on constructing the criterion that Sue records. In the process, they come very close to the way Aristotle expresses it.

Scott's contributions, though they seem to go against the mainstream of the discussion, have made significant contributions to it. His initial comment, "all these contradict the other ones," sets in motion the strategy of contrasting and comparing, a strategy that is followed throughout, even in the final collaborative turns of the discussion. Second, his insistence on considering the courage of people undertaking something "in the first place," without the benefit of training, helps the group to make the important qualification that what is a "usual" situation for trained people may be quite dangerous for others.

Clearly all students involved have made important contributions to the discussion. Working together, the group has advanced its members' understanding of one dimension of courage from a rather general impression to a more complex and more explicitly defined concept. However, two important questions still remain. First, how is it that students who are unable to develop abstract criteria independently are able to do so in a group? In a sense, the group clarified its own thinking. But how does that clarification take place? When the individuals in this particular group were presented with a comparable scenario involving the way expertise diminishes danger, none of them made a response comparable to the criterion they developed as a group. In fact, of over 250 high school students responding independently to the courage scenarios, fewer than 3% made use of the criterion that the group above devised. What happens in the group?

A VYGOTSKIAN PERSPECTIVE

Vygotsky's (1978) *Mind in Society* provides some insight into the processes at work here. First of all, although the students, working independently, do not make use of the criteria that the group manages to state explicitly in the discussion above, they are able to make decisions about whether people in each situation presented are or are not courageous. And they are able to provide concrete reasons for their decisions. For example, in turn 7 Scott stipulates that these men are courageous because they are doing a job, a job he associates with the job in scenario #2. For Scott, it is a fairly concrete matter. In turn 9 Amy gives another concrete reason, this time, however, to support the opposite point of view. "No," she says, "it's different. You're not putting yourself in front of a bullet." The task, then, is not completely out of the reach of the students involved. They are able to make decisions supported by relatively concrete reasons.

The task is within Vygotsky's "zone of proximal development" for these students. If students were unable to make judgments about the courage of characters in the scenarios and give reasons in their support, they certainly would be unable to arrive at an explicit rule even with the aid of the scenarios and peer discussion. In this instance, students can make such decisions, have the guidance of the instructional set and the support of peer-group discussion, and are able, therefore, to devise explicit criteria.

The question remains, however, of how it is that the students are able to clarify their thinking in this group discussion. By what mechanism are they able to arrive at an abstract principle that is new to all of them? Here Vygotsky's idea of "mediation" is useful. Vygotsky (1978) argues that language or signs enable children to move beyond the direct perception of data within a sensory field. The use of signs or words enables children to "single out separate elements, thereby overcoming the natural structure of the sensory field and forming new (artificially introduced and dynamic) structural centers. The child begins to perceive the world not only through his eyes but also through his speech" (p. 32).

The same, of course, might be said of verbal fields, the kind of material under discussion by the students in the group above. The speech of the various students contributing to the discussion provides continually changing perspectives by establishing new structural centers. The changing of these structural centers appears to be what allows the development of the criterion at the end. For example, in the very first turn Scott moves away from the consideration of the details provided in the scenario to a generalization that requires the group to consider this scenario in contrast to all of the others. In turn 3 he focuses the contrast between scenario #6, the one in question, and scenario #2, the one about the security agent. In turn 4 Keith changes the structural center by focusing on experience and the fact that these men are "not actually putting themselves at risk."

Amy, in turn 9, makes use of what both boys have said previously. She uses contrast and develops a new structural center focusing on the difference between the experience of the firefighters and that of the Secret Service agent who must throw himself in the line of fire. Keith then provides a somewhat different structural center, enabling the students to bring in additional information from their experience about automobiles and automobile accidents. Next Sue focuses on the specific evidence of experience in the scenario: "He has fought many oil fires it says." Immediately following, Amy changes the structural center again by focusing on the difference between the Secret Service agent scenario and that of the firefighters with her sarcastic comment that implies the impossibility of gaining experience from throwing oneself in the line of fire. Indeed, almost every turn in the discussion serves the purpose of mediating new understandings or conceptions of the scenario. Simply the expression of alternative ideas provides possible perspectives from which to think about the events in question.

Recent research (Hillocks, in progress a; Smagorinsky, 1991) suggests that students, working on their own, are unable to examine an incident from a number of points of view and devise criteria related to their judgment of it before instruction. However, after the kind of instruction described above, they appear better able to think systematically about an example and to develop explicit criteria independently.

Vygotsky (1978) might call this movement from group to independent process the "internal reconstruction of an external operation" or "internalization" (p. 56). According to Vygotsky, internalization of processes takes place in the learner's "zone of proximal development" when the learners have been provided with guidance by skilled adults or peers. He points out that "the classics of psychological literature, such as the works by Binet and others, assume that development is always a prerequisite for learning and that if a child's mental functions (intellectual operations) have not matured to the extent that he is capable of learning a particular subject, then no instruction will prove useful" (p. 80). This assumption, according to Vygotsky, led to the fear that "premature instruction" would harm learners, perhaps even traumatizing them, thereby inhibiting future learning. In Vygotsky's view, these assumptions result in concentrating on "finding the lower threshold of learning ability" (p. 80).

However, as Vygotsky points out and as research on teaching writing indicates (Hillocks, 1986a), learning appears to precede development. That is, students are able to work at higher levels with the guidance and support of adults or the collaboration of peers than they can independently. The processes internalized during such guided or collaborative work provide for a new level of development. In Vygotsky's (1978) words, "the only 'good learning' is that which is in advance of development" (p. 89).

What appears to happen in environmental instruction, then, is that various components of the teaching provide an environment in which students can move well beyond the levels of their independent functioning. The higher-level processes made possible by the support of the instructional environment and externalized in the group collaboration become internalized and a part of the student's repertoire of strategies that can be called upon later in independent situations. As these processes take place, "learning awakens a variety of internal developmental processes that are able to operate only when the child is interacting with the people in his environment and in cooperation with his peers" (Vygotsky, 1978, p. 90).

I believe that something else is involved as well. When John Diekhoff came into our Milton class that very hot August day, my guess is he had something in mind besides engaging us in discussion of concepts important to the study of Milton. I am sure he hoped we would enjoy the process of thinking about Milton, that we would develop a disposition to think about such issues. In a sense that is what real teaching is all about, helping students learn to enjoy the process of thinking through complex problems because that gives them the power and the confidence to undertake new problems in new situations without the structure of the classroom environment.

Chapter Five

The Composing Process: A Model

When I first began teaching, teachers of writing had just moved beyond assuming that teaching grammar was tantamount to teaching writing. In my district, there was a standing order from the superintendent's office that every English teacher from ninth grade up was to maintain a file of each student's writing. Due to the efforts of the assistant superintendent, our supervisors expected to inspect the files and find evidence that students had written once a week. To allow this, our board had set the English class size at 22 for ninth grade and up. (Seventh and eighth graders were presumed to need grammar first, and those class sizes stayed at 29 to 33.) This nearly met the National Council of Teachers of English recommendation of 100 students per day. Unfortunately, that superintendent died shortly after my arrival, and teacher load mushroomed to 150 or more students per day, in five classes.

At the time, even with all the recommendations for "a theme a week," there was little recognition that learning to write was a matter of learning the processes of writing. As English teachers, we were expected only to make assignments, collect the results, comment on them, and file them for future inspection. And inspected they were. It was a start, at least.

Research over the last two and a half decades has indicated the benefits of involving students in what I will call the general writing processes. Even more important for substantial growth in writing is learning the more specific procedures required in a full range of particular writing tasks. What follows will examine a theoretical model of elements in the composing process, findings of research on processes in writing, the ideas of declarative and procedural knowledge, and the implications of all these for practice.

ELEMENTS IN THE COMPOSING PROCESS

Many teachers of writing act as though writing is best done under some sort of compulsion, involving surrender to mysterious psychic powers that take over the task of producing text. They believe that this state may be attained in a number of ways and order classroom activities accordingly, dimming lights, listening to emotive music, writing freely without inhibition, encouraging certain group encounter activities to raise the emotional awareness of the participants. I once witnessed a high school class in which the teacher had erected a tent in the middle of the floor. She asked her students to enter the tent in groups, hold hands, and meditate. She then asked them to write. Teachers talk about these activities as "getting the creative juices flowing." They are modern equivalents of invoking the muse, compulsive in the sense of giving up authority to the spirit that rules creation.

There is plenty of testimony that appears to support the idea of creation coming in an almost somnambulistic state. Bernard McCabe (1971) compiles evidence from several authors. My favorite story of this kind is from A. E. Housman (1933), who tells about the genesis of one poem.

> Having drunk a pint of beer at luncheon—beer is a sedative to the brain, and my afternoons are the least intellectual portion of my life—I would go out for a walk of two or three hours. As I went along, thinking of nothing in particular, only looking at things around me and following the progress of the seasons, there would flow into my mind, with sudden and unaccountable emotion, sometimes a line or two of verse, sometimes a whole stanza at once, accompanied, not preceded, by a vague notion of the poem which they were destined to form a part of. Then there would usually be a lull of an hour or so, then perhaps the spring would bubble up again. I say bubble up, because, so far as I could make out, the source of the suggestions thus proffered to the brain was an abyss which I have had occasion to mention, the pit of the stomach. When I got home I wrote them down, leaving gaps, and hoping that further inspiration might be forthcoming another day. Sometimes it was, if I took my walks in a receptive and expectant frame of mind; but sometimes the poem had to be taken in hand and completed by the brain, which was apt to be a matter of trouble and anxiety, involving trial and disappointment, and sometimes ending in failure. I happen to remember distinctly the genesis of the piece which stands last in my first volume. Two of the stanzas, I do not say which, came into my head, just as they are printed, while I was crossing the corner of Hampstead Heath between the Spaniard's Inn and the Footpath to Temple Fortune. A third stanza came with a little coaxing after tea. One more was needed, but it did not come: I had to turn to and compose it myself, and that was a laborious business. I wrote it thirteen times and it was more than a twelvemonth before I got it right. (pp. 48–50)

William Blake (1906) writes, not about a single poem, but about "an immense number of verses."

> I have in these three years composed an immense number of verses on One Grand Theme, similar to Homer's *Iliad* or Milton's *Paradise Lost,* the Persons & Machinery entirely new to the Inhabitants of Earth (some of the

> persons Excepted). I have written this Poem from immediate Dictation, twelve or sometimes twenty or thirty lines at a time without Premeditation & even against My Will; the Time it has taken in writing was thus render'd Non-Existent, & an immense Poem Exists which seems to be the Labour of long Life, all produced without Labour or Study. (pp. 115–116)

Perkins (1981) argues that such evidence is highly suspect. He cites the case of Coleridge's claims about composing "Kubla Khan," inspired by the images of a dream, awakening from which, he "instantly and eagerly" wrote down the poem as it had appeared to him in the dream. Perkins cites the work of John Livingstone Lowes (1926), who demonstrates convincingly that the imagery of the poem derives from several sources in Coleridge's extensive reading. A later discovery of an earlier manuscript of the poem presents a different story of the poem's composition and suggests that, contrary to Coleridge's public claims, the poem actually went through more than one draft (Schneider, 1953).

Still, McCabe compiles evidence from Joseph Conrad, Goethe, T. S. Eliot, Tolstoy, and others, who all speak of writing as though in trance-like states with little or no conscious awareness. It is hard to believe that all of them are making up that experience. Perhaps the experience appears to be like that to them. Why might that be? It is interesting to speculate that perhaps, when skilled writers are in the midst of production that is going well, their concentration is elevated to the level of what Csikszentmihalyi (1990) calls the "flow" experience. He writes:

> One of the most frequently mentioned dimensions of the flow experience is that, while it lasts, one is able to forget all the unpleasant aspects of life. This feature of flow is an important by-product of the fact that enjoyable activities require a complete focusing of attention on the task at hand—thus leaving no room in the mind for irrelevant information. (p. 58)

Some theorists and teachers appear to hope to activate such states in their students but believe that activation involves no more than allowing students to write what they can. They appear to believe that such states are the result of something akin to inspiration and presume that attention to structure and content distracts from some innate expressive ability. In doing so, they ignore Csikszentmihalyi's full description of the flow experience as involving skill, challenge, clear objectives, and immediate feedback through self-monitoring.

We have all had that kind of experience, if not as writers, as readers. If we wish to see our students experience "flow" in writing, then our teaching will focus on ensuring that students reach the level of skill (in the sense of using the full symbol system of written language) that will allow them to engage in it. On the other hand, if we believe writing is the result of inspiration, there is little we can do about it in schools other than turn on the music and hope that the muses are invoked.

The Control of Writing

Most writing is purposive. Writers wish to convey something to an audience, themselves or others. And they ordinarily hope to have a certain affective impact on the audience. Although writing is purposive in this sense, not all of its elements are under conscious control.

Like anything else we do, some elements are part of our tacit knowledge. We do not have to think about them. If we do, our performance is bound to suffer. Think about controlling each muscle as you tie a knot in a string. If you are able to do it at all, your performance will slow down considerably. As a musician, if I think about the precise control of each of my fingers in a quickly played passage, I destroy my performance. Hartwell (1985) demonstrates that native speakers of English have tacit knowledge of very complex rules of word order in English noun phrases but are unable to explain them. At the same time, once such rules are explained, they find it very difficult to apply them in a deliberate way. This is not to say that tacit knowledge was always tacit. On the contrary, the evidence is that things that have become second nature at some point were once complex and required painstaking, step-by-step effort.

Certain circumstances external to the writer appear to influence the process. Many writers, for example, testify that the environment in which writing takes place is very important to their productivity. Tolstoy (Goldenveizer, 1969) claims:

> I always write in the morning. I was pleased to hear lately that Rousseau too, after he got up in the morning, went for a short walk and sat down to work. In the morning one's head is particularly fresh. The best thoughts most often come in the morning after waking, while still in bed or during the walk. Many writers work at night. Dostoevsky always wrote at night. (p. 160)

This idea of the impact of the immediate environment on writing (time, circumstances, physical surroundings) remains essentially unexplored by researchers and unused by classroom teachers. McCabe (1971) had his students consider systematically the circumstances under which they wrote and did their best writing. They wrote accounts of their own writing processes that considered the environments in which they wrote. My experience with this idea is that it appears to give students greater control over their writing processes.

The language the writer uses and the culture that produces it exert powerful controls on writers, though they are likely to be unaware of the influence. The examples cited from Heath's work in Chapter One illustrate the kinds of influences that environment may have.

Current critical theory argues the linguistic indeterminacy of texts, the idea that no text can convey meaning in such a way that it cannot be interpreted in some way other than the writer intended. As we have seen, Derrida, in particular, has argued that lurking beneath the surface of both written and oral texts are other texts or meanings, some that may not even be available to the writer, as when a story develops a plot with mythic implications. Graff (1992b) refers to these as "other texts waiting to get out." One way to think about this is that we can never say everything necessary to cover all the challenges that might be directed at our texts. When someone challenges what we have said, we produce another text in response, one that might have been part of the first—which happens to be the case for the last two sentences in this passage.

Viewed from the vantage point of current-traditional rhetoric and texts such as Warriner's (1988), these considerations appear to offer unavoidable difficulties for writing. Viewed from another perspective, however, they provide an invaluable advantage to writers willing to explore their own words in search of meanings.

Purposive Writing

Despite these elements that lie outside the writer's conscious control, we assume that most elements of writing are purposive. To assume otherwise is to assume also that teaching or curriculum can have little legitimate effect on writing. Any attempt we make to teach something about writing assumes a purpose or intent that is to some extent conscious. When Calkins (1979, 1981) writes about helping children find "leads"—statements that put the reader into the middle of the action—she assumes that the child wishes to achieve some effect on an audience through the use of that lead. Otherwise, it clearly would make no difference to the writer what the lead is. Even a suggestion so trivial as how to spell a word assumes a conscious purpose. Anyone, other than the writer, suggesting revisions assumes that the writing is purposive and that the reviser knows what the purpose is. If it is not purposive, then revision can be little more than random changes.

This idea has some important implications for the use of journals, free writing, or other writing situations intended to generate expressive writing. If the writing that results is outside the writer's control, in the sense above, the teacher has no basis for making suggestions about it until the writer has made a decision about using such writing to express something to an audience, at which time it becomes purposive.

Necessarily, most of the writing that concerns us in schools and college writing classes is purposive. When we do concentrate on elements that seem outside the writer's control, we do so in service of the purposive. The term ***purposive,*** as I intend it here, is much broader than Britton and colleagues' (1975) category of transactional writing. Purposive writing includes all writing that is intended to communicate to or have some impact on an audience, even if the only audience is the writer.

BASICS IN THE PROCESS MODEL

McCabe (1971) points out that the composing situation of purposive writing entails several important variables of which the three most obvious are the writer, the audience, and the composition. These variables, or their counterpart in spoken language, occur in traditional speech communications models, such as Jakobson's (1960). However, in Jakobson's model the focus is on individual utterances and how the function of an utterance varies with the focus of the speaker's attention. For example, when the speaker's attention is focused on him- or herself, the function of the utterance is emotive. When the focus is on the "addressee," the function of the utterance is "conative." When the focus is on the context, the function is referential, and so on. Britton and his colleagues (1975) point out, I think rightly, that while speakers shift attention from one utterance to another, "a writer sets out to do one thing in a way that speakers seldom do: in other words that one of the differences between speech and writing lies in the sustained attitude that a writer takes with regard to the features in a situation" (p. 14).

If we view the writer as preparing a piece of writing for an audience, additional important variables in the model are the relationships between writer and audience, writer and piece of writing, and the audience and the piece of writing. At the very least, the writer has some impression of the needs, knowledge, and disposition of the audience and some idea of the impact the writing is to have on the audience.

Writer/Audience Relationships. Writer/audience relationships include the writer's general knowledge of the audience and the more specific information resulting from particular relationships, as in the cases of friends, lovers, bosses and employees, and so forth. In certain cases, attributes of the audience will be researched in great detail, as is the case in mass-market advertising. In some cases, the writer's knowledge of audience may be little more than a set of assumptions about an idealized reader. In others, a writer will have information about an audience's knowledgeability, interests, and dispositions.

In any information-oriented writing, knowing what the audience already knows will make a big difference in what is expressed and what is not. When a writer can assume a knowledge base shared with an audience, much can be left unsaid that would have to be made explicit for a less knowledgeable audience. Predicting what is likely to interest an audience or how to catch its interest is also important. Certainly, advertisers take it to be so. Finally, the disposition of the audience, including level of skepticism, what the audience views as pleasurable and painful, desirable and undesirable, and so on cannot be ignored.

Recognition of the audience's knowledge, interests, and dispositions seems clearly to have an impact on writing. Yet recognizing them is never the focus of serious attention in school and college writing textbooks. If texts such as Warriner's (1988) mention audience it is virtually only in passing and by admonition, without providing students any help in learning to think about audiences.

Writing/Audience Relationships. Further, the skilled writer is likely to be concerned with the actual interrelationships between the piece of writing and the audience. It is for that reason that writers often seek readers' reactions to their manuscripts in progress. Jerzy Kosinski used to tell a story of calling telephone operators late at night when he was new to America and the English language, to read them passages from a novel he was working on to get their responses to his language. He also told of reading an early version of *The Painted Bird* to a group of women on Long Island who had survived the terrors of World War II. They recommended that he eliminate some of the most vivid passages describing the worst horrors because they thought no one would believe him. He claims to have followed their advice (personal communication, 1969).

It is common practice in academic circles to ask colleagues to read papers and books prior to submitting them for publication. Reviews resulting from submission to journals and presses also serve that purpose. In classrooms, many have recognized the value of using peer response groups, and researchers have examined the impact of such groups (S. Freedman, 1987).

This variable of considering audience/writing relationships appears to hold even when the audience is the self. As Steve Witte (1992) points out, people construct grocery lists according to the way they navigate the aisles and counters of the grocery store. Certainly that is true for me. I know that if I have an item out of place, I am likely to forget it until I have completed the tour of the entire grocery store. Finding I have missed the item, I have to make my way back through the crowds of customers and carts again. That knowledge about my own behavior in relationship to the grocery list influences my construction of future grocery lists.

Writer/Writing Relationships. Writers often view their words as representing themselves. That is why they become upset when someone attacks their words. They see the attack as directed against themselves rather than against the words they have uttered. The writer is likely to have some disposition toward writing as both a process and a product. Although such general dispositions as writing apprehension have been examined with some care, we know very little about the effect of writers' dispositions, as they write, on the particular piece of writing.

The Writing Situation

McCabe's (1971) model points out what the example of the grocery list clearly implies, that every writing takes place in what he calls an "immediate situation" to differentiate it from the wider environment in which it takes place. The immediate situation includes the conditions surrounding the inception, process, and anticipated reception of the writing. In the classroom, the writing situation includes the manner of the assignment, preparation for the writing, the time available, discussions with others about the subject, resources available, the reviewing process, and so forth. My grocery list is situated in terms of my purposes and the particular store at which I shop. Were I to shop in a different supermarket, the construction of my list would be of very little use.

In the case of professional and academic writing, the specific dimensions of a writing task are likely to be governed to a greater or lesser degree by the writer's perception of the relevant issues in the field, earlier publications about those issues, and discussions with colleagues or others concerned with the same issues. Such discussions and publications provide the texts from which the writer draws and provide the basis for the intertextuality common to any writing.

Not only the substance, the issues involved, but the actual shape of the writing will have been heavily influenced by the immediate situation of the writing. My grocery lists, though not identical, look very similar from one week to the next. In fact, as I write them out, I find myself recalling the structure and even the content of previous lists as well as my memory of the store layout, a kind of text in itself. ("Let's see, green peppers and tomatoes are first. Which aisle has chutney? That is in two different places. Heaven knows why.") In the case of professional and academic writing, the appropriate genres are also situated, and learning them, as Berkenkotter and Huckin point out, requires "immersion into the culture, and a lengthy period of apprenticeship and enculturation" (1993, p. 487).

While every piece of writing is situated, writers may see themselves as involved in the particularities of the situation to greater or lesser degrees. That is, the writing is undertaken within some framework that involves the writer's purpose (whether it be his or her purpose or an assigned purpose), the particular contingencies surrounding that purpose, the audiences, and the writer's relationship to all of these. In the case of the grocery list, my purpose is to get everything in the right order to save time getting through the store. That is, the situation, even without an audience other than the writer, has the effect of dictating the structure of the writing.

Other situations may have far more important consequences for the writer. For example, a few years ago I had the opportunity of interviewing a senior loan officer at a very large bank who had been assigned the task of evaluating a loan application from a multinational corporation that included farms, food processing plants, manufacturing plants, and other businesses. The corporation had defaulted on its payment of an earlier loan for millions of dollars but had submitted a request for an extension and an additional loan. The loan officer explained that because the initial loan was so large, the bank would consider the additional loan in order to enhance the possibility of recovering its earlier investment.

The writing task facing the officer required a recommendation involving a series of arguments: one assessing the corporation's performance with the initial loan, one evaluating its current viability (including assessments of its productivity, markets, current financial structure, management, and so forth), and one predicting its potential for recovery and continued viability. The officer felt a keen sense of responsibility in this task. Not only would he have to convince his superiors that his recommendation was valid, but it would have to prove so in the end for his continued well-being at the bank. Although his recommendation would be meticulously reviewed by his superiors, its success or failure would become part of his record.

This loan officer was only slightly less involved in the immediate situation than is a lawyer who must present arguments to a jury. A teacher preparing a sheet of directions for students to follow in some project is likely to feel intimately involved in the presentation of the sheet to the class. In each case, the writers are likely to have planned their writing with very concrete ideas in mind concerning the needs and likely responses of particular participants, including highly specific expectations of certain passages of the writing.

Writers facing other writing tasks will not be so involved in the immediate situation of the writing. Historians, writers for the popular press, news writers, biographers, and so forth, while concerned with audience response, will not see themselves as involved in the particular presentational situation. The publication of material in periodical or book form places the writer at one remove from the immediate situation of reception that we see in the bank, courtroom, and classroom.

Research suggests that at most levels of schooling, the writing situations encountered by the great majority of students are of a single kind (Applebee, 1981; Britton et al., 1975; Hillocks, 1992): The writer's audience is almost always the teacher, and the teacher almost always sets the purpose of the writing and responds to the writing with a grade. Even though there is an immediacy to this writing and certainly consequences for the writer, the richness of nonschool settings that comes through discussion, reading, and informal talk is usually, though not necessarily, missing.

The General Environment

In addition to the immediate situation, McCabe's model also indicates the need to consider that any act of writing takes place in a wider environment, namely that of the culture (or possibly cultures) and its institutions in which the writing takes place. The environment of the broader culture and its institutions supplies many of the basic tools of writing, tools that, as already noted, lie outside the writer's conscious control: the language and all that it entails, including category systems, archetypes, stereotypes, and certain assumptions about how knowing and thinking proceed. It is at this level of the writing situation that cultural criticism is likely to make significant contributions.

The Impulse to Write

The writer's impulse to write may come from within the writer as a result of the writer's perceptions of a particular situation (in which the writer may or may not feel directly involved), from a desire to recapture some idea or experience in language, or from some mysterious inner prompting that the writer may be unable to explain; or it may arise in response to something in the broader environment. The impulse may stem from two or more of these working in concert.

Most writing in school originates in the specific situation of a classroom. That is, the writer produces in response to an assignment. Much writing in workplaces also appears to be in response to the particularities of workplace situations, often to assignments. The computer specialist who writes a memo recommending the use of new software, the bank officer who writes a recommendation to extend or deny a loan, the teacher who writes periodic evaluations of students, all write in response to an assignment that is part and parcel of the job. Such assignments are very often quite specific. The bank officer is assigned a particular loan application to review. The computer specialist may be asked to examine a particular software program. Other writing assignments are far more generalized. Academics in research universities are expected to publish the results of their inquiries. However, what those inquiries are will be up to the academic. Any case that a lawyer takes on will require some writing, but the lawyer will have some leeway in deciding which cases to undertake.

Some writers have suggested that school assignments are so restrictive that they cannot be successful (e.g., Graves, 1981, 1983). They argue that students should always select their own topics. The important issue seems to be whether or not a writer can internalize an impulse coming from the outside. Can a writer in a workplace take ownership of the assignment? Can the bank officer or the computer expert come to feel responsible for writing sound recommendations? It would certainly seem so.

Can students take ownership of classroom assignments? To date we have little or no systematic research on this question. However, over the last several years, seventh and eighth graders in Chicago public schools, taught by M.A.T. students at the University of Chicago, have responded very favorably to a highly structured assignment asking them to imagine being chased through the dark streets of the South Side and suddenly jumping behind a dumpster to hide as the chaser approaches and to write about this imagined scenario in concrete detail. Not only is the writing very strong, but students choose this assignment as their favorite even over writing in which they had high levels of control over the subject matter, suggesting that students are at least sometimes able to take ownership of topics that do not originate with them (Rian, 1992).

It is also clear that the impulse to write may spring from doubts and questions of the sort that give rise to systematic inquiry. My guess is that for many successful academic writers, identifying an intriguing question is nearly concomitant with the impulse to write. As Brenda Shapiro points out, "Research and writing are absolutely integrated" (personal interview, 1993). If research gives an article form, as Shapiro suggests, the initial question probably begins that process.

All of this suggests the need to develop learning environments that, at least occasionally, include all or most of these elements. Simulations such as those devised by Troyka and Nudelman (1975), E. M. Anderson and Hamel (1991), and McCann (1994) build many of these elements. They include the wider environment of the problem as understood by the participants, the immediate situation for which students prepare arguments, and all of the writer/audience/text relationships discussed above. That is, students prepare arguments as representatives of a particular group with a more or less common perspective on the problem, knowing, in general, what the perspectives of others are and needing to be thoughtful about how others will respond to what they say. In addition, the simulations include opportunities to respond to other arguments and perspectives and to reconsider and reformulate ideas. Such simulations provide a far richer task environment than the ordinary classroom assignment. Considering the elements in some communications model, whether this or another, will provide guidance in developing richer learning environments.

COMPOSING PROCESSES

Once the impulse to write is in place, the composing process brings the writer's repertoire of knowledge and strategies into play. Research on the composing process indicates that writing is an enormously complex task, demanding the use of at least four types of knowledge: knowledge of the content to be written about; procedural knowledge that enables the manipulation of content; knowledge of discourse structures, including the schemata underlying various writing tasks (e.g., story, argument), syntactic forms, and the conventions of punctuation and usage; and the procedural knowledge that enables the instantiation of discourse of a particular type (Hillocks, 1986b).

While McCabe's model indicates the array of elements involved in the writing process, Bereiter (1980) posits hierarchical levels in the composing process once it is engaged. In my adaptation of this model, I conceive of higher levels as being necessarily engaged in the production of each of the lower levels. At the same time, the process is recursive. For example, when one writes a particular word as part of a composition, that word is necessarily governed by the purposes and constraints that govern the whole. We can think of the writing of each word as an occasion for evaluating the whole. That is, a word *may* trigger an association that leads to changing the purpose of the writing.

Before proceeding with an explication of my adaptation of this model, two caveats are in order. First, the model, as presented here, should not be interpreted as a representation of a rule-driven process (see J. D. Williams, 1993). That is, one level does not lead inexorably to the next. During the composing process, writers appear to move effortlessly up and down the hierarchy, not only from higher levels to lower, but from lower to higher. Work at any lower level, even editing, appears to permit a move to any higher level.

Such ease in movement appears to be the result of the writer's entertaining several levels simultaneously. I have said earlier that when one writes a word, it is a word that is part of a sentence and part of the whole piece viewed in light of its purposes and constraints. Thus, working at the level of generating sentences or editing, the larger patterns of the work (purpose, substance, genre, etc.) are implicated and may be assumed to be present in a network of associations related to the writing task. This presence appears to permit reexamination of any part of the piece, the whole piece, or even the knowledge structures underlying it.

The model of processing I am suggesting has much in common with what James D. Williams (1993) calls an association model. According to Williams, longer discourse, such as pieces of writing, "probably involve multiple, interconnected mental models of 'audience,' 'aims,' 'sentence patterns,' 'premises,' and so forth, all competing with and simultaneously reinforcing one another." The idea is that the writer generates features of the text suggested by the mental models involved. "As a text develops, it must be matched against the mental models that govern it, until . . . all the proper elements are in place" (pp. 563–564).

The second caveat is that although the levels are hierarchical, they should not be taken to represent a rigid stage theory. On the contrary, the research of Flower and Hayes (1980, 1981; Hayes & Flower, 1980), Bereiter and Scardamalia and their colleagues (e.g., Bereiter, 1980; Bereiter & Scardamalia, 1982; Scardamalia & Bereiter, 1983; Scardamalia et al., 1982), and others strongly indicates that the processes and subprocesses of composing are not only hierarchically related but recursive. That is to say, any decision making allows for continuous review of what has already been decided. For example, the act of writing any set of words in a composition requires a review of what has already been written. This review demands a return to higher-level processes, leading again to working through lower-level processes.

Purposes and Constraints

At the top of the hierarchy are the writer's purposes and the constraints that govern the composing process and its product. These result from the writer's construction of the immediate situation and the impulse to write. Bearing in mind that purposes and constraints are closely linked in practice, consider them separately for a moment.

Constraints. The constraints derive from the writer's construction of the variables in the immediate situation. Ideally, the writer considers all the elements discussed above: the audience, the immediate situation, and the relationships between writer and audience, writing and audience, and writer and writing, and the writing task itself. These considerations have a powerful impact on purpose as they become more and more specific in the writer's mind.

Suppose, for example, that the director of freshman English, untenured assistant Professor Straits, wishes to propose a reform in the freshman writing program at Dire University. She knows her audience consists of the chair of the English Department, who believes one cannot teach writing to anyone; the dean of humanities, who constantly cries "poor house" when asked for funds to upgrade teaching but who spends to increase the visibility of the scholarship and research in his division; most of the tenured faculty in the English Department, who view the freshman writing program as a means of supporting graduate students in literature; the graduate assistants, the majority of whom do not wish to spend any more time on their freshman classes than absolutely necessary; and a few allies among the faculty and graduate assistants who not only enjoy teaching in the program but see value in it as a means of helping improve writing and introducing students to the humanities at Dire U. In addition, she is also aware that any proposal she makes will reflect on her, allowing the interested parties to construct their version of her ethos. At the same time, she wants any proposal she develops to represent what she believes will truly be helpful to the writing program.

Clearly, the constraints here are such that Professor Straits might be better off resigning from her position as director of writing, at least until she becomes tenured. If she decides to go ahead with her proposal, she will have to think about winning over at least some of the factions involved and at least one powerbroker.

The constraints combined with her purpose will have a powerful influence on the substance of the proposal. How she sets it forth will be important as well, but secondary to the ideas. She may envisage a plan with dimensions that seek to give the department greater visibility and that arguably strengthen scholarship. It will have to appeal to the graduate assistants, perhaps simply as a way of improving their own marketability at first. Ultimately, however, she will have to appeal to their intellectual interests and win more allies among the tenured faculty. The options selected for the plan may be those thought best able to improve the program, provide visibility, and increase opportunities for advancing scholarship.

Purposes. Although we ordinarily speak of the writer's purpose as singular; it is useful to think of every piece of writing as having three kinds of purpose, which are unified in the execution. One of the major purposes has to do with the substance of the writing, one with the audience, and one with the writer. Writers may work with the same set of data with quite different results because their intent and methods differ. For example, one literary critic may write about the novel *Tom Jones* with the intent of examining the underlying framework of the novel's ethical arguments. Another critic, however, might not be concerned with the question of ethics at all, but rather with the nature of the plot. Others will be concerned with different substantive purposes.

By substantive purpose, I mean the set of data that the writer wishes to deal with conjoined with the writer's interpretations or transformations of that data, the intent to treat a certain set of data in a certain way. In essence, this purpose represents the inventive, imaginative, and problem-solving dimensions of writing, all of which were called for in the English Coalition Conference of a few years ago (Lloyd-Jones & Lunsford, 1989). Such a purpose holds for every piece of writing, though the strategies may differ from one kind to another, just as Tolkien's substantive purposes differ from his famous article "Beowulf: The Monsters and the Critics" (1936) to *The Hobbit* (1966).

The second dimension of the writer's purpose has to do with how the writer intends the audience to respond to the substance of the piece. The desired response may be one of cool detachment, governed by logic or, at least, apparent logic. Or it may be an emotional, highly involved response, in which the reader laughs and cries with the characters. Or it may be the detached, bemused response engendered by satire. Or it may be some combination of these. This response amounts to a stance or disposition that the writer invites the reader to assume toward the content.

Closely related to this reader-oriented response is the hoped-for writer-oriented response: in classical terms, the ethos of the text and writer, or, in modern terms, the persona of the implied author. Whatever we call it, readers construct some view of the writer from the language of the text and the stance it appears to purport. Writers ignore such cues to the reader at their peril. Yet I have never seen any attention to ethos in any secondary school writing program and no more than an announcement of it in college material, not anything that we might expect most students to learn from.

To summarize, the writer hopes that the reader will construct the substantive meaning of the piece within fairly narrow boundaries and react to it affectively in terms of developing some disposition toward the work and the author. In this sense, all writing is persuasive. The dispositions toward the work and writer are of very great importance because they control the way an audience responds to the substantive dimensions of the writing. I will refer to these internal responses as the primary effect.

The writer may also want the audience to take some action as a result of reading the piece of writing—answering a letter, providing financial support, voting for candidate X or Y, buying a product, and so forth. This effect, which I will refer to as secondary, is not always a part of the writer's purpose. Popular novels, for example, are typically dependent upon their primary effects for their success. Most advertisements, on the other hand, have clearly intended secondary effects. It is a mistake to think that only writing of a certain type can have secondary effects, can result in people doing things beyond responding internally to the work. Poems, fables, satires, novels are all capable of persuading people to action. *Uncle Tom's Cabin* and *The Jungle* each had a secondary effect that has had a lasting impact on American society.

Discourse Knowledge and Strategies

At the next level of his model, Bereiter posits what he calls genre schemata. The idea is that a writer, depending on the purposes and constraints, elects to write some particular kind of piece: a letter to the editor, a scholarly analysis, a satire. This election prompts some particular processing of content that is appropriate to the genre schemata. However, it is just as reasonable to suppose that thinking about the data in particular ways results in the selection of the genre schemata. Certainly, as we have seen, writers regard thinking about the substance as guiding the final shape of their writing.

Once the writer selects the particular genre schemata, however, it appears to limit the kinds of processing the writer engages in. If Professor Straits elects to write a satire, her processing is likely to focus on discovering ironies, hypocrisies, and injustices rather than on, say, surveying the teaching practices in the program.

At the same time, it seems clear that knowledge of genre schemata contributes in significant ways to the processing of substance. For example, research suggests that knowledge of form (schemata) enables young children to produce elementary stories (Stein & Trabasso, 1982). Emig (1971) argues that form learned in school (e.g., the five-paragraph theme) enables high school students to produce compositions quickly and easily, if superficially.

Unfortunately, current writing texts focus on learning the characteristics of what the texts define as types of writing but are mainly types of "expository" writing and structures such as "the paragraph." The texts then ask students to generate pieces of writing with those characteristics, with little or no attention to procedures for generating them. The result is that very few students are able to learn much from such presentations. What is important is learning the procedures for generating a variety of kinds of writing, however they be named. Chapter Six will return to these ideas in greater detail.

Theory and Strategies of Inquiry

At the next level in his model, Bereiter places what he calls the "content processor." In Bereiter's model, content processing is subservient to purpose and the selection of a genre schemata. However, the testimony of various writers indicates that the act of processing data directly influences purpose. Any academic researcher knows that as the data open up to scrutiny, many possibilities for writing and publication become evident. In addition, data processing may influence discourse choices. Therefore it seems unreasonable to limit content processing as Bereiter has done.

Rather, we need to view every human as engaged in inquiry at some level of expertise. Even as people go about their daily living, their contacts with various aspects of their environments necessarily require inquiry. For Dewey, inquiry begins in experiences that evoke questions or, in his word, *doubt.* The experience need not be in a laboratory. It might be at the breakfast table when the toaster turns out darker toast than expected. For a teacher, it might be any of the hundreds of problematic situations that one encounters in a classroom. For me, at this moment, it has to do with how I will be able to put this chapter together in a meaningful way.

Just what is meant by *inquiry* here? What are its strategies? Briefly, inquiry involves a number of strategies that range from observing and attempting to construct an interpretation of the observations to imagining what could be. It includes comparing, contrasting, testing, evaluating, and hypothesizing—and interpreting the results of all these. Such a list as there is space to present here is suggestive rather than exhaustive.

It is important to note that the range of substantive purposes available to a writer will depend almost entirely on the strategies of inquiry a writer has available for dealing with the subject. Thus a writer concerned about some causal relationship will be limited by the writer's own conception of cause-and-effect relationships and the strategies available to that writer for dealing with such problems. Similarly, a writer concerned with providing an extended definition of some complex concept is likely to be limited by the strategies available to that writer for dealing with such concepts. In some cases, of course, thinkers invent the necessary strategies for dealing with their substantive concerns, as Newton invented calculus for dealing with planetary motion, but for the most part we use strategies already in our repertoires. Chapter Six will deal more extensively with the nature of that repertoire.

The point here is the importance of inquiry for writing. It lies at the heart of writing of any kind. It is not merely useful for producing the content of a particular piece of writing; rather, in many cases, it is responsible for the impulse to write and for the kind of writing.

Gist Units

Research by Hayes and Flower (1980; Flower & Hayes, 1980) suggests that as a result of thinking about purposes, constraints, content, and type of writing, writers produce abstract chunks of discourse, what Bereiter (1980) calls gist units. A gist unit is a generally circumscribed unit of content which has not been laid out in words but for which the writer has ideas about content and purpose. In writing this chapter, for example, I knew in advance what most of the major units were to be. But as the writing progressed, the gist units multiplied, subdivided, and so on. Outlines set out a list of gist units, thereby providing an overall picture of the writing plan.

Semantic, Verbatim, and Graphemic Units

Research by Matsuhashi (1981) and Bereiter, Fine, and Gartshore (1979) suggests that the composing of written sentences involves three fairly distinct stages. To begin with, writers appear to have a general notion of what is to be written (semantic units) and proceed to work out the specific lexical items to produce what Bereiter calls a verbatim unit, a sequence of words not yet recorded but that the writer can state upon request. Writing these words produces graphemic units, which are often different from the verbatim units announced orally.

Matsuhashi's research indicates that in developing a long sentence, writers work with semantic units, which become clauses or phrases. They work out the first phrases or clauses explicitly, having only a general idea of what will follow. After recording the first unit, they pause to plan the remainder. The semantic units appear to include keys to the kind of structure to be produced, though not the specific lexical items. That is, while the semantic unit may necessitate that a certain kind of relationship be established (e.g., temporal, cause-and-effect), it allows for choice among a variety of specific syntactic and lexical structures. At this level a writer may review alternative constructions and choose one in light of its appropriateness to purposes, content, and form.

Verbatim units are the lexical strings that writers hold in mind as they record what they wish to write. Graphemic units are the recorded versions of them. Verbatim units differ slightly from graphemic units. According to Bereiter and colleagues (1979), the differences between the two are in the direction of "correctness." Thus writers do not simply record verbatim units but edit them during recording, sometimes omitting, adding, or changing a word, sometimes making "corrections" in usage.

Editing appears at two levels: as lexical units are transformed into graphemic units and following their production. This involves the correction of spelling or usage, the addition and deletion of words of phrases, the restructuring of syntax, and so forth.

Revision

Before leaving this model of composing, we need to consider the role that revision plays in it. We tend to think of revision as what writers do to improve written texts. Research indicates that changes take place at the lowest and topmost levels of the hierarchy discussed above. Minor "revision" or editing takes place as verbatim units become graphemic units and after graphemic units have been recorded. Flower and Hayes (1981) show, at the other extreme, a young man changing his purpose, form, and content after reconsidering his audience.

As we all know, most revisions that students make are at the lower levels. Bridwell's (1980) high school seniors, for example, made an average of 61 revisions per piece of writing. The vast majority of those revisions were cosmetic and mechanical. About 19.6% were revisions at the sentence or multisentence level. She found no revisions at the level of the whole composition. No students changed basic purposes, content, or form. We should not be shocked by these findings. How many of us, after producing a first draft, scrap the entire manuscript? We may do it occasionally, but not often.

Large-scale revision, the reconstruction of a whole discourse or some extensive part of it, appears to involve the reexamination of the whole product, or some part of it, in light of purposes, content, and genre schemata. What provokes larger-scale revisions has not been studied in any detail, but we can surmise that major revisions come about because of changes, even minor ones, in the writer's environment. These may involve receiving new information, means of processing, or insights into the discourse structures used. The sources of such new information are most likely to be some experience related to the topic at hand (e.g., reading a related article or book) or feedback from an audience. Otherwise, however, the impulse to revise must come from the writer, from recalling something forgotten during the writing, from recognizing some anomaly or discrepancy in the text, from the invention of a new way of fulfilling the purpose, and so on.

However, revision takes place at many points during the composing process, not only after some written draft has been composed. If, as suggested in Chapter Two, inquiry shapes writing even as we are in the midst of simply thinking about a problem, and if we remember Derrida's suggestion that nothing is not a text, then we will have to see revision as integral to composing. In an extensive research project, our earliest glimmerings of ideas and our early conversations are tantamount to drafts that are revised again and again, perhaps only in our heads, as we add each new piece of the problem and rethink what we have thought earlier. In this sense, revision is not simply a part of the writing process, but an essential dynamic of inquiry, the art of moving beyond what we have already thought.

IMPLICATIONS FOR TEACHING

If we accept this model as a reasonable representation of the composing process, we must ask what its implications are for teaching. Although many of these will be taken up in the chapters that follow, a brief review of the implications will be useful here.

1. If nonconscious elements in writing are as important and unavoidable as this model suggests, we need to take advantage of them more than we do. Free writing and journal writing as means of generating content and language that helps to reveal purposes to the writer are important in this regard. Finally, the writing environment (where, when, under what conditions) appears to be very important in the writing process. Part of a writing program ought to be aimed at providing opportunities for students to mon-

itor their own writing processes and environments with the goal of bringing those elements of writing under conscious control when possible.

2. If the three sets of relationships among writer, audience, and writing are as important as they appear, then writing programs need to do far more with them than simply admonish students to keep the audience in mind as they write. Asking students to imagine an audience is not enough. However, allowing classroom written discourse to evolve from real or simulated situations in which different groups have different voices and opinions appears to have a powerful effect on student writing.
3. Inquiry has been excluded from writing courses except for the "research paper," which, in many high schools at least, is really only an exercise in copying from library sources, not inquiry at all in the sense I intend here. Yet in my meta-analysis of research on teaching writing, approaches that involved students in active, original inquiry, even on a small scale, had far and away the most powerful effects on student writing (Hillocks, 1986a; see the Appendix for more information). Yet textbooks have largely ignored it, only admonishing students to collect data or brainstorm, suggestions implying that there is no need for hands-on inquiry.
4. Finally, if the range of possible audience responses is as broad as even this limited picture of discourse possibilities suggests, then our writing programs at the college and secondary levels are, in my opinion, far too narrow to be of maximum benefit to students. The writing-to-explain that has dominated textbooks since the turn of the century, as Berlin (1984) points out, teaches an epistemological stance that is inadequate. In assuming that reality is directly transferable to the page through the mechanism of language, teachers and students alike accept the corollaries that genuine differences in opinion do not exist and that perceived realities need not be argued, only reported. To accept this point of view is to undercut the idea of critical thinking, and to undercut it, as they say in the movies, "with extreme prejudice." The implication for practice is surely to expand the repertoire.

Chapter Six

The Writer's Repertoire: Inquiry and Discourse

Most teachers of writing seem intuitively aware that writing involves knowledge of both certain means of processing data (what I will refer to as inquiry) and discourse knowledge. In the following transcription, an excerpt from a two-hour class, a college freshman writing teacher begins preparing his students for their next writing assignment, an in-class comparison and evaluation of "two entertainment events": two movies, two TV programs of a comparable type, two music albums of comparable type, or two poems or short stories. After explaining the conditions of writing and the choices above in great detail, Professor James, as I shall call him, turns to how to make an evaluation and to the features he expects in this kind of writing. As he proceeds, his goal is to build on existing student knowledge.

PROFESSOR JAMES: The purpose of today's and probably a good portion of Wednesday's class is to get you thinking about what's involved in an evaluation. And that is after all the mode of writing, the particular strategy that you're going to be using right now; it's a technique, it's a purpose you have in mind. *Mode* incorporates all of that into its definition. A mode is both a method for, a strategy for doing something, or also involves a purpose. What do you think you're trying to do when you evaluate something? Give me your commonsense definition of what the problem in evaluation is. The problem for you doing an evaluation, what literally are you doing? Sam?

SAM: Studying something in order to put a grade on it.

PROFESSOR JAMES: That's a start; you're studying something in order to put a grade on it. The grade is the evaluation. What is the grade? What does the grade do? Diane?

DIANE: Comparison?

PROFESSOR JAMES: It may come from a comparison . . . It's rating or ranking the thing you are doing with something else, higher or lower. Essentially, though, what's at the heart of an evaluation? What is, what's the purpose?

SHIJUANA: Comparison.

PROFESSOR JAMES: Behind an evaluation?

CARLOS: Comparison.

PROFESSOR JAMES: Comparison is a way to perhaps do an evaluation, but what is behind it? What's your outcome when you finally accomplish an evaluation, what have you done? Beth?

BETH: How well you think it . . . how well . . .

PROFESSOR JAMES: You've introduced the term *well.* What's at the heart of the term *well?*

ROBERTO: The worth. Evaluation to me would mean the worth of what it is, what was it worth, the value of its . . .

PROFESSOR JAMES: Value, value. That's what's in the term, the term *well.* The amount of value. You're making a value judgment. How well does something work, how good is it? What's it worth, what value does it have? That's what lies at the heart of evaluation. . . . [He reiterates and elaborates] Now. Go to the next step . . . How are you going to make that judgment? [Professor James provides an example, "part 26" of *Friday the Thirteenth,* and elaborates for several lines of transcript before returning to the question.] What would you do to render judgment on that movie? Shijuana?

SHIJUANA: A summary of what you thought about it?

PROFESSOR JAMES: A summary of what you thought about it. What you thought about it is certainly involved, but why would that necessarily be an evaluation, if you just gave me a summary of what you thought about it? Oh, I thought that Jason was a pretty scary person, . . . I thought that the theater was cold . . . Yeah, you may have come up with a whole series of things you thought about while you were seeing the movie, but what would render some of those things part of an evaluation?

CAROL: You compare the good and the bad in the movie?

PROFESSOR JAMES: You compare the good, how do you *know* there's a good there?

SHIJUANA: You know if a movie is good or bad.

PROFESSOR JAMES: You know if a movie is good. How do you know if a movie is good or bad?

SHIJUANA: If you like it.

PROFESSOR JAMES: If you like it. Why would you like it? Because it's good. [Students laugh]

SHIJUANA: It's something you know right if you understand.

PROFESSOR JAMES: OK. Squeeze this as much as you can. How do you know if a movie is good or bad? You don't just know. How do you know?

ROBERTO: If you holler and scream. If there's something you will holler and scream, you know.

PROFESSOR JAMES: The hollering and screaming, if it's not meant to be a serious movie, meant to be a horror movie or a scare movie, . . . the hollering and screaming is an indication that, hey, that movie was scary. [He elaborates this idea at length.] But how do we know that? What? We know that because we started to appeal to something, we started to use something that jumps at you. What we started to use has a fancy name. The term is *criteria*. Criteria are characteristics by which we can judge something [He writes this on the board] to be worth more. There. Characteristics by which we can evaluate. So we can judge something to be good or bad. Now we know . . . there are certain things a good horror movie does . . . We want to judge whether this is a good horror movie or not. So we tried to come up with a list of what the characteristics are of good horror movies. [No list was developed before or after this point]

From general talk about the need to develop criteria for judging movies in particular genres—for example, horror—Professor James moves to "criteria appropriate to movies in general." About 25 lines later, he gives an example of a criterion:

> You look at the actors. You look at the acting, in effect. Hell, you're going to go see a movie, you look at the acting, were they good or not, were they funny or not, if it was supposed to be a comedy. That would be the genre of the movie, comedy. You look at the quality of the acting, OK? What else might you look at in addition to the acting?

Eventually, Professor James provides two more criteria for judging movies, setting and plot. He makes a summary statement:

> Do you want to tell me this is a good movie? Tell me about the acting. Why was it good acting? Why was it a good story? One of you mentioned another characteristic of movies. The setting. Was it a believable setting?

He provides examples of how he would evaluate movies in each of these areas before proceeding to criteria for the other "entertainment events" and concluding class with a homework assignment to read three examples of evaluations and the "characteristics of very effectively written evaluation essays," all of which appear in the text.

Clearly, Professor James is concerned with the extension or development of his students' repertoires in both discourse knowledge and inquiry. Class time goes to his explanations of both, as it does in many classes. He believes that if he explains how to do an evaluation, students will be able to do it. In that sense, the emphasis that I place on learning the strategies of inquiry is not altogether new to writing programs. However, Professor James's explanations of how to conduct an evaluation turn quickly into explications of the features required in the assigned writing: "Do you want to tell me this is a good movie? Tell me about the acting. Why was it good acting?" The question of how one evaluates the quality of acting goes unanswered. In fact, it may not be answerable except in general ways outside the presence of concrete examples. How does one discriminate between the acting of John Wayne in anything and Dustin Hoffman in *Rainman*?

The students in this class must learn both strategies of inquiry and those for instantiating certain kinds of writing from their teacher's descriptions of the writing. After they have been told what to do, they have an opportunity to use what they have learned. But it is the first *and* last chance for them. If they did not understand what the teacher meant by *criteria* and how they should be used, they will not have an opportunity to learn it in practice. Four hours of class time will be devoted to telling students how to write an evaluation. In the following class, they will have to do it, after which the teacher will evaluate their performances.

The remainder of this chapter argues that writers need two kinds of knowledge: strategies for inquiring into the substance of writing and strategies for producing various kinds of discourse. Then it will explore the range of tasks in which those strategies appear. It will argue that, in both cases, the important knowledge is procedural. There is a place for declarative knowledge as a means of talking about writing and thinking reflectively about doing it. But it cannot substitute for learning the procedures in action. The special pedagogical art is inventing activities that will engage students at the appropriate level, their "zones of proximal development," activities that will enable learning that procedural knowledge. I will deal with such invention in Chapter Eight.

INQUIRY: PROCEDURES FOR THE SUBSTANTIVE

In the preceding chapter, I argued that the substantive, which has been largely ignored in writing programs in favor of discourse knowledge, requires a central position in the teaching of writing. It is often responsible for the impulse to write. We do not sit down to write an essay, we sit down to write an essay about a particular subject. The essay, as a type of writing, is incidental to the project of writing about the subject. Further, our purposes and subject shape the final form of the writing in very important ways. While abstract notions of discourse provide initial shape to the writing, our representations of the content (including all its details and the relationships among them) result in the specifics of the final form. Finally, the quality of the writing must be judged on how well or interestingly the content has been constructed or represented. An essay, a poem, a novel may exhibit all the features that such discourse requires for excellence, but if the representation of content is inadequate or uninteresting, the piece fails.

Teaching Writing and Inquiry

Teaching writing has a venerable history of assuming that the demands of content will be taken care of elsewhere. A good deal of what we do comes to us from Aristotle, who seemed to set content aside, though certainly not to ignore it. In the *Rhetoric* (1932), he provides a fairly lengthy summary of ethical principles appearing in the *Nichomachean Ethics,* important to arguing policy, and outlines five common subjects of deliberation that effective orators should have at their command: "(1) ways and means; (2) war and peace; next, (3) national defense; (4) imports and exports; finally, (5) legislation" (p. 23). For each of these the orator must know the subject, not only from the perspective of his own country, but from the perspective of others. Further, Aristotle was very forceful in insisting on specific knowledge:

> Now, first of all, let this be understood: whatever the subject on which we have to speak or reason—whether the argument concerns public affairs or anything else—we must have some knowledge, if not a complete one, of the facts. Without it you would have no materials from which to construct an argument. How, let me ask, could we advise the Athenians whether they should go to war or not if we did not know their forces, whether these were military or naval or both? The size of these forces, what were the public revenues, and who were the friends and foes of the state, what wars it had waged, and with what success—and so on? (p. 156)

This knowledge was to be acquired in other fields and imported for use in writing. If we believe that knowledge is not simply imported from the outside, but constructed by us even when we borrow the constructions of others, then writers must have the means of constructing their own knowledge. I propose that inquiry must become part of the writing program, which is not, by any means, to limit its role in other areas of education.

We cannot expect to teach the specialized strategies of inquiry that appear in the various fields, of course. But several of what I will call basic strategies of inquiry appear in every field that I can think of, including mathematics, I am told by colleagues who should know. To illustrate these strategies, let me take, as an example, the investigation of a body, as reported by Ross and Robins (1991), discovered in 1984 in a peat bog some 30 miles east of Liverpool, England—a body that had been slain close to 2,000 years before.

The Body in the Bog: The Report

Peat is an excellent preserver of parts of human remains, and bodies up to 2,000 years old have been recovered from European peat bogs. In particular, the skin tends to be well preserved by chemicals in the peat, similar to tannins, that turn the skin to a supple form of leather. At the same time, the acids in the ground water of the bogs dissolve bones and internal organs.

When a well-preserved human leg was found among peat that had been extracted for drying, an archaeologist was called in and began the search for further remains. He soon discovered a flap of skin protruding from the edge of the peat, where an excavator had cut through. The body was removed from the bog, still encased in peat, and shipped to a laboratory for careful study. X-rays of the mass showed the vague outline of a crouching body. As the body emerged from the peat, it was carefully sampled for radio-carbon dating.

The skin and hair had been remarkably well preserved. Most of the body's insides had dissolved, except for a few long bones, the stomach, and part of the small intestine. The latter contained a dark brown pulpy substance, remains of the man's last meal. (The digestive tract has a natural resistance to acid, helping it survive while other organs decay.) Except for a fox fur arm band, the body was naked. The bog man's facial features were quite apparent, despite the deterioration of bone. Careful examination of the skin revealed that the man had been very muscular. His fingernails were in good condition, not chipped or broken, and could be described as well manicured.

Previous X-ray scanning of the skin had shown the outline of the body's skeletal structure, indicating that his skull had been fractured at the crown and at the base, and that his neck had been broken "in a manner entirely consistent with death by hanging" (Ross & Robins, p. 26). Examination of the skin supported what the X-ray revealed. There were several obvious marks of wounds to his body, any one of which might have caused his death. Two lacerations at the crown of the skull and one at the base came from blows by a fairly sharp, heavy instrument, such as an axe, that could easily have caused the skull fractures.

When investigators pulled the head back, they found a knotted cord of animal sinew around the neck, "fitted so tightly that it had sunk deeply into the skin, leaving clear ligature marks on the front and both sides of the neck" (p. 27). This knotted sinew, the investigators thought, was clearly a garrote, a knotted cord intended to crush the windpipe. When a stick is inserted between the cord and the side of the neck and rotated, the cord digs rapidly into the skin, crushing the windpipe and snapping the spinal column.

When the investigators lifted the head to remove the garrote, they found another wound, "a deep and narrow incision, made with a very sharp and pointed blade that had been stabbed into the jugular with surgical precision" (p. 28). The effect of such a wound would be to empty the body of blood, if it were still alive. Other investigators studying the detailed history of the bog from pollen grains concluded that, after his final wound, the bog man had been dropped into water about a meter deep, rather than into the bog itself, a kind of ritual drowning.

Basic Strategies of Inquiry

Assumptions and Prior Knowledge. Even the abbreviated "report" above, though it appears to be an account of observation, is filled with assumptions and inferences, even apart from the radio-carbon dating techniques. Perhaps the most basic assumptions are that the actions of human beings are meaningful and that bodies, even though long dead, can reveal secrets if subjected to very close examination. Such assumptions are based on other experiences of a similar kind. They say, for example, that remains of bodies exhumed in the past have revealed evidence providing the basis for inferences about the life and times of their possessors. Therefore this body may. They say, the activities of human beings are patterned. If we find any evidence of activity, it may provide the basis for inferences about the patterns. Therefore we may learn something about the lives of people in that time and place. Such assumptions are based on what Dewey would call warrantable assertions.

Questions and Interpretations. The observations, as represented above, seem straightforward enough, but even they are interpretations based on other warranted assertions that have come from experience of one kind or another: Something in the shape and look of what is recovered reminds the researchers of a human being; what they know about leather suggests that this substance is leather-like; what they already know about anatomy and death and killing suggests that these wounds are wounds and that they may have been lethal. The questions that we naturally ask about our sensory intake result in interpretations in light of our existing experience.

All of these inferences or interpretations are based on the kind of general knowledge that most of us have. To make them, we begin with a question, search our memories for what we already know, and compare our new observations to that prior knowledge. We ask: Is this like something in our experience, or is it different, and in either case what does it mean? Deciding what it is we see is not much different from what seem to be higher-level interpretations. Interpreting the blows to the skull as those of a sharp, heavy instrument depends on detailed prior knowledge of such blows. Confirming that hypothesis will involve comparison of the wounds found here to those found in situations in which the wounds are known to have been delivered by a sharp, heavy instrument. The garrote seems self-explanatory, but it is so only if you know what a garrote is in the first place, or can find out.

Ross and Robins (1991) describe what might appear to many to be no more than a hole in the throat as "a deep and narrow incision, made with a very sharp and pointed blade that had been stabbed into the jugular with surgical precision" (p. 28). Such an assertion is based on a great deal of information about the specific characteristics of stab wounds, their direction, and the kinds of instruments that make them.

Testing Interpretations. Interpretations such as these, hypotheses we might call them, must remain open to review. In an inquiry, everything remains a working hypothesis until we believe that the evidence not only supports it, but rules out the possibility of other interpretations. Still, even a supported hypothesis is never "true" with absolute certainty. It would be more accurate to say that there is high probability that the stab wound to the throat was made by a very sharp instrument used with surgical precision. The tentative nature of inquiry requires that our assertions remain open to reexamination in light of new evidence. That is why Dewey uses the expression *warranted assertion*—to indicate openness to review.

Two of the major inferences about the bog man were based on special studies made to test their validity. A casual observer might note that his fingernails were in good condition, possibly even manicured. From this casual observation, one might assume that the bog man did no manual labor. Since Celtic civilization had few labor-saving devices, it might be assumed that this bog man was an aristocrat. But is such an inference warranted on the basis of casual observation? Some more rigorous test seemed necessary. Brothwell (1987) carried out studies of the condition of the fingernails of living people in various occupations and compared them to the bog man's and those of other bodies found in bogs. He was able to link "good diet and non-manual occupation with the quality of the nails" (Ross & Robins, 1991, p. 42), both indicators of aristocracy.

When scientists examined the bog man's last meal, they found that it was made up almost entirely of finely ground primitive wheat, rye, and barley (along with some bran and chaff), apparently cooked as bread, some of which had been burned or scorched. People who knew about Celtic customs and ritual immediately inferred that the scorched bread suggested association with "a Celtic calendar festival and a sacrificial death" (Ross & Robins, 1991, p.

13). However, the contents in other bog body guts were a coarse-grain mixture, with a variety of seeds mixed in, apparently eaten as porridge. Two basic questions arose: Had the grains been made into a cake or bread and had they been burned in some manner?

Scientists had been using a technique called electron spin resonance (ESR) for measuring the thermal history of various ancient foods. It could reveal both how high cooking temperatures had been and how long the food had been cooked. To do this, the scientists had to conduct "lengthy comparison experiments" on the modern counterparts of the grains involved. These experiments with grains cooked in particular ways and at a range of particular temperatures provided the basis for making inferences about the ancient cooking of the bog man's cereal. That is, for example, if ESR had *x* results for modern counterparts cooked as bread at 200 degrees, and if ESR had similar results for an ancient sample, it could be inferred that the ancient sample had been cooked in the same way and at the same temperature. ESR, then, is an aid to human observation, but the basic strategies for interpreting the data remain the same: comparison and contrast. The conclusion, in this study, by the way, was that the grain had been cooked as flat cake, much like the modern Scottish oatcake, at 200 degrees, but that a part of it had been scorched at 400 degrees.

Imagining. But there is more to inquiry than all of this. When it comes to asking what to make of the data and the inferences thus far, something else must enter in. We have the body of a man, probably an aristocrat, recovered from a peat bog, a man who, having eaten a scorched oatcake, suffered three violent wounds, any of which might have killed him, and was cast into a pool of water as if to drown. No other bog body discovered had been subjected to such a violent, three-way death. In fact, there were very few similarities between this bog man and the others. Ross and Robins pursue the rest of the story by asking a series of questions and making a series of imaginative leaps, imagining the people, what they might have thought, and what the circumstances might have been that would bring about this sacrifice.

The key imaginative leap seems to have been the recognition that this was not simply a ritual death, but a very special one, betokened by the aristocratic status of the victim, the three mortal wounds, the fox fur, and other details. Following up hunches, testing them against a variety of evidence, discarding some and accepting others, they develop a plausible theory of the events that led to this sacrifice of a young man in his prime, probably a Druid prince who went willingly to his death as a dying-and-reviving king to propitiate three major gods of the Celtic pantheon, at a time when the Celtic world in Britain seemed about to be devastated.

Ross and Robins admit that much of their theory is "conjectural" and, in doing so, prepare the way for new evidence. Their theory is a structure of what Dewey calls "warranted assertions," in their minds "the best explanation of the data." In developing that theory, they use what I regard as all the basic strategies of inquiry: careful observation and representation in language of phenomena observed, questioning at every stage, comparison and contrast of the phenomena with what is already known (prior knowledge), interpretation leading to tentative hypotheses, testing of tentative hypotheses through formal tests such as those used with ESR above, evaluations by examining hypotheses in light of additional data and competing hypotheses, and imagining.

Imagining may seem to be the most important strategy of all, but it cannot appear without at least some of the others. It is dependent on them. Perhaps one of the most famous imaginative leaps occurs in the story of Archimedes and the king's golden crown. Even if it is apocryphal, it illustrates how a flash of insight comes after arduous thought through an associative process. This insight led to the discovery of a method of measuring specific gravity. The king of Syracuse had given his craftsmen a specific amount of gold to make a crown, but he suspected that they had stolen some by substituting silver so that the final crown weighed the same as the initial amount of gold. How could the king be certain that no gold had been taken? He asked Archimedes for an answer. Archimedes knew that the volume of a certain weight of silver would be greater than the same weight of gold. However, the crown was so intricately made with curves, peaks, and spires that its volume could not be measured using conventional means. How to know for certain, then, if the gold had actually been diluted?

Archimedes did not know but continued to mull over the problem. One day in the public baths, he noticed that as he immersed himself in his tub, the water overflowed, running out of the tub. In a flash of association, he realized that the volume of the crown could be measured by immersing it in a vessel full of water and measuring the overflow. The story is that Archimedes, ecstatic at this discovery, lept from the tub and, still naked, ran through the streets shouting, *"Eureka! Eureka!"* ("I have found it! I have found it!")

It is a mistake to think that Archimedes' leap came easily. It is based on knowledge of the relative weights and volume of gold and silver, an understanding of reasoning about proportions, and considerable thought about how to measure the volume of the crown. Without that knowledge and what amounts to problem formulation, Archimedes would be no more adept at leaping to the solution of the problem than the rest of us.

Many teachers use methods that encourage imagination: role playing of various kinds in the context of developing arguments from various perspectives; role playing to invent characters and their actions in problem situations; writing about being in an imaginary place under certain conditions; writing from the point of view of a literary character or of some inanimate object;

playing various games, including signifying, to develop metaphor. All these involve imaginative leaps, but they also involve considerable preparation. Simply listening to music or sitting in a tent holding hands with classmates is unlikely to provide the basis for imaginative insight.

Shared Strategies

The strategies outlined above are shared across fields. They are not exclusive to any one field. They certainly generalize to the areas of thinking, analysis, or problem solving in which an active citizen in a democracy engages. The objects of observation and the specific means of observing will vary from one field to another, but the necessity for observing, questioning, and constructing representations and interpretations will remain constant. Specific tests of hypotheses will vary markedly from field to field, but not the need to test.

Many people argue that the processes of inquiry of given disciplines are learned as people become engaged in the disciplines (Berkenkotter & Huckin, 1993). No question about it, especially when the disciplines use specialized techniques for observation and interpreting what is observed. (Did you ever see an X-ray as a doctor explained it to you, and you nodded as though you could also make something meaningful out of what really appeared to you to be a smudge with a funny shape?) Disciplines have rules of evidence and rules about warranting arguments, usually involving the approved procedures for conducting arguments. And people know the issues in the field and what their colleagues are doing and thinking. All undeniable.

Engaging in the strategies of inquiry that I am proposing here will certainly not provide a sufficient base for becoming an organic chemist, a linguist, an anthropologist, a theoretical physicist, and certainly not an economist. And some fields are so filled with gobbledygook that the very act of becoming socialized in them places one entirely out of communication with anyone outside the field, which, come to think of it, may be just as well.

Unfortunately, focusing on the socialization factor of entering a discipline neglects the necessary knowledge of what used to be called "general education." Such inquiry allows one to evaluate the events and times, problems and aspirations, proposals and programs that we all encounter in everyday life, even if we are only a little awake to the world around us. Beyond that, they provide the necessary basis for beginning to understand disciplines other than our own. They provide the basis for breaking down the insularity of the highly "socialized" disciplines and permitting the interdisciplinary work that we so badly need. But these are other arguments that need to be taken up elsewhere.

Many are beginning to realize the importance of including inquiry in the curriculum. Even state agencies are experimenting with assessments that emphasize explorations of problems over a period of time. In Texas, these "performance" assessments are concentrated in science and focus on students looking into a problem from a variety of perspectives over several weeks. The participants in the English Coalition Conference stated that students of writing need help "in mastering techniques for discovering and testing . . . information to develop ideas" (Lloyd-Jones & Lunsford, 1989, p. 21). The final report of the secondary strand of the English Coalition Conference, *English for the Nineties and Beyond* (Johannessen, 1987), puts the case even more strongly, stating that students must "learn to be inquirers, experimenters, and problem solvers" (p. 6), not only to become more effective writers and readers but to become fully participating citizens in a rapidly changing world.

Research on Inquiry and Writing

Despite the significant body of research examining the relationship of inquiry to various measures of effectiveness in writing, writing programs and textbooks at the high school and college levels have, until recently, ignored content and the procedures for constructing it almost entirely. Even now, content receives only a nod with shallow directions to students to "gather information" or "brainstorm for ideas."

This research shows consistently that beginning writers, at whatever level, do not develop the content of their writing. Bereiter and Scardamalia (1982) show that when youngsters come to school, they have the schema for conversation, but not one for writing. In conversation, a turn by one partner prompts a comment by the other. In writing, no conversational partner exists to prompt additional content. The result is that when children are asked to write on a particular topic, they produce about as much as a normal conversational burst would include. When they are asked to say more, they produce about another conversational burst. Providing a series of "contentless prompts" indicates that children have far more content available for writing than they actually use. They must learn that, in writing, there is no partner to call forth information. In part, this may indicate a need to learn how writing differs from conversation. In part, it may involve learning how to recall content without prompts from conversational partners.

A study by V. Anderson, Bereiter, and Smart (1980) involved helping students conduct memory searches. In 12 writing sessions they asked students to write a list of all single words that might be important to a topic before they began writing. This procedure, comparable to brainstorming but done independently, provided children with the means for conducting a memory search, for they wrote longer compositions at the end of training even when they were not requested to write out the list of single words. Other techniques such as brainstorming, "clustering," and "mapping" (e.g., Buckley & Boyle, 1983) may have similar effects.

Inquiry, however, involves more than memory searches. Several studies engage students in observing carefully and representing their sensory perceptions. These students show large gains in the effective use of detail in later independent writing (Fichteneau, 1968; Hillocks, 1979, 1982). Others involve students in analyzing data for use in developing arguments (claims, evidence, warrants, qualifications, counterarguments, and so forth). Students in these studies show large gains in developing arguments more fully and effectively (e.g., Hamel, 1990; Anderson & Hamel, 1991; Hillocks et al., 1983; McCleary, 1979; Troyka, 1973; Widvey, 1971). In general, as a synthesis of studies on teaching writing reveals, engagement in these strategies has the most powerful impact on subsequent writing of all approaches examined (Hillocks, 1984, 1986a), with effect sizes several times those of the competing approaches. Given the evidence and the arguments, there can be little doubt that teachers of writing need to incorporate inquiry into their curricula systematically.

A Theory of Inquiry

If we do incorporate inquiry into the curriculum, what will be its theoretical base? We can no longer accept the realist view that reality is knowable directly and, therefore, directly transferable from one mind to another through the agency of language. Nor, I think, can we accept the subjectivism of Guba, who states that, "Realities are multiple, and they exist in people's minds" (1990, p. 26). As I have argued in Chapter Three, our daily actions demonstrate that we accept a reality outside ourselves and that we come to know that reality well enough to base actions on that knowledge. We need a pragmatic inquiry, one that allows us to make sense of the world and to assess the sense we have made. Dewey (1938) provides just such a base.

Dewey begins by arguing that inquiry has biological roots:

> Living may be regarded as a continual rhythm of disequilibrations and recoveries of equilibrium. . . . The state of disturbed equilibration constitutes *need*. The movement toward its restoration is search and exploration. The recovery is fulfillment and satisfaction. (p. 27)

The pattern of inquiry that Dewey sees in everyday living is comparable in important ways to the pattern of more systematic inquiry that I believe we must reintegrate into the teaching of writing, both as part of the writing curriculum (perhaps part of all curricula) and as part of pedagogical practice.

We will need to base our theory of inquiry on the assumption that human observation and interpretation are inherently subjective, embedded as they are in personal experience, cultural conditioning, and language. If, then, it is impossible to "capture reality" directly, how is it possible to believe that any of our thinking is meaningful? How is it we can act or conduct any inquiry with any confidence? Dewey, in *Logic: The Theory of Inquiry* (1938), poses the question differently. He states that science has recognized the impossibility of knowing the objects of our senses "directly," that "science has destroyed the idea that objects as such are eternal substances," and that it "has also destroyed the notion of immutable kinds marked off from one another by fixed essences" (p. 127). He asks, if a "logical subject," a word or words,

> cannot be identified either with an object or sense-datum directly given to judgment for qualification through predication, nor yet with an ontological "substance," what is meant by being an object substantial *in any sense* that makes it capable of serving as a subject? (p. 127)

That is, if the language we use to think about the world around us cannot be said to represent reality directly, how can we conduct any logical inquiry?

Dewey's solution: If the subject of inquiry is "grounded" in explicit relations to other terms and meets certain conditions, it "constitutes a substantial object in the logical sense of that term" (p. 127). To meet these conditions, the subject (of inquiry) must be linked to a variety of other terms that (1) "delimit and describe the problem in such a way as to indicate a possible solution" and (2) imply how "new data, instituted by observational operations" in the service of some "provisional predicate," or hypothesis, "(representing a possible solution), will unite with its subject-matter to form a coherent whole" (p. 128). If these conditions have been met, the subject can serve as a term in a logical system about which logical determinations can be made. At the same time, "the subject is existential" (p. 127). That is, it has reference to the existential rather than simply the conceptual (pp. 351 ff.).

At the level of personal experience, we constantly "ground" subjects in sets of explicit relations to other terms in the same system. We can plan a trip to a country that we have never seen and know very little about. How is this possible? We develop a plan that consists of a series of propositions that relate our general knowledge of travel (the more we have of which, the better), our more specific knowledge of the country involved, our general knowledge of monetary systems, details gleaned from talks with friends, and so forth. These propositions may have little "truth" to them, but if we have taken the time to think about them and relate them to one another, they provide a matrix of ideas, what Dewey calls "the ground of inference to a declarative proposition that such and such an act is the one best calculated to produce the desired issue under the factual conditions ascertained" (p. 162).

Our travel plans become a subject of inquiry and assume a logical position in that system. As such, logical operations can be conducted on it. These operations engender predictions that serve to test the logic of the structures that give rise to them. Because the subject of the inquiry is existential, the results of the inquiry can serve as a guide to action or to inquiry in action. In other words, we have a basis for making, testing, and revising hypotheses.

Dewey argues that good conclusions may be reached from premises that may not be true. Inquiry can begin from a state of ignorance. Indeed, it must. "It suffices to have hypothetical (conditional) material such that it directs inquiry into channels in which new material, factual and conceptual, is disclosed" (p. 142). Such, in my experience, are often the plans of teaching, research, and travel.

Dewey calls the result of inquiry *warranted* assertion because, for him, the terms *knowledge* and *belief* are ambiguous and suggest a finality that is inappropriate. For Dewey, the term *warranted assertion* implies both the unsettled character of the product of inquiry and the understanding that such outcomes may be "resources" for further inquiry. "The use of a term that designates a potentiality rather than an actuality involves recognition that all special conclusions of special inquiries are parts of an enterprise that is continually renewed, or is a going concern." Inquiry, then, is what "warrants assertion" (p. 9). It provides the arguments upon which we base our further thinking and action.

Dewey argues that inquiry must be a continuing project for two reasons: (1) the difficulty of knowing whether any two situations are alike in practice and (2) the necessary assumption that any inquiry influences the environment in which it takes place. Any teacher understands the first. Any carefully planned lesson is likely to have somewhat different effects in different classes. The classes can never be equated on all variables. For teachers, the second is also obvious. Any attempt to teach anything necessarily influences the possibilities of future teaching. Effective teaching should make learning the next thing easier. Poor teaching is likely to result in greater inattentiveness, misunderstanding, and so forth. The same principles apply elsewhere.

Dewey argues that "as special problems are resolved, new ones tend to emerge. There is no such thing as a final settlement, because every settlement introduces the conditions of some degree of a new unsettling" (p. 35). These assumptions have important implications for practice as well as for the model of inquiry that informs our writing curriculum.

DISCOURSE KNOWLEDGE

In schools and colleges, we have precious little time to devote to the teaching of writing. We cannot teach everything. What we ought to teach is a central question. For over two decades, some writers have fought against teaching any discourse knowledge at all. They felt it was necessary to have only some inspirational activity to stimulate the imagination (Parker, 1979). Anything else would be too confining. That perspective has not disappeared. We have other disputes about how discourse knowledge is acquired or best acquired (see Fahnestock, 1993; A. Freedman, 1993; J. M. Williams & Colomb, 1993). And we have disputes, at both the college and high school level, about what kinds or types of writing ought to be included in the curriculum. Writers say that argument is neglected; others say that we have too great an emphasis on narrative. Still others say that the types of writing that dominate textbooks and writing assessments are rubbish. These types come to us from current-traditional rhetoric (responsible for the heavy emphasis on exposition in colleges and schools), which has been roundly and rightly attacked for a number of reasons (e.g., Berlin, 1984).

If we are to deal with the problem of what to teach, we must have an analysis of what there is to teach. If we have an analysis we can trust, we can proceed to make more sensible decisions about curriculum. First, should we teach discourse knowledge at all?

Should We Teach Discourse Knowledge?

One objection to teaching knowledge about discourse is that it leads to formulaic writing. At one level, writers probably use relatively formulaic patterns to help them generate pieces of discourse, such as some business letters, memos, and letters of recommendation (P. V. Anderson, 1985), and the five-paragraph theme that Emig (1971) found her students using. At another level, however, discourse knowledge appears to operate in the composing process in a way that is not at all formulaic.

An example appeared in a study my students and I conducted a few years ago. We asked the youngsters attending a summer writing workshop at the University of Chicago to do the following: "Write about an experience, real or imaginary, that is important to you for some reason. Write about it so specifically that someone else reading what you have written will see what you saw and feel what you felt." Of the 40 students writing in a large classroom, my graduate students and I observed a stratified random sample of 19 during the writing. As each of the youngsters concluded writing, one of the graduate students took the writer to another room to talk about what had just been written. The first questions in the interview asked the writers what they considered writing about before they actually began writing. Eighteen of the 19 students observed considered content of some kind first. That is, they thought of a summer vacation, a trip to an amusement park, a school-related adventure, or some other specific experience.

One 14-year-old boy, however, said that he did not know what he was going to write when he began. He did, however, know the kind of story he wished to write—one that would be mysterious and puzzling and that would have a surprise ending, "a twist," he called it. The story begins with the line, "Where's the floor?" He chose that line, he says, because he thought it would get people's attention. He claims he did not know what would come next, that for him writing the story enabled him to discover what would happen next.

The story develops in the first-person as a nightmarish dream sequence and ends with a double ironic twist. The writer in his interview was able to describe the kind of story he wanted to write in his own words and to compare what he had done to certain stories by Edgar Allan Poe. When the story was rated holistically, it received the highest rating from three raters. Here was a complex first-person narrative with ironic twists written in 50 minutes by a young man who claimed that he did not know what the content of the story would be when he began it. Here is a case in which discourse knowledge apparently guided written production, but not at all in a formulaic way.

P. V. Anderson (1985) points out:

> Discussion of forms is unpopular at present because of the movement in composition pedagogy . . . away from an approach that focuses on the characteristics of good writing to one that focuses on the processes by which good writing is created. As a result, discussion of the forms of writing tends to be scorned. (pp. 11–12)

Anderson outlines several reasons why attention to "forms" is important: (1) The competent use of conventional forms in a job setting marks one as a "bona fide member of the culture of the workplace" (p. 12); (2) conventional forms help readers know what to expect as they read; and (3) knowledge of form probably operates as an integral part of the composing process, as strongly suggested by the example above.

The discourse types and tasks that find their way into school and college classrooms are based on some theory of discourse. The influence of these theories comes to bear through textbooks and increasingly through statewide assessments of writing. These theories may not always be adequate and, because they wield such influence, need to be examined carefully. The questions for examining any theory, as enumerated in Chapter Three, are useful here. Is it systematic and comprehensive? Does it explain relationships among the types of discourse examined? Does it have predictive power?

Current-Traditional Rhetoric

In "current-traditional rhetoric," purpose has always been associated with the "forms" of writing: to describe, to narrate, to explain, and to persuade. According to James A. Berlin (1984), this typology devolved from the rhetoric of George Campbell and other Scottish Common Sense Realists and, for the past 200 years, has dominated college composition programs. Without question, it has also dominated composition in the secondary schools and is the organizing principle underlying most state-ordained assessments of writing.

For nearly the last half of the twentieth century, Warriner's (1988) *English Composition and Grammar* has dominated the teaching of writing in American high schools, not only by virtue of the numbers sold (I am told that Warriner's is the best-selling textbook ever published), but by its power to influence other texts, many of which have tried to out-Warriner Warriner.

In the 1988 edition (which retains material from the 1951 edition), we find the following list of forms and purposes:

> *Narrative* writing tells a story or relates a series of events.
> *Expository* writing gives information or explains.
> *Descriptive* writing describes a person, place or thing.
> *Persuasive* writing attempts to persuade or convince. (p. 4)

This list of forms sets up the essential organization of the composition section of the text, which discusses writing paragraphs of each type and then full compositions of each type.

This four-part analysis of purpose in writing is rife with problems. Berlin (1984) points out that it is based on a mechanistic eighteenth-century psychology that posits faculties (the emotions, will, understanding, reason, and imagination) that function "independently of each other . . . and depend upon sensory experience; they are receptacles or muscles or malleable surfaces brought into play by experience. They do not shape experience but are shaped by it" (pp. 62–63). The epistemological ramifications are clear: given these assumptions, the mind is able to grasp the sensory input directly with no interpretation, no transformation, and no bias. As I have argued in Chapter Three, such a stance is simply not acceptable from the point of view of modern psychology or philosophy.

One of the chief problems with the typology is that its categories are not mutually exclusive. In fact, they overlap to a point that eliminates their usefulness as categories. Persuasive writing is supposed to be one of four distinct categories, but any purposive writing seeks to persuade, at the very least to convince the reader to accept its premises, to suspend disbelief, to accept certain conventions of discourse, or more simply to read on or listen. Consider the problem of narration and exposition. If a narration relates a series of events and exposition gives information, then what is an account of the attack on Pearl Harbor? If it is both and possibly also a description, then the categories are not useful. Fables clearly tell a story, but their ostensible purpose is to persuade. The point should be clear: The categories are hopelessly confused and, therefore, of little use in the analysis of writing tasks.

Perhaps even more important, this typology suggests that writing begins with an abstract notion of purpose, for example, to persuade. In Warriner's text, it always does. According to this book, making such a decision requires no context, no issue, no audience. The writer simply says, "Gee! I think I'll write a persuasive essay. Now, what shall I write a persuasive essay about?" Eighteen of the 19 students in our sample above began with content. Ability to begin with the abstract is very rare.

Perhaps novelists, editors, and other professional writers decide first to write an example of the genre with which they earn a living and worry about the subject later. But ordinarily, people write arguments because they have something to argue. They write narratives because they have a story they want to tell. For most writing the substantive purpose comes first. It is a safe bet that even professionals who write within a genre feel far more comfortable when they have an "idea," what amounts to a substantive purpose. The young man who wrote the Poe-like story found his content very soon. Our records indicate that he began his draft within three minutes of the assignment.

An Alternative Theory of Discourse: Purpose

As already indicated in Chapter Six, it is useful to think of purpose as having three dimensions, a substantive one, one that has to do with the intended impact on the audience, and one that has to do with the desired audience view of the writer. The substantive purpose is the writer's construction of some topic as the writer wishes to convey it to an audience. Substantive purposes will be capable of infinite variation, depending on the choice of topic and its treatment. The third purpose, the projected ethos, is also widely varied, perhaps as widely as personalities can be, but nonetheless identifiable and revisable (Hatch, Hill, & Hayes, 1993).

The second dimension of purpose has to do with the impact the writer hopes to have on the audience as the audience reads and thinks about the writing. I will argue that there are four basic kinds of audience response that appear in relatively pure form at times but that can appear in mixed form as well. Each of these affective responses may be thought of as the kind of persuasive force that the writer brings to bear on the audience.

As an illustration, consider the problem of Professor Straits (in Chapter Six) and the obstacles she faces in trying to bring about change in the freshman English program with a penny-pinching dean, a chair who believes no one can teach writing to anyone, a recalcitrant faculty, and only a few allies. If she has a sense of humor, it is conceivable that she would at least toy with the idea of writing a satire, perhaps one on the model of Swift's "Modest Proposal," proposing the indentured servitude of freshmen to faculty and graduate students so that the latter would have more time to work as productive scholars and arguing that this proximity of freshmen to great minds would benefit the frosh in countless ways that the ordinary freshman writing course could not begin to match.

As the frosh scrubbed floors and cooked meals, they could observe brainstorming, drafting, and revising by masters. What better modeling could one hope for? Since the freshman program focuses on a reader full of prose models now, models already fully developed, this change would allow for observation of the actual process involved in developing such models. Professor Straits might argue that such a plan has precedent in the current graduate program. Certainly, the graduate program has released the regular faculty from hours of drudgery and allowed the grad students to observe great minds at work. No one on the faculty wants to abandon this valuable program. This modest proposal would simply move a known quantity to the freshman level. The innovation would surely draw attention from other universities and make Dire U a model to be emulated.

After toying with the idea, perhaps even writing a draft, and after considering that her tenure decision is only two years away, Professor Straits might abandon it. She might consider writing a novel about the writing program, developing characters and a plot that would allow her readers to empathize with at least one character, eliciting still another kind of affective response. A novel might reveal aspects of problems in the program and gain sympathy for certain points of view through the characters who represent them in a way that other sorts of writing could not. This approach worked for Upton Sinclair in writing *The Jungle.*

In the end, however, Professor Straits is likely to return to her original idea of a serious proposal. She might propose a course for new graduate assistants in conjunction with a workshop in which groups of graduate assistants teach one writing course as a team. While a different graduate assistant would teach each day, the others would observe each class, participate in discussions evaluating each day's work, and work on plans and the revision of plans collaboratively. The course might have a dual focus: theory and research in the teaching of writing. The major goal would be to help the graduate assistants become more confident, effective, and reflective as teachers of writing.

For this proposal, Professor Straits desires a serious response. It will involve no hints that it is not to be taken seriously. It will involve little or no irony and no exaggeration or caricature, certainly not of the dean or department chair. It will present a clear, well-developed line of argument with support for each contention, even those relating to the design of the workshop. It will probably indicate one or more means of assessing the impact of the course and workshop on the graduate assistants' thinking or teaching or both. It will be written to indicate confidence, equanimity, and a sincere desire to evaluate the impact of the proposed program.

To consider these different possibilities, I will draw on McCabe's (1971) analysis of purpose, purpose that I have dubbed *affective.* Each of the possibilities that Professor Straits considers illustrates a different intended basic affective response. The novel evokes an involved empathic response, through the details of characters interacting in plots, details that allow readers to evoke their own memory stores and thereby enter into the imaginative world of the characters. The satire, on the other hand, through a variety of cues (Booth, 1974), lets the reader know that it will be necessary to reconstruct the apparent message of the work. Its irony and exaggeration pushes the reader back, warning that it is not to be taken seriously even while certain of its details evoke memories that might engender an empathic response, thus creating instead a detached response. McCabe (1971) argues that any work that focuses the reader's attention on the relationship of parts creates a detached response. For that reason, he calls it the opus-oriented response.

I would add that such a response is mandated by the need to reconstruct the meaning. That is, when we recognize irony at work and stop to reconstruct the meaning (cf. M. W. Smith, 1989), we also recognize that an empathic response is inappropriate. But when we fail to recognize the irony, as I did in reading *Huckleberry Finn* as a child, we may respond with empathy. Similarly, the conventions of jokes, fairy tales, and fables demand that we respond to the work as a whole with a detached response.

The serious proposal intends to promote a different kind of detached response, one that focuses the reader's attention on the information, piece by piece, and the links between the pieces. In the words of Martin Joos (1967), the language of such texts

> endeavors to employ only logical links [as opposed to personal links to reality] kept entirely within the text, and displays those logical links with sedulous care. . . . The grammar tolerates no ellipsis and cultivates elaborateness; the semantics is fussy. Background information is woven into the text in complex sentences. Exempt from interruption, the text organizes itself into paragraphs; the paragraphs are linked explicitly. (p. 37)

The fourth general kind of affective impact is one that demands an involved response, not indirectly through association as do the novel and other genres, but directly through threats and promises directed to the various drive systems. Propaganda and nearly all advertising fall into this category.

These four categories should not imply that a piece of writing necessarily promotes a single affective response. Many do. But many writers have been able to combine two or more quite different affective responses. Bakhtin (1981) argues that the novel as a genre remains alive because of its ability to assimilate other genres. He indicates its ability to integrate the empathic with the parodic. *Huckleberry Finn,* for example, allows us to empathize with Huck (my only response in three readings during the summers of my twelfth, thirteenth, and fourteenth years) while bringing into play several kinds of satire.

To summarize, purpose is not the unitary phenomenon that current traditional rhetoric suggests it is. Purpose, at the very least, involves the substantive and the affective as well as considerations of ethos, all refined by the variety of factors involved in the situation surrounding the writing and sometimes giving rise to it.

THE BASIC STRUCTURES

Current-traditional rhetoric provided more than a view of purpose. As Professor James says at the beginning of this chapter, the idea of "mode" of writing implies both a purpose and a method, a structure. Hence, the common allusion to "forms" of writing. The problem is that, with the exception of narrative, current-traditional rhetoric does not present anything that can be considered formal properties of these forms. What can be meant by the "form" of persuasive writing? Still, it seems intuitively obvious that something like these basic "forms" exists.

Several years ago, reading, at the same period in time, the work of story grammarians (Stein & Glenn, 1979; Stein & Trabasso, 1982) and Toulmin's work on argument (1958), it struck me that certain basic structures of discourse exist in a kind of irreducible form in very young children's oral discourse. Miller (1982; Miller & Sperry, 1988) has shown that mothers socialize their children through the use of stories. Her research suggests that they actually teach children how to tell stories by questioning them about a series of events. Story grammarians say that children by age 5 or 6 have learned the basic grammar of simple stories. As my neighbor's children frequently illustrate, even 6- or 7-year-olds have learned the basic structure of arguments:

OLDER BROTHER: I want an ice cream cone!
MOTHER: It is almost lunch time.
OLDER BROTHER: But Missy has one.
MOTHER: You'll have to wait.
OLDER BROTHER: But that's not fair!
MOTHER: You'll have to wait.
OLDER BROTHER: But you said we should be equal. If she can have a cone, so can I. You said so!

What we have here besides a shouting match is an argument by Older Brother that includes, in Toulmin's terms, a claim, evidence, a warrant, and backing, in that order. This is a structure that children learn very early and use in this minimal form and, occasionally, in more elaborate versions.

At first I saw only these two basic structures clearly. Jerome Bruner (1990) seemed to agree, claiming that there were two irreducible types of discourse that represented two kinds of thinking: narrative and paradigmatic. It seemed that these were demonstrably different in structure. The structure of narrative is governed by consistent agency, chronological order, and some indication of how one event is related to the next, beyond mere chronology. That is, some agent or set of related agents engages in a sequence of actions that lead one to the other in some way. *The Anglo Saxon Chronicle*, taken as a whole, is not a narrative in this sense. It is more like a list. A list of school holidays in chronological order is not a narrative. The structure of argument, on the other hand, has little or nothing to do with chronology or agency except incidentally. It involves a proposition with supporting data and other statements that tie the two together.

As I thought about it, it seemed that there had to be other basic structures. One of these others, one that is neither narrative nor argument, is what I will call topical. Topical discourse depends upon association for its structure. Sometimes the topic is set out in an abstract statement followed by more concrete statements, but not for purposes of support. Sometimes, however, all statements are at the same level of abstraction, such that the topic must be inferred. But the statements are linked by collocation (Halliday & Hasan, 1976). Applebee (1978) reports finding this kind of discourse in his study of children's stories. He calls such structures "piles." In professional writing such structures occur in travel books, encyclopedia entries, wildlife manuals, catalogues, and so forth. Writing textbooks label them descriptive or expository.

The fourth candidate for basic structure status in this analysis is the list, although it may be a subcategory of topical structures. The importance of lists was initially suggested to me by Bernard McCabe, who pointed out that our current school theories of discourse could not account for telephone books and dictionaries. Steve Witte's article (1992) on situated writing uses grocery lists as an example and has convinced me that lists may be a basic structure. Parents teach children to make lists. (What happened today? What do you want for your birthday?) In certain respects lists are similar to topical discourse, but there are key differences. Lists may be construed as part of a single sentence, usually in an object or predicate nominative position, as in, "For my birthday, I want *a, b, c, d,* and so forth." However, in their actual state as answers to questions, for instance, they may be devoid of such syntax. The only relationship among the items on the list is the hypothetical verb. The items need have no intrinsic relationship to one another.

I suggest three criteria for deciding whether a structure is basic or not.

First, it can appear in what might be called a kernel form of a few sentences, but we still recognize its structure. Second, it appears in this kernel form in the language of very young children. Third, in its kernel form, it does not overlap with the others. (Even a list of towns visited in chronological order would be construed as a list, rather than a narrative.) Fourth, it can serve as the organizing structure for much larger, more complex structures. Fifth, the kernel form and expansions of it appear in subordinate positions in larger, more complex structures. That is, a narrative might incorporate arguments developed by the narrator or by characters. At the same time, an argument might include minimal narratives as evidence or to make a point in some other way.

Finally, any of these basic structures, although perhaps not in the minimal form, can produce any of the basic affective responses. This is fairly obvious with narrative and argument. If we can make the case for lists, the point is made. Certainly, lists have an informational function, eliciting a detached response. I would not have my grocery list any other way. Can lists generate any other response? Poets and song writers know they can, and they use lists to generate empathic responses. A case in point is the song "My Favorite Things" from *The Sound of Music.* According to Elliott (1960), one of the earliest forms of satire was the list of curses or invective used to drive scapegoats from communities during the ritual of ablution. Such lists of invective occur in various domestic and even international disputes, when one party threatens another with a list of scurrilous names. The intended effect of the list is to frighten the recipient in a very direct way. The abuse leads one to expect, directly or indirectly, bodily harm or worse. Finally, the satiric technique of presenting a list in which one item contrasts with all the others, thereby undercutting its implications (zeugma), demands the opus-oriented response. A famous example occurs in Pope's "The Rape of the Lock" in the description of Belinda's dressing table:

> Here files of pins extend their shining rows,
> Puffs, powders, patches, Bibles, billet-doux.

Placing *Bibles* in this list strongly implies that Belinda ranks her religion along with the other accouterments of appearance.

I do not wish to pretend that this set of four structures is exhaustive. There must be others. I simply do not know what they are.

The Writing Curriculum

At another level of analysis, specific genres can be seen as fitting within this framework of structures and responses. Almost any research article, for example, has the overriding structure of argument mixed with topical and narrative structures, with the intended response being detached, information-oriented. These specialized genres tend to be field-dependent and learned, as Berkenkotter and Huckin (1993) argue, through a long process of socialization in the field. As such, they are likely to have limited value and interest to secondary school students and college freshmen, most of whom are far from selecting a field of learning to call their own.

Decisions about what specific genres to include in college and school curricula need to be based on three sets of considerations: the appropriateness of the genre to the students; its usefulness in attaining other curricular goals; and its generalizability to other writing tasks. For example, the kind of extended definition discussed in Chapter Four is demonstrably appropriate to high school students, given effective instruction. It is of particular value if some part of the school curriculum is focused on the analysis of values because it enables students to think rigorously about their own ideas of whatever values are the focus of attention. Finally, the strategies learned for extended definition, namely, the specifying of criterion statements and the various uses of examples, are transferable to a variety of other writing tasks. These considerations suggest that the role of specific genres in writing programs will vary from school to school and college to college as students and curricula vary.

It is still necessary to consider the scope of the writing curriculum. We can do that without specifying the specific genres involved. If the sets of basic structures and intended affective responses are comprehensive, they provide an overview of writing and, therefore, a means of thinking about the writing curriculum. Genres can be shown to fit within the categories of the structures and responses outlined above. Therefore, our curricular concerns may be addressed through that model.

Even a cursory examination of textbooks reveals that argument is reserved for nearly the last place in the twelfth-grade text (see Warriner, 1988). And there is no attention to opus-oriented writing such as satire or the situation comedies that inundate our TV sets. And despite the recommendations of so many "experts," most teachers do not even deal with writing about personal experience in a way that involves empathic response. (In Illinois the state writing assessment almost demands that a student write about personal experience in the expository mode.)

Raymond Williams (1983), in *Writing in Society,* tells us that no society has been so dominated by writing as this one, through the agency of the TV and cinema. Yet the schools ignore the very kinds of writing that these media feed upon: narratives for empathic and opus-oriented response.

As Berlin (1984) points out, for a variety of reasons, "exposition, 'setting forth' what is inductively discovered (narration and description are similarly conceived), becomes the central concern of writing classes" (p. 63). If we assume that knowledge may be directly discovered, argument is unnecessary.

According to Berlin, freshman English in American colleges, by the end of the nineteenth century, had become a technical writing course. And to prepare students for college, secondary schools followed suit. That situation needs to be redressed.

There are components other than general processes, discourse, and inquiry to consider in the writing curriculum, namely, the place of grammar, usage, semantics, and even language history. I simply recognize them here and note that many sources deal with them.

PROCEDURAL KNOWLEDGE

The classroom with which this chapter opened is typical of many classrooms at the high school and college levels. They focus on what I have called declarative knowledge. That is, texts and teachers tell students about the features of discourse and sometimes about the general procedures to use in producing written discourse. Think about learning how to swim through this lecture method: four hours of explanation of how to do the crawl, into the pool for the final test on that stroke, and a written evaluation. Not too many of us would learn to swim.

Students certainly learn something about the nature of written discourse through such teaching. They may learn that a "good" paragraph should have a topic sentence (though according to Braddock [1974] few actually do in the textbook sense) or that arguments consist of propositions supported by reasons. But those same students may not be able to generate a "good" paragraph or a developed argument. In fact, Flower and Hayes (1981) report that when writers first focus on the final form of discourse and try to produce its parts, as the texts would have them do, they short-circuit the normal generating processes and become mired in an unmanageable task that blocks writing.

It is one thing to identify the characteristics of a piece of writing but quite another to produce an example of the type. McCann (1989) indicates that sixth graders rank-ordered arguments of varying quality in the same way as adult experts. But they were unable to produce arguments of high quality. Knowledge of discourse, then, appears to have two dimensions: declarative knowledge, which enables identification of characteristics, and procedural knowledge, which enables production. This turns out to be a very important distinction.

The evidence is that declarative knowledge, descriptions of types of discourse along with descriptions of procedures to follow, has only a very weak effect or no effect on improving student writing. In a meta-analysis of teaching writing (Hillocks, 1984, 1986a), the two foci of instruction most dependent on teaching as telling had the weakest effects. Those with significantly stronger effects engage students in the procedures involved. They do not rely on simply stating what the procedures are and then later asking students to use them in a single piece, usually for the first and last time. Rather, the approaches with the stronger effects, call them "procedural approaches," engaged students in a series of activities in which they used the procedures at some level short of independence, with various kinds of support as described in Chapter Four, prior to using them independently (see the Appendix for more information).

At least one writer (A. Freedman, 1993) has taken this as evidence and warrant to inveigh against what she calls "explicit teaching," arguing that procedures cannot be taught explicitly. In fact Freedman, in adapting a model from Ellis (1990) based on research on second language acquisition, argues that explicit teaching of writing is only effective under certain highly restricted conditions. Further, she states that "explicit knowledge is conscious and declarative; implicit is unconscious and procedural. . . . These two kinds of knowledge do not interact" (p. 242).

Although she cites my findings (Hillocks, 1986a) in support of this idea, those findings cannot support such a contention. Indeed, one criteria for selecting studies for inclusion in the inquiry group (the group of studies, as it turned out, with the greatest gains) was that goals and criteria be explicit. Further, when goals were not specific and when students were not focused on learning particular procedures (natural process treatments), gains in writing were not significantly different from those for presentational teaching in which students were consistently taught through lecture.

To make a procedure as explicit as possible is not to make it unlearnable, as Freedman suggests. If the explanation is clear and specific and concurrent or nearly concurrent with the learner's attempts to do it, then the explanation will be helpful. If, on the other hand, the explanation comes days or even hours before an actual attempt at the procedure, it is likely to be of little use. Consider learning how to use the clutch on a standard transmission. My dad's explanation, by itself, would have done little good. His explanation, combined with my trying (and stalling the car fairly frequently) and his coaching, finally did the trick by the end of our second session. On the other hand, had he chosen simply to demonstrate, I would have been in trouble. It would have taken a long time to perceive exactly what the relationships of the pedals had to be.

Learning to produce the *legato* necessary for Debussy's "Dr. Gradus ad Parnassum" was comparable. My teacher demonstrated in detail, explained the effect I was supposed to be after, asked me to try it, then made as verbally explicit as she could what I was to do: "Don't attack the notes. Use more pressure, but it has to be even. Don't release too quickly. Keep it smooth. More pressure here! Lean in to it. You're getting it!" She would sing with me to help me get the emotional quality. That is explicit to my mind. And I am convinced that being explicit is important. However, explicitness is not worth a dead cow in a dairy farm if it is removed from actually using the procedure at some level of sophistication.

What this chapter has tried to do is to outline the kinds of procedural knowledge that writers need to have in their repertoires. The remaining chapters will deal with attempting to teach them. That is, they will be explicitly declarative about procedural knowledge. Here's hoping the price of dead cows from dairy farms appreciates.

Chapter Seven

The Art of Planning I: Some Basics

I once worked in a factory that made rear-end gear assemblies for trucks. My job was to deliver the large ring gears and the matched pinions to about 20 machine operators, who plopped them on their machines to grind them within some desired tolerance. The floor supervisor could plan exactly the night's production with very little effort. Ring gears of different sizes required different speeds to grind within the desired tolerance; the men could change gears for grinding in a certain length of time; checking to insure that desired tolerances had been attained was a matter of inserting a go-no-go gauge; barring any unexpected occurrences, such as a machine operator showing up drunk and surly, the supervisor could tell exactly how many gears of each size would be produced by the end of the seven-and-a-half hour shift. The margin of human error was very narrow. Planning of that sort is about as close to algorithmic as we can get with human beings; there is nothing to it.

Planning for effective teaching, on the other hand, is an art. There are no algorithms, only a wide range of theoretical guidelines suggesting what practice might look like and examples of planning that were more or less effective for particular groups of students. When lecture predominates, as in the profile described in Chapter Two, teaching comes very close to the algorithmic. However, as Socrates warned in the *Phaedrus:* "It shows great folly . . . to suppose that one can transmit or acquire clear and certain knowledge of an art through the medium of writing" (Plato, 1973, p. 97). Derrida would point out that a spoken text has little advantage over the written. I, therefore, approach this task with some trepidation.

THE GOALS OF PLANNING

Writing is an art. Learning an art is learning how, when, and for what purpose to use procedures that are the province of that art. The crucial factors in beginning to acquire such knowledge appear to be having some knowledge of the purposes of such procedures, trying them at some level with some notion of a desired result, a disposition to continue trying when attempts appear to yield only distant approximations, a teacher who both encourages and provides other views of performance than the learner is capable of, and some source that provides models and guidelines. The major goal of planning will be to create an environment in which all of these are present.

Donald Schön (1987) speaks of reflective practitioners as using "frame experiments" that are based on thoughtful analysis of previous experience in comparable situations. Reflective planning and teaching involves, in Schön's words, "a kind of reflection-in-action that goes beyond statable rules—not only by devising new methods of reasoning . . . , but also by constructing and testing new categories of understanding, strategies of action, and ways of framing problems" (p. 39). I would take the matter of reflection a step farther for teachers, especially at the planning stage. The thoughtful teacher, in searching for ways to help students learn more effectively, will plan real trials (what researchers call quasi-experiments), determine what effect they have, even as the trial goes forward, and consider new options as a result.

More specifically, the goal of planning will be to invent materials and activities that will engage students in using specific processes and strategies relevant to particular writing tasks. The aim is to develop an environment like that described in Chapter Four, comparable in many ways to what Schön calls a practicum. "The work of the practicum is accomplished through some combination of the student's learning by doing [and] her interactions with coaches and fellow students. . . . In simulated, partial, or protected form, they engage in the practice they wish to learn." Schön makes the point that learners in a practicum practice both in the sense of engaging in what practitioners do, and "also practice, as one practices the piano, the analogues in their fields of the pianist's scales and arpeggios" (p. 38).

Since this kind of planning is time-consuming, demanding of intellectual energy, and frustrating while it is in process, it makes sense to examine the major objection to it: that the kinds of activities recommended here are too time-consuming. The critics say they have too much to cover to devote class sessions to group discussions similar to those in Chapter Four. There is some truth in what they say. We can do the math. A college class meeting 3 hours a week for 16 weeks is thought to provide 48 hours of instruction. But it doesn't. Each class only meets for 50 minutes, which brings the total time to 40 hours, about one week's full-time work. Our records show that even in the most efficiently run classes some of this time goes to tardiness, record keeping, the telling of favorite jokes and stories, and conferring with one student while everyone else waits. The records indicate a loss of 5 to 30 minutes in classes that are supposed to be 80 minutes and 5 to 25 minutes in 50-minute classes (Hillocks, in progress a). In secondary schools, most of which offer 180 days of school and 40-minute classes, the time crunch is even worse. Even if English teachers tried to spend one-half of each year on teaching writing, with 40-minute classes and time lost for administrative tasks, announcements, attendance taking, and interruptions for assemblies, class pictures, fire drills, pep rallies, field trips, and so forth, a teacher will be lucky to have 40 to 50 hours left for teaching writing. Why bother to spend enormous time and energy planning under such circumstances?

I can think of one major reason. Our evidence strongly indicates that covering many types of writing by lecturing about them or "leading class discussions" about them, what I refer to as presentational teaching, has little or no impact on the way students write (Hillocks, 1986a; see the Appendix). It is far more productive to "cover" fewer "types" of writing in the kind of practicum suggested, where available data show that gains in writing are many times greater. In other words, if students are not learning when the teacher "covers" all that material, then covering the material is unproductive.

To be of use, the ultimate writing curricula, what we spend our time planning for our own students, will have to be designed in light of what a theory of discourse has to say about particular writing tasks, the current performance of specific students in terms of those tasks, a theory of composing, and a theory of teaching and learning. In this chapter, I will turn first to the theory of discourse and specific writing tasks, then to the analysis of current student performance, and finally to the setting of goals in light of both these.

WRITING TASKS IN THE CURRICULUM

A theory of discourse provides, among other things, an analysis of different types and genres of discourse. It may recognize the existence of odes, panegyrics, tankas, and cinquains, but our pedagogical theory may eliminate them from the curriculum in favor of haiku, blues, and free verse. That is, our theory of discourse cannot, in itself, justify what is to appear in the curriculum.

We require a value-laden theory that helps us to reason about which writing tasks are more important for various students at different times. The pedagogical theory argues which types ought to be included in the curriculum on the basis of arguments concerned with the key educational goals, the generalizability of the knowledge, and the appropriateness and appeal of the tasks to students. At the moment we have only a set of assumptions about what ought to be taught, assumptions that have never been seriously examined. Rather than undertake a full-scale analysis of this sort, this section will focus on three writing tasks to illustrate the kind of arguments required. The examples include empathic narrative of personal experience, argument, and satire.

Personal Narrative

We live in an age, says Raymond Williams (1983), when "drama, in quite new ways, is built into the rhythms of everyday life." He points out that we now have "drama as habitual experience: more in a week, in many cases, than most human beings would previously have seen in a lifetime" (p. 12). We are inundated by this kind of writing and the other kinds that go along with it. How many different narratives can one tap into, without reading, at any given time in the United States or in any developed or even undeveloped country of the world? Narratives dominate TV from news to commercials. They provide the content of many popular songs and, even when they do not, a narrative is likely to show up in the video version.

Yet the most important narratives are the narratives of our own lives. Our stories, as we construe them, make us what we are. The narratives we already hold provide the context, values, and assumptions by which we construe the new. Yet each new story influences the existing mix, renewing the context, questioning the assumptions, molding the values. Retelling those stories in a formulaic way adds nothing to the mix. But retelling them to sift their meanings by bringing their details into one focus or another involves reexamining how our stories came to be—what we brought to them and what the world brought to us; reconsidering what we think we care about; putting the articulated story in the perspective of other stories; in short, reinventing the self in a variety of significant ways. Such storytelling fosters the soul. Surely such writing has the potential for meeting the important goals of self-discovery and personal growth.

Personal narrative has more mundane justifications, however. It is highly generalizable to other kinds of writing. Narrative is a key structure in almost every sort of writing. Research reports provide a narrative of what the researcher or the subjects of observation did. Closely argued court decisions often provide detailed narratives of the events leading up to the need for a decision. Aristotle's definitions in the *Nichomachean Ethics* present brief narratives with details carefully chosen to illustrate distinctions between true virtues and seeming virtues. Even business reports and manuals include narratives. For qualitative researchers, narrative is an important research tool. Indeed, many qualitative researchers strive to include the kinds of detail that make the resulting documents empathic (see, for example, the work of Lewis, 1959, 1961).

Although there are no surveys that I know of to determine what kinds of writing students most like to do, many teachers believe that students enjoy writing about their own experience (Graves, 1983). Certainly the experience of my students and me over the past 15 years in working with inner-city students on personal narrative confirms our belief in the appeal of such writing. Our approach has been to work toward the kind of detail that engenders empathic response.

Not all school programs teach personal narrative in that way. The scoring rubric of the Illinois state writing assessment encourages writing about personal experience in the expository mode, complete with what amounts to a topic sentence: "The most important experience of my life . . . ." In addition, the rubric assesses heavy penalties for weak organization, a sure sign of which, according to the scoring guide, is one-sentence paragraphs. If a composition exhibits more than one or two-single sentence paragraphs, it is judged to exhibit weak organization, automatically limiting its possible score. Under such circumstances, what teacher will encourage the use of dialogue, which conventionally results in many one-sentence paragraphs?

Writing that achieves empathic response is arguably the most important kind of writing in our culture. If we include TV and cinematic productions, as does Raymond Williams (1983), there is no question of its wide ranging importance and influence. I have heard people claim that there is "no audience" for personal empathic writing about personal experience. Anyone who visits bookstores or even airport bookracks cannot help but see empathic writing about personal experience. Memoirs and autobiographies abound. Making it as a celebrity nowadays entails writing a memoir of some sort, or having someone do it for you.

Most of our students will not become celebrities and write memoirs. However, what students may or may not become has never been a good basis for deciding what ought to be included in the curriculum. One major concern in schools is with developing potential, providing the bases from which students may grow. A second has been with providing the tools for understanding the culture. If our writing program is to fulfill either of these broad goals, it must include writing for empathic response, both to develop potential and to better understand how such writing operates in the culture.

Beyond that, empathic writing has auxiliary purposes as well. Because students engage with their own stories and like to hear the stories of others, personal narrative can be used in a variety of ways to involve students in high-level discussion of complex ideas and emotions. Many years ago, in teaching *Oedipus Rex,* I was concerned that my students would not feel empathy with Oedipus. I hit upon the idea of asking them to think about "a time when you did something that you were really sorry about but could not change. It was done and you could do nothing about it." I told an experience of mine. They listed some of theirs. We talked a little. They wrote. They gave every evidence of being able to understand Oedipus' plight. At their request, we ended the unit with a student-edited, -produced, and -directed 55-minute version of the play on the school stage, complete with masks for every character.

More recently, my students have used personal narrative to engage in concepts of tenacity, the hero, loyalty and betrayal, justice, conflicts of value, and so forth. The personal-experience texts become part of the textual experience of the class and provide an important sense of ownership in the topic and materials under study. The usefulness of personal empathic narrative and its appeal to students, it seems to me, can hardly be questioned. I would argue that it should be included in every level of the curriculum.

Argument

As I have defined it in Chapter Six, argument is a basic structure of discourse that filters through everything we speak or write. As a basic structure, it does not have the specific, set characteristics of a genre such as fable or even the personal-experience narrative or any of the specific types of satire. Rather its basic features (claim, grounds, warrant, etc.) may take one of several forms, but at the same time they are infinitely malleable, appearing as satire (see, e.g., Swift's "Modest Proposal," Burn's "Holy Willie's Prayer," etc.), advertising and propaganda, some news writing, and research reports. Argument is often incorporated into various forms of popular empathic writing, such as Philip Friedman's (1992) novel *Inadmissible Evidence,* about a murder trial in which guilt must be argued on the basis of circumstantial evidence, without even the reader's being privy to "who really did it."

Certain writers have argued that expert writing is field-dependent, suggesting, in essence, that if you do not know the field, you cannot make a relevant argument. Such writers seem to suggest that one cannot make an argument at all unless one knows the field. Even a moment's reflection suggests that this cannot be the case. While it is certainly the case that a layperson is unlikely to be able to frame an argument supporting some hypothesis about the effect of certain vitamins on the coagulation of the blood, it is equally true that during the founding of the United States, ordinary citizens, none of whom could be considered experts in American constitutional law, made telling arguments in framing the U.S. constitution. Clearly, all argument does not depend on arcane knowledge.

As I have suggested earlier, constructing arguments is closely tied to conducting inquiry and to epistemological assumptions. The strategies of inquiry are inextricably engaged in the development of argument. As we set out to conduct an inquiry, we necessarily conduct an argument, an argument whose claim is continually reshaped by our changing perceptions of the problem, its data, and its context. The more we work with a problem, the more likely we are to deconstruct and reconstruct our thinking about it. This is part of the recursive composing process, part of revising.

We work toward what Dewey called warranted assertions (see Chapter Six) in our inquiries and in our arguments. The process of developing a thoughtful argument cannot be undertaken without the analysis and interpretation of data, the definition of concepts and ideas, the developing and testing of hypotheses, and the imagining of new relationships and other points of view. Many who argue avoid the process of inquiry. They seem to begin with arguments picked up from various sources regarded as authoritative, with claims and sometimes grounds, warrants, and backing in place, but unexamined and shrouded in a Teflon coat that wards off even the most persistent warnings of need for further inquiry. It is with all these conditions in mind that we need to approach the teaching of argument.

Taught as the dry analysis of claims, grounds, warrants, qualifications, counterarguments, and so forth, argument is likely to have little appeal to students. But everyone engages in arguments. Everyone is concerned about issues, and students at all levels, I am convinced, want to engage in discussion of those that they see as relevant. I still remember in considerable detail a rain-filled Scout weekend at which one of our leaders posed an ethical question for discussion. As I recall, it had to do with a messenger carrying a vital directive to a commanding officer near a raging battle in World War II. If the messenger reached the officer on time, the officer would be able to act to save the lives of hundreds of his troops. If not, they would certainly die. The messenger, speeding down the road on a motorcycle, suddenly sees a child standing at a spot in the road ahead, with a rock outcropping on the left and a steep cliff on the right. If the messenger swerves to avoid the child, he may be killed himself, but he will surely lose not only precious time but the motorcycle, which is his only means of getting the message through on time. What should he do, swerve and risk the lives of hundreds of men or run the child down?

I remember that we probed every dimension to find some way out of the dilemma. When every try was disallowed, we had to examine the moral issues involved. My guess is that that was the first time most of us had ever engaged in the serious, extended discussion of any difficult moral issue. Mr. Holloway let us deal with the problem, only setting limits to what the messenger could do with the motorcycle to avoid hitting the child. We were excited and exhilarated. When we had come to some conclusion (I forget what it was), we demanded another problem. The experience provided an important opportunity to me. I learned that I could think about serious issues in a sustained, logical way and, moreover, that I liked doing it. Experience indicates that most students respond in the same way to appropriate problems. In the process, they learn about the structure of arguments and how to develop them.

Because argument is central to our writing, our culture, and our knowing, and because it is accessible and appealing to students, there is no doubt that it demands inclusion in the curriculum.

Satire

Satire is not so easily defended. I discovered many years ago that a significant number of English teachers could not understand why anyone would want to include satire as a major focus of study in English, especially at the ninth-grade level. I remember one young woman saying to me, "I never even studied that in college." At the time, I defended the decision with three arguments: Satire is all around us (novels, cartoons, TV shows, cinema); secondary and college students tend to miss the point unless the satire lacks any subtlety (e.g., *Mad Magazine*); when students begin to recognize the signals and reconstruct the meanings, they enjoy it. I still hold with those ideas.

Over the years, I have come to see satire not simply as a separate genre, but as one that shares many of its strategies with what we tend to think of as distinctly different genres. Satire occurs in novels, plays, short stories, and poetry that would certainly not be labeled satiric. MacPherson's *Marvin's Room,* a play about aging and dying, incorporates satiric scenes but is far from being a satiric play. Bakhtin (1981) comments on the "ability" of the novel to parody other genres: "The novel parodies other genres (precisely in their role as genres); it exposes the conventionality of their forms and their language; it squeezes out some genres and incorporates others into its own peculiar structure, reformulating and re-accentuating them" (p. 5). But the novel also manages to criticize itself. "Throughout its entire history there is a consistent parodying or travestying of dominant or fashionable novels that attempt to become models for the genre" (p. 6).

In the process of this "novelization of other genres," Bakhtin argues

> They become more free and flexible, their language renews itself by incorporating extraliterary heteroglossia and the "novelistic" layers of literary language, they become dialogized, permeated with laughter, irony, humor, elements of self-parody and finally—this is the most important thing—the novel inserts into these other genres an indeterminacy, a certain semantic openendedness, a living contact with unfinished, still-evolving contemporary reality (the openended present). (p. 7)

Satire is the key to this ambience of renewal, this reinvention not only of the self (to return to an earlier theme), but of ways to see and use language and genre. It offers resources that encourage, perhaps demand, seeing in different ways, resources that are tapped in no other writing done in school: all the tools of the satirist—diatribe, exaggeration, understatement, symbolism, irony, travesty, and parody.

If all these arguments fail (as they surely will with high school teachers who want more grammar), we can argue simply that satire is fun. There is a lot to be said for fun in developing talent, as Bloom (1985) points out. Sometimes fun is enough. If you do not recognize the fun in satire, you may have to go a long way to find it, and your fate may be that of the elephant in the fable that Cam Amos wrote when he was in the seventh grade. So take this to heart.

The Unhappy Elephant

by Cam Amos

An elephant who lived in the jungle became very dissatisfied with his life. He was not happy living with the herd and thought that the life of an elephant was too hard for him. Tired of moving tree trunks, he left to seek happiness in the world.

After traveling many miles, he saw a group of monkeys chattering happily while sailing from tree to tree, across a deep ravine. He asked them if it was enjoyable and easy, and they answered him, "It was indeed both."

So he went to one of the trees that was very close to the ravine, wrapped his tail around the overhanging branch, and sailed over the cliff, crashing to the bottom and killing himself.

MORAL: When seeking happiness, never try to make a monkey out of yourself.

EXAMINING STUDENT PERFORMANCE

We need to know what students do as writers, for both planning and the evaluation of our own teaching. Further, we need to track progress over the course of our teaching. To do that we need a theory of quality for each writing task. At the very least, the theory must include (1) a conception of the range of features of the type, (2) an understanding of how the features work together to achieve the substantive and affective purposes, and (3) a conception of how audience response may be affected by variations in the features and the way they work together.

At the beginning of a year or term, our students are likely to be new to us. We cannot begin planning, except with general outlines, until we know what students do as writers. Any writing sample we collect will indicate the performance of particular students on that occasion under the set of conditions imposed by the sampling. People frequently refer to the result as an indication of the students' ability level, allowing the term *ability* to suggest some abstract set of characteristics that are somehow unchangeable, impervious to teaching and other influences.

The word *performance,* however, implies changeability. Everyone knows that performance changes from one day to another. We believe that teaching can change performance. If Verita's first composition (in Chapter One) had been indicative of some unchanging ability, we should not expect to see anything like her second, which appears in Chapter Ten. At the same time, we all believe that ability underlies performance. If performance varied without reference to ability, we might all expect to play basketball like Michael Jordan at least once, if we played often enough. Anyone who has my athletic ability will not bet on it. At the same time, we believe that teaching can change ability. Learning, as Vygotsky points out, precedes development, the development of ability.

We need to begin with a writing sample that can provide guidance for our teaching, regarding it as indicative of current performance under the conditions imposed by our collection. As we proceed with teaching, we will collect more and more samples that will allow tracking of changes in ability and performance. The important idea is that not only do performances change, but abilities develop with effective teaching. As students become better writers, our scales and guidelines need to become more and more demanding. If the Vygotskian principle that learning precedes development holds, students will only improve if we raise the standard of our teaching, helping them learn more sophisticated strategies for writing. Our research supports that.

Our judgments of performance and ability are necessarily based on our construction of the features and qualities of writing. It is no simple matter to decide on this range of features and qualities. To some extent, the theory depends upon the culture in which the writing is produced. Smitherman (1986) argues that the writing of African American students displays many features of oral culture, which academicians consider to be weaknesses, for example, repetition. It is important to be alert to these differences as we plan our teaching strategies and evaluations.

A second problem arises from the fact that different writing tasks involve different qualities. We do not judge a haiku on the same basis that we judge an argument. A satiric narrative will have different qualities from an empathic one or it will not work as a satire. There are some qualities that seem, at first glance, to be qualities we look for regardless of the writing task: the use of accepted conventions for edited writing, clarity of syntax as described by J. M. Williams (1981), and so forth. We commonly talk about qualities such as specificity, focus, and organization. Even these, however, are not applicable to every writing task in the same way. It is necessary to consider criteria for each writing task included in the curriculum. I will confine the discussion here to empathic narrative about personal experience.

Personal Narrative

Ordinarily, it is useful to examine a range of papers thought to display, in varying degrees, the features and qualities of a particular writing task. The following pair of narratives will be useful in this effort. They were written in a

Chicago seventh-grade class, officially designated a "low-level language arts class," that my students and I teach in the fall. Twenty-five of 29 students in the class were African American. Both pieces were written under test conditions—that is, without help from other students or the teacher—over two class periods in response to the following prompt: "Write about an experience that is important to you for some reason. Write about it in as much detail as you can, so that a person reading it will see what you saw and feel what you felt."

The following example is from Maurice, an African American boy who was the biggest seventh grader I had ever seen in more than 25 years of working with seventh graders. The class included two ordinary-sized seventh-grade boys who were fond of punching whoever happened to be sitting near them. I suggested we seat one on either side of Maurice. The punching stopped. Maurice was a solemn boy, dejected perhaps, clearly not very happy to be in school, but not hostile. He wrote:

> Last night when I left school I went home and talked on the phone for about one hour and then I went out front and talked to friends and then came back upstairs and talked on the phone again and then we went to the store and bout some candy and we went home to my house and watch tv for a couple of hours and played around a while then my mother came home from work we went to my grandmother's house for a party it was my mother's birthday we had pizza, lasagna and cake and ice cream and pop and my mother's sister she came over and they went out to party and then we went home and we got to watch movies on tv until really late like 2 in the morning

Despite the fact that Maurice had two successive class periods for writing this paper, it includes only 135 words, with the word *and* making up 12% of the total. Details of the kind we hoped for are nonexistent. There are no allusions to his own personal feelings. Although it is chronologically organized, the focus is diffuse. The passage of time connects the narrative. Finally, the paper includes no punctuation, not even at the end. It was the weakest performance in this class. In other classes, we have received even fewer words. Recently, one seventh grader wrote two lines—which he then studiously erased.

Compare this piece by Maurice to a story by Ranakea, an African American girl in the same class who was in many ways the opposite of Maurice, bubbling over with energy, always smiling, clearly happy to be in school, and hard-working. While my students and I considered Maurice's story the weakest in the class, Ranakea's was pretty clearly the strongest.

The Night I Went to Wisconsin Dells

> This summer 1988 on Friday night at 9:30 p.m. my parents decided to go on a trip to Wisconsin Dells. We packed our bags and loaded the car. We headed out to the highway and the first time my father paid the toll was $1.20 and the next toll was 40 cents. My father drove for 3 hours, but we didn't make it to Wisconsin Dells because my father made a wrong turn and we were heading our way back to Chicago! So my father turned around and said "we'll go to lake Geneva because it was a shorter ride. I fell asleep and my mother did to, finally I woke up and we were at a Motel.
>
> It was $60.00 for one night and all it was a little cottage and all of us couldn't sleep in one bed so father slept on a cot me and my mother slept in the bed. I was so excited because my Grandfather work down in lake Geneva he owned a barbecue pit called Gino's. He sold ribs, chicken, fish, bread pudding, salad, and all the drinks you want. We went there for a little while then I went shopping with my mother to be some biking shorts, Gym Shoes, and a T-Shirt.
>
> Then we kept riding and went to Wisconsin dells. We found a hotel at Wisconsin dells 6:00 a.m. in the morning. So then we all took showers put on our new clothes and headed out to explore Wisconsin. We got on the boat ride call the upper dells at 2:00 p.m. and I saw a lot interesting that God made and nature did together it was beautiful! I rock formation trees that were growing out of the rocks it was a extrodinary. Then after all that we had a 17 year old captain it was fun. Then it was time to go back home to Chicago and we made it home at 12:00 p.m.

Like Maurice's piece, this composition is essentially a chronicle, similar to what Graves (1983) calls a bed-to-bed story, but not a story that depicts a character in attempting to do something. Things happen and the actors go along with the happenings. Although there are volitional statements, the consequences related to them are not very important to what follows. For example, when Ranakea tells us that they "headed out to explore Wisconsin," the action has no special determinant or consequence. The only result is expressed in some generalized response to what she sees, a response that remains unrelated to the other events of her chronicle. One event is held to another only by means of the trip. This noncausality appears to be very common when inexperienced writers write about a trip.

Ranakea's piece does include detail, specific times, the price of the tolls and the room, what is served at her grandfather's barbecue pit, her shopping list. But her details are not the kind that elicit empathic responses. They are simply details that make the trip more believable. She is not at all shy about telling us how she feels about things: the wonders of the Dells, the 17-year-old captain. Her writing displays a pleasant, good-humored exuberance that suggests she will be fun to watch develop.

By way of contrast, Arne Kildegaard's paper, in Chapter One, is a much more complex narrative than it at first appears. We can analyze it as three interlocking episodes. Stein and Glenn (1979) define an episode as consisting of a statement of setting that includes ongoing action (e.g., "one day I was leaving school"), an initiating event (e.g., "when I saw a big shiny Cadillac"), an attempt that includes goal formation (e.g., "without knowing why I scratched an obscenity on it"), a consequence of the action (e.g., "I end up being towed by the ear to the principal's office"), and a response to the consequence (e.g., "I really felt bad because I didn't know why I'd done it").

The first serves for the initiating event of the second episode in which the narrator sits at home (setting) trying to figure why he did it (attempt). The consequence is the father's statement as he turns the light out that night. The response to that consequence is implied in the title of the story. This consequence is really a third elliptical episode, with its major elements clearly implied in the rest of the story. This episode belongs to the parents. For them the setting and ongoing action are the son's reaction to what he has done. Their "attempt" is to let him suffer but to assure him that they love him without qualification. The consequence is implied in the title and, if we think of the real-life rhetorical situation with its multiple audiences, in the very writing of the story.

This story is very complex by seventh-grade standards, even high school standards. Most personal experience stories that I have seen at these levels include only a single episode. When they do include more, the episodes are related, as Ranakea's is, by simple addition. First, a character undertakes one attempt, then another. When other characters appear, they usually remain part of the setting. They ordinarily do not undertake any action independent of the main character, particularly one that intersects with the action of the main character.

In addition, the story strategically uses concrete detail, dialogue, statements, and implications of personal response. Each appears to be selected carefully to convey a central impression. The writer provides an *in medias res* beginning, another fairly unusual feature. The understatement of the ending is quite remarkable for a seventh grader. All these features lead a variety of readers to judge it as outstanding.

As strong as this piece is, it is important to remember that a great range of personal writing exists beyond it. There is always more to help students learn to do. Several years ago, I taught a class composed of juniors and seniors at the University of Chicago Laboratory Schools. For the most part the students enrolled were what I judged to be fairly competent writers, although only a few had learned to make effective use of details in their writing. I set as the major goal of the class the writing of an essay based on personal experience intended for publication in a periodical that had been researched by the writer (through the *Writer's Market,* a query, and reading) and that might reasonably be expected to be interested in the proposed article.

A fairly wide variety of pieces emerged, one about running as the only female on a boys' track team, one about how to hitchhike in Europe, and a composition about an experience working as a volunteer at an archaeological site on the Illinois River (a large prehistoric burial mound). Susan Hack, the author of the latter, sent and sold her piece to the *Midwestern Magazine* of *The Chicago Sun Times* (1977).

What is particularly powerful about this piece (and why I think it is superior to Arne's) is its remarkable interweaving of sharp detail in a focus that allows Susan to take us through a particular day's work at the site, explaining what goes on and why, while formulating every sentence so that each seems to contribute to the ominous judgment of its final one, a tactic that makes it an argument ensconced within a narrative. It appears below as the final draft (she did several) that she turned in to me. *The Sun Times* editors requested an opening paragraph that explained her presence at the dig, which I have not included.

A Matter of Time*

by Susan Hack

Shortly after 6:30, in the half-light of the early morning, the tan school bus, bearing its load of sleepy excavators, arrives at the main trench of the Koster archeological site. Located on a farm which lies nestled in a small cul-de-sac along the east wall of the Illinois River Valley, the site is one of the best known and most extensively studied excavations in the world. But to the crew, up since 5:30 and who face some nine hours of meticulous, slow work under the gruelling heat of the August sun, this is of little interest. Eyes closed, they try to savor the last few precious seconds of sleep before the bus stops and their work day begins.

In the same moment that the bumpy motion of the bus is brought to a halt, all eyes fly open. Everyone stands, grabs his gear, and stumbles, shivering, out of the bus and into the chill of the morning air. Although it cannot be more than fifty degrees, nearly everyone is dressed in shorts and a t-shirt. Each of us knows that while we

---

*Reprinted by permission. *Chicago Sun Times* © 1994.

freeze now, in an hour, the sun will be high enough to shine directly into the trench, that by 10:30, we will be sweating with the heat, and that by noon, the sun will burn unmercifully onto our backs, already cramped and stiff with hours of kneeling and stooping over the squares of earth we are to excavate. At this time, the heat and the incessant buzzing of the wasps and horseflies gathered along the small pools of stagnant water which have collected in the pockets of the black plastic sheeting lining the walls and floor of the trench, become almost unbearable. One feels the sun draining away one's physical energy as it draws the sweat from each pore of the body, while the noisy buzz of the insects, along with the knowledge that there are hours left to go, reduces the mind to a state of uncertain numbness as vague feelings of uneasiness and irritation play erratically along the darker edges of fatigue.

At this stage, it becomes very easy to leave discipline behind and fall into the lulling rhythm of the trowel-work. At Koster, each six-foot square is taken down in two-inch levels. Every object over a quarter of an inch in any dimension is saved in carefully labeled debris bags, and, in many cases, must be meticulously recorded onto numerous forms and maps. Archeology is a destructive process, for in the excavation, the archeological record is destroyed. Thus, a sense of scientific responsibility is essential if the record is not to be lost forever. But when the mind becomes dulled with the heat and the noise, the artifacts and the mapping become the obstacles rather than the objectives. Lost in the pleasant rhythm of troweling, it is easy to forget the heat and the insects. One becomes obsessed with perfecting the troweling technique-scrape, sweep back the loose dirt with your free hand, and scrape again, each time attempting to shave a thin, perfect roll of earth from the ground and pausing only to place the collected piles of loose earth into a nearby bushel-basket. But underlying the relief is a gnawing sense of frantic urgency. The floor of the square must be made smooth and flat as quickly as possible so as to fill out all the forms and perform all the other rituals which enable one to begin another level and escape all the unpleasantness once more.

But for now, with all this ahead of us, we are somewhat optimistic, shaking the last remnants of sleep on the short walk to the site. Arriving at the trench, a rectangular pit thirty yards wide, forty long, and some thirty feet deep, we pause at the edge, looking down to see if any damage has been done by the short rain of the night before. But no, from the top, the tarps protecting the squares look secure. We file down the narrow stairway leading to the floor below, ready to begin another day's excavation. A few people remain behind on the surface to light up a cigarette, a last luxury before entering the pit.

Grabbing a few bushel baskets and debris bags, I head for my square in the northwestern quarter of the site. After untarping it, I equip myself with the various archeological paraphernalia—trowel, carpenter's ruler, line level, etc.—which I will need for the day, and set to work. A gentle breeze, though cold, feels good on my face as it wafts down into the trench, blowing the sleep from my eyes. I smile at my square-partner. Perhaps it won't be so hot today after all.

For me, the morning passes somewhat uneventfully. Among the usual bits of shell, bone and chips of chert, I find two things of particular interest—a large fragment of a shattered stone tool (probably a scraper) and the small lower jawbone, teeth intact, of a raccoon which wandered the forests and marshes of this valley some eight thousand years ago, before ending up as somebody's dinner. Eight thousand years. It is only later than I can comprehend the magnitude of the figure. Time means nothing in the trench. Each scrape of the trowel takes a year from the earth's surface; every inch is a century. It is an odd sensation to look up from the floor of the trench. One sees only blue sky and the tops of the trees which surround the site. Our horizon is limited by the edges of the trench and we can only look up into the curious eyes of the frequent tourist, staring down with wonder, as from some distant future, into the time machine of Koster. We cannot see what they see at the surface—nothing of their present or their horizons, only the empty blue beyond their heads. Even this is too much. After a few minutes, the brightness of the sun sends pinpoints of brilliant pain into our eyes and back into our brains. We must look away, blinking, and turn once more to the mottled brown surface of our small squares of earth.

Shortly before lunch, a halt is called. As frequently happens at Koster, a human bone has been found. Along with a few others, I leave my square and walk over to where the find has been made. At this site, it is not uncommon to find human bones disarticulated from the rest of the skeleton. Of particular interest, however, is that lying next to the partially exposed end of this tibia, the large bone of the lower leg, is the fibula, the companion bone, and a portion of the foot suggesting the presence of the complete skeleton. Thus, while the rest of us break for lunch, the site supervisors call in the osteologist and together they pore over the bones, deciding the strategy for the excavation of the burial. By the time the rest of us return, they have determined, from the positions of the exposed bones alone, the position of the entire skeleton, noting with wry humour that the steel datum-post has been driven through the rib cage and into the cavity which once contained the heart.

To protect the bones from being dried out in the sun after lying in an ideal environment of alkaline soil for so long, the entire burial must be excavated today. Thus, by midafternoon, the entire skeleton has been uncovered and is ready to be mapped and removed. Taking a break, I walk over to the burial square and peek under the makeshift tent which has been erected to protect the bones from the sun. Apart from museum exhibits, I have never seen a "real" burial and along with a few other initiates, I study it in fascination. Fully articulated, the skeleton lies in a semi-fetal position. The knees, spread slightly apart, are drawn up towards the chest. The left arm lies across the chest, the hand clutching at the throat, while the right arm is flung up about the head. The skull, tilted to the left, away from our inquisitive faces, is crushed slightly about the forehead (whether from the weight of eight thousand years of earth or some unknown injury will be determined in the Lab, along with the other details of this individual's physical history) while the jaws are separated, locked in a macabre grin or perhaps the distortion of extreme and utter pain. We are told by the osteologist that it is the body of a man about twenty-seven years old, the approximate age of many people working here. Lying on his back, he looks slightly ridiculous and we laugh.

Yet it occurs to me now that ours was a nervous laugh. We looked down on the body of this man, old beyond memory, from our perspective in time with some apprehension. After eight thousand years of secrecy and, perhaps, peace, we had exposed him. The drawn-up knees, the averted gaze of those empty orbits, the arm flung up, perhaps to stay our stares, suggested an air, not of ridicule, but of protest, an attempt to hide, to get away. We had intruded, unwelcomed, into his time, his place, his way of life. We had uncovered the remains of his camps, his tools, his fires and now, finally, we had dug into his last refuge of secrecy, of privacy, and had exposed him in his nakedness. Remembering my laughter over a joke someone had made about the datum-post sticking like a silver stake into his heart, protecting us from his vengeful ghost, it occurs to me that for me, at least, there was no joke; that incorporated into the wish, not quite so insincere, for the exorcism of the spirit which had inhabited those bones, was a vague fear and an unmentioned plea for forgiveness.

Susan's apparently straightforward narrative, examined from the perspective of story grammar, or my version of it, turns out to be quite complex. It is a chain of minor episodes (arriving, dealing with the heat, working the square, and so forth), each linked to the others by sharing some part with episodes before or after but, at the same time, organized within an encompassing episode that sets the goal as understanding the meaning of the dig, coming to grips with the "vague feelings of uneasiness and irritation [that] play erratically along the darker edges of fatigue."

Not only are the details precise, but the language of their presentation packs an emotional wallop. Further, she presents them so that they resonate with other details in other parts of the story. Look again at some of the details from Susan Hack's writing:

> the heat and the incessant buzzing of the wasps and horseflies gathered along the small pools of stagnant water which have collected in the pockets of the black plastic sheeting lining the walls and floor of the trench, become almost unbearable.

As I reread it, this detail, powerful in itself, resonates with two major themes of the whole. It establishes the theme of distaste and uneasiness that culminates in the final paragraph and the theme of intrusiveness that permeates the entire piece (for the flies, wasps, black plastic, and pools of water are all intrusive). If we wanted to push this a bit further (and why not?), we could see the flies and wasps as playing a role in relationship to the excavators parallel to that of the excavators to those whose graves they disturb, parasites both.

Or consider Susan's description of the skeleton. Why is it so powerful? It begins, midparagraph, as a straightforward, almost technical description and continues rather matter of factly until the words *clutching* and *flung* in the third sentence, words that warn us something more is involved than a technical description. The precise detail remains, of course, but the phrase "away from our inquisitive faces" clearly connects this passage to the theme of intrusion. The fourth sentence, serving as a kind of crescendoing exclamation, not only states the mystery of the man's death, but uses it to imply a commentary on the intrusion of the excavation, for the "macabre grin or . . . the distortion of extreme and utter pain" seem to be directed at the excavators.

In other words, many of the details in this piece have multiple functions. Apart from moving the basic narrative along, each contributes to various layers of meaning developed in the piece. In my judgment and in the judgment of the editors who bought the piece, at professional rates, nothing is extraneous; everything counts. Susan Hack's work demonstrates that such tightly woven, forceful work is not out of the reach of high school and college students.

However, Arne's composition along with the pieces by Maurice, Verita, and Ranakea constitute the rough outline of a scale for holistic scoring that is more reasonable for use in research with high school and college students. (If Susan Hack's paper were the benchmark paper for a score of five, that score would seldom be used, an observation that indicates the need for a more complex scale for more sophisticated writers.) On the other hand, the pretest pieces by Maurice and Verita are representative of the weakest pieces we receive from seventh graders, as well as high school and college students. Ranakea's piece stands midway between those and Arne's piece, a 3 on a 5-point scale, because although it was without the sharp focus and tightly related events of a strong empathic narrative, it did include specific detail and expressions of personal response.

I have used such a scale in formal research (Hillocks, 1979, 1982) and informally nearly every year to evaluate the impact of our teaching on seventh graders and versions of it to examine change in the writing of classes of high school students and freshmen in four-year colleges and universities and in community colleges. Although the scale is very useful, the score in itself, apart from the description, is no use at all for teaching. However, this scale, or some other, can be used as a guide in identifying the features of personal writing produced by a group of students. In doing that, the scale also becomes a guide in setting the objectives for teaching. If we see, for example, that none of our seventh graders use dialogue or indicate personal response, except in very general ways, then using dialogue and indicating response may become goals. For individuals, one piece of writing is certainly inadequate for any remotely definitive judgment. But a single writing assignment for a class as a whole is quite reliable and very useful.

SETTING DIRECTIONS AND GOALS FOR TEACHING

In light of what I have argued about the knowledge necessary for effective writing, the goals of a writing program will include objectives that reflect the full panoply of knowledge required for effective writing: abilities and dispositions to use writing process strategies, the conventions of standard edited prose, and general knowledge about discourse that appears useful across writing tasks. Here, however, we are concerned about the objectives related to particular writing tasks.

In Chapter Four and in the chapters on inquiry, I indicated that a common characteristic of effective teaching of writing is clear objectives, clear not only to the teacher but also to the students. Significantly, clear objectives are a condition for what Csikszentmihalyi (1990) calls flow experience. Specific descriptions of writing, along with examples such as those above, are imperative to determining what those objectives will be and, therefore, to effective planning.

For some people, the terms *objectives* or *goals* connote limitation, as in the matter of the number of ring gears to be ground in a single factory shift, 30 say, no more, no less. In teaching, however, our specific goals indicate the direction in which we hope teaching will help students move. A specific goal for Maurice's class (as well as Verita's, Ranakea's, and Susan Hack's) was the effective use of specific detail. We will be very happy if Maurice moves to the level of specificity in Ranakea's pretest paper. But if he moves to Susan Hack's level, so much the better. Obviously, no one would limit the potential extent of student gain.

What is important is determining the qualities that are important to the writing task. Donald Schön (1987) points out that "skillful designing depends on a designer's ability to recognize and appreciate desirable or undesirable design qualities" (p. 159). Even more important is knowing how to produce the desirable qualities. The same is true for writing. While it is clearly important for writers to recognize the qualities of good writing, as those qualities vary from task to task, they also need to produce them if they are to be effective. This is the difference between declarative and procedural knowledge.

When we set objectives, we attempt to determine specifically what those qualities are. At the same time, the verbal statement of the goal must remain relatively abstract to allow for countless variations that will qualify as meeting it. The abstraction of the goal, therefore, prohibits the kind of specification we might expect in a laboratory. Still, we can indicate what will count as success through the attendant examples. Determining what meets the objective remains a matter of judgment, based on some construction of the abstract statement in light of its concrete examples. If two teachers construct the objective differently, refer to different concrete examples, they will judge the results of teaching differently. Another way of saying this is that different standards result in different judgments, and inevitably in different teaching emphases and differences in what students learn.

Consider, for a moment, two different constructions of the objective about specific details. Compare the following two teacher comments, collected in a pilot study, in response to Ranakea's paper, which appears earlier in this chapter. The teachers had been asked to comment on the quality of the paper and the direction they thought teaching should take as a result of what they saw in the paper.

> Teacher 1: This is quite a good paper in terms of content. She has included many different specifics about the trip, and gives the reader a good idea of what was involved. She tells how much the tolls were, what times they arrived and left, and so on. I would commend the

paper for that. I believe that this child is ready for a workshop approach in class. She should choose topics that interest her and share her writing with peers. This is what I would do.

Teacher 2: I like this writer's peppy style. It helps to reveal the excitement she felt about the trip. I would hope she will continue to develop it. The piece as a whole is not very strong, mainly because it lacks focus. The details she includes do not contribute much. I would encourage her to use more precise detail and more detail in the service of some more particular event or mood, maybe her flirtation with the "seventeen year old captain."

The first teacher, who thinks the content is fine, will focus on a workshop approach, which will not involve specified teaching. The notion is that writing more will result in improvement. The second teacher will deal with the development of content with special attention to detail and focus. One sees the content as fine, the other as problematic and something to improve upon. The difference in the perception of content is striking. The second teacher is likely to provide instruction that will lead to better focus and integrated details. The first teacher is likely to ignore differences in content, leaving the student to discover not only the desirable qualities but the procedures for generating them on her own.

The objectives we set will indicate the desired qualities, the direction of learning; the concrete examples indicate the range of what we hope for. More than that, however, the statement of the central task objectives stipulates what is essential and helps to establish it for continual and automatic reference during teaching. Without the objectives and the underlying specific references that give them meaning, reflective practice is impossible. Without them, the teacher has nothing against which to judge current observed performance of the students.

What will the written objectives look like, then? They can take many forms. I encourage my students to use a simple statement about the writing task followed by a list of criteria that indicate the desirable qualities. For example, one might read as follows:

Write empathic narratives about personal experience. The narrative should

1. Focus on a particular experience in which the main character attempts to do something or is the recipient of some action or both
2. Make use of specific, concrete detail including details of the

senses, dialogue, figurative language, and statements indicating personal physical and emotional responses
3. Use detail so as to develop empathy with the character
4. Select and present details so that they contribute to the focus of the narrative

This statement includes most of what I discussed earlier. It is necessarily abstract, but combined with examples it provides a guide to the qualities we hope to help students learn to produce in their narratives.

Talk of clear objectives, however, raises red flags for some people. Many associate the term with behavioral psychology and the Tyler (1949) curriculum rationale, which they assume leads to mechanistic teaching (see, e.g., Cain, 1989). They appear to believe that working toward some goal in teaching and specifying or predicting what the outcomes ought to be lead to rigidity in teaching, a tendency to ignore the real needs of students, and a lack of insight into the teaching process (Cain, 1989). In a certain sense, Cain and critics like her are right, especially if we restrict our thinking to what passes for clear objectives (what Cain refers to as behavioral objectives) in curriculum guides.

What constitutes a clear objective? What appear to be the clearest "behavioral" objectives are, in fact, often the most vague or the most trivial. Simple statements (e.g., "to write better paragraphs" or "to write a short story") are not simply useless, but harmful. They hide the complexity of the tasks they represent. When they stand alone, as they generally do, they provide no help in conceptualizing either the task or the instruction it requires. As a result, they suggest that some sort of simple-minded planning will suffice to help students reach the goals they purport to convey.

On the other hand, statements of broad general purposes that may seem to pass as objectives for teaching are not very useful either. For example, the student teacher of whom Cain approves makes the following general statements of goals or objectives for teaching Shakespeare's *Henry IV, Part I:* "Through the study of literary works, we may increase our understanding of the commonality of human emotions as well as the range of differences in human experience. By reading and responding to a piece from a different time and culture, students move beyond their own experience to become aware of values, beliefs, and experiences different from their own as well as to recognize the universality of human emotions and reactions." This statement certainly represents a worthwhile goal.

As it stands, however, it is a goal difficult to translate into classroom activities likely to prompt meaningful discussions of the complex questions involved. In fact, Cain nowhere indicates that this goal is ever taken seriously. If it were taken seriously, one would expect the teacher to ruminate about it, at least considering how to raise such questions as (1) what we think the emotions are today and how they were viewed in Shakespeare's time; (2) what constitutes a universal "reaction"; (3) whether or not people from different cultures react in the same way to the same phenomena, or whether reactions are culturally dependent; and (4) how to involve students in thinking about the "universality of human emotions and reactions."

Cain's account of the teacher's thinking and planning indicates no such ruminations. Such global goals, though well intended, tend to serve as window dressing: They look good, they don't cost much, and they do not reveal what's really in the shop. Worse, they often seduce the planner into believing that something important is happening. The planner in Cain's study appears to believe that certain broad values are inherent in the literary work and readily transferable to readers upon the act of reading, viewed as a relatively passive process. Such belief ignores the idea that the reader constructs meaning from texts. Meanings do not transfer directly from the text to the student's head, especially not the meanings the teacher has constructed for herself.

If Cain's teacher expects students even to recognize the "universality of human emotions and reactions," the goal must be translated into specific activities that can result in meaningful discussion and writing. For example, consider as a test case Act 5, Scene 4 of *Henry IV, Part I,* a key scene in the play taught by Cain's teachers. In this scene Falstaff feigns dying at the hands of Douglas and then rationalizes his deceit. Students might focus on Falstaff's speech after he has feigned death, interpret the scene to determine what emotions they think are involved, consider the extent to which Falstaff's reaction might be considered universal and why, and so forth.

Imagine how Maurice and Verita would fare if the stated goals remained abstract, rather than made concrete through specific activities, examples, various indications from their teachers, and eventually their own writing. What would happen to their writing if they heard only the abstract goals? Their experience would be not unlike that of the students whose teachers are profiled in Chapter Two, students who show no gains in writing (Hillocks, 1992, in progress a).

Chapter Eight

The Art of Planning II: Inventing Gateway Activities

Imagine a fifth-grade classroom, racially mixed, a student teacher in charge. The first thing you notice is that desks are all pushed to the edges of the room. The children are huddled in small groups on the floor. They and the student teacher are all within an area marked off by masking tape, roughly in the shape of a ship. The student teacher is wearing a ship captain's cap. There is a lot happening at once. Most groups are talking earnestly among themselves. But one group besieges the captain, pleading for something from the sound of their voices. They speak gibberish, with one or two words of English thrown in: cold milk, porridge, water. Their urgency and distress are expressed in many nonverbal ways, in facial expressions, posture, movements of hands, arms, and even legs. As the group becomes more and more insistent, the captain orders them away abruptly, but another group approaches, clearly needing or wanting something.

When all groups have been turned away by the captain, the captain's demeanor and voice change. She becomes the student teacher again. The students drop the role they have been playing and, at the teacher's request, return to their desks and move them back to the classroom formation. She asks her 26 students to stay in the role of the person they have just dramatized and to write that person's thoughts and feelings in a poem, a diary entry, or a letter. The students, who had been thoroughly engaged in playing their roles, now sit quietly at their desks to write.

The class has been studying immigration to the United States with a particular focus on Ellis Island to help make the immigrant experience more concrete. Marjorie Hillocks, the student teacher and my daughter (in an elementary school teacher education program at the University of Chicago), has engaged the class in other activities that demand a kind of imaginative leap and that have served as preparation for this. In one of these, students looked at and talked about pictures of objects left at Ellis Island, thought about an object that they believed they would take if they had to leave home as emigrants, drew pictures of them, described the objects to the class, explained why they would take them, and wrote about them.

Marjorie's main goal in using the creative dramatics activity was to help students make the imaginative leap into emigrant shoes. Her belief is that without such activities, the students may learn what the immigrants to the U.S. suffered, but they will understand it only as a distant set of facts that will be easily forgotten. The collaborating teacher regularly integrates the learning activities of her classes so that social studies and language arts flow into one another. So the writing activity followed naturally.

Did this activity, involving what I have called an imaginative leap, work, or at least appear to? Some students wrote more than others; some wrote more effectively than others. But all wrote from the point of view of another person enduring difficult circumstances, something of an accomplishment in itself. In my experience even college students find writing from another point of view difficult without preparation. The following two pieces are representative of the quality of the class's written responses.

I Cry

by Rebecca Meredith

I cry out in need,
a cry for air.
I can hardly breathe.
My throat aches with pain,
my heart aches with grief.
The dusty air is in my chest,
it's like a test for death.
I never should have left my country,
never.

The Long Voyage

by Matt Brent

Being tormented by the captain, who herself didn't have to ask for anything, but I can see all these people besides us who are suffering and getting frustrated because no one speaks their language except the people in their family. Unfortunately, I can understand some English but cannot speak it. My only words are, "COLD MILK." Sometimes I wish I had stayed home where everybody speaks our language.

If I live through this, I will be all thankful to the Lord. Besides

> the captain, the rest of the voyage has been fairly good. I can only act out my thoughts to the others on the ship who have different languages.
>
> Now my baby's whooping cough is worse, and the captain won't do a thing about it.

Clearly, the activity worked for these students. They seem to have some insight into the plight of immigrants, and the writing produced as a first draft is impressive. The impact extended beyond the boundaries of the immediate unit of instruction. Toward the end of the school year, after Marjorie had completed her stint, the students studied mythology, and wrote and produced a play based on what they had learned about the Greek gods and demigods. In addition, however, they wanted to write and produce another play about the problems of immigration. Their play told the story of an immigrant family, one of whose children was forbidden entry into the United States for medical reasons, and the anguished decision-making process involved. It seemed clear to me, as I watched their play, that their imaginative experiences (their inquiry) earlier in the year had carried over into their writing and production of the play.

This activity concentrated on inquiry, ways of thinking about substantive issues that would become the material of the writing. Students had other classroom experiences that provided understanding of the kinds of discourse involved: letters, poetry, journal entries, and plays. Effective teaching of writing must involve both.

INVENTING GATEWAY ACTIVITIES

In one sense, what follows is *the* crucial section of this book. Theories of discourse, inquiry, learning, and teaching are useless if we cannot invent the activities that will engage our students in using, and therefore learning, the strategies essential to certain writing tasks. These activities provide the circumstances and support that enable them to use strategies that they would otherwise not be able to use. Because writing involves both substantive and affective purposes, our activities will have to involve students in appropriate strategies of inquiry and ways of generating discourse features. I will refer to these as *gateway activities.* In Chapter Three, I referred to Serres's (1982) metaphor for thinking about knowledge: the journey. Gateway activities open up new journeys. The problem for this chapter is: How does one invent them?

A sequence for teaching writing may include many different activities. Most may be described as standard: listening to teacher explanations, reading a model piece of writing, drafting a piece, providing feedback to a peer, revising, and so forth. While these activities are important to achieving the goals of the sequence, they cannot, in themselves, engage students systematically in using strategies that are beyond their reach for independent use. The gateway activities, on the other hand, engage students in using difficult production strategies with varying levels of support and lead eventually to independence. The standard activities prepare for and reinforce that learning.

The success of gateway activities is heavily dependent upon effective design, which requires attempting to predict problems that might occur and rectifying them beforehand, a kind of reflection-in-design. Unfortunately, not all problems are predictable, a condition that requires reflection-in-practice and the continuation of design. In neither case are there any rules to follow. There are guidelines from theory, research, and experience, but no rules.

The initial problem is the hardest: generating the activity. What are the key production strategies for generating activities that will enable students to learn production strategies for various writing tasks? That is the key question. Every year my students set out to invent these key activities, and many of them have subsequently published them (see, e.g., Johannessen, 1992; Johannessen, Kahn, & Walter, 1982; Kahn, Johannessen, & Walter, 1984; Lee, 1993; Smagorinsky, McCann, & Kern, 1987; M. W. Smith, 1984, 1991; Stern, 1995). However, I can never tell them how to do it, exactly. The best I can do is indicate general strategies that have proved useful to others in devising successful gateway activities and engage students in the production of others, first relatively simple ones, later more complex ones. The invention of these activities is not complete without careful evaluation. Our key production strategies have been to

1. Determine, as well as we can, the essential features and strategies of the writing tasks;
2. Invent gateway activities that enable students to engage in those strategies;
3. Evaluate these introspectively;
4. Develop sequences, including standard activities that will prepare for and reinforce the gateway activities and that will enable students to develop the full range of strategies, including the more general writing processes, required by the particular writing task;
5. Put our inventions into practice so that they may be assessed and redesigned as necessary; and
6. Evaluate the full sequence.

This chapter will be concerned with the first three of these, Chapter Nine with the fourth, and Chapter Ten with the fifth and sixth.

FROM TASK ANALYSIS TO ACTIVITY: THE FABLE

Features of Fables

Let us take the satiric fable as an example. The features and qualities of fables are probably well known to anyone reading this book. In the satiric fable, the moral comes at the expense of some animal displaying a human foible or vice. The stories are brief, the animals are characterized in a few strokes, one animal displays a vice or foible in its actions, and if there is another, it usually serves as foil or trickster. Occasionally, there are several animals, but ordinarily only one displays the vice or foible, as in James Thurber's "The Scotty Who Knew Too Much." The Scotty's arrogance leads him into serious trouble and then into rationalizing his failures. The skunk, the porcupine, and the farm dog are foils that reveal the Scotty's foibles by contrast. When the second animal has the role of trickster, it often takes advantage of vices and foibles, as does the crafty fox in "The Fox and the Crow," flattering the crow's voice, thereby enticing the crow to sing and, as a result, drop his cheese into the fox's waiting mouth.

One quite tricky feature of the fable for students is the plot. Unlike personal-experience writing in which, for students at least, the plot is no trouble, being dictated by the experience as recalled, the plot of the successful satiric fable turns on the objectionable trait, which brings the downfall or embarrassment of the character who possesses it. The play between the character's disposition and behavior and later fate provides the impact of the fable.

Production Strategies

Knowing all this and more about fables does not provide a clue about the processes of generating one. How does one begin? At least, what are some of the strategies involved in generating even parts of the fable? Unfortunately, for writing a fable and for most other writing, there is little or no research that will reveal the requisite task specific processes. However, we can speculate about the processes of production, on the basis of our own introspective experience in producing an example of the type. The goal in this speculation is to discover possible procedures for producing an example of the type.

In the case of the fable, teachers frequently suggest beginning with a moral. That suggestion, however, asks us to generate a list of the morals familiar to us. When I do that, I immediately think of Ben Franklin, Aesop, and James Thurber. The moral I think of may not be one I want to write about. If it is part of an existing fable, the existing fable may be such a strong stimulus that it is difficult for me to think of a new one. Years ago, my students were frustrated with that approach. I also gave them situations to use if they could not think of one of their own, but I realized that doing so provided what Bereiter and Scardamalia (1987) call "substantive facilitation." I was doing a major part of the task for them.

Another salient feature of the fable is the human foible portrayed by some personified animal, a feature that brings about the downfall or embarrassment of the animal. A possibility for generating a fable might be to explore the nature of foibles or vices that the writer finds loathsome or, at least, irritating, to consider how people with such a foible act, to think of possible animals that might represent such a foible, and to consider how that foible might bring about the animal's fall. This is a process of inquiry into what writers already know.

Evaluating Possible Procedures

There are three ways to evaluate such possibilities: Consider whether it is reasonable to assume that a writer of successful fables might have begun that way; try to generate a piece of writing using that approach; and try it on students. For obvious reasons, these evaluations ought to be made in that order. We will take them one at a time.

It seems very reasonable to assume that Aesop and Thurber may have been inspired by people exhibiting despicable vices and foibles. Can you imagine Aesop observing some wealthy, self-satisfied businessman trying again and again to attain some property or office, but failing to, finding fault with that which he had hither to eagerly sought? And so, perhaps, "The Fox and the Grapes" was born. Can you imagine Thurber being disgusted by some cocky, know-it-all bully who had no respect for anyone but himself? Some such person might well have given rise to "The Scotty Who Knew Too Much." In my mind, it is at least conceivable that some such process of suggestion led to the writing of their fables.

The next level of evaluation is to try the procedure personally. If it will not work for the teacher, it is a travesty to subject students to it. What traits irritate me? Hypocrisy, pomposity that goes with a false sense of one's knowledge, pretentiousness of various kinds, and so forth. Since hypocrisy is at the top of my list, I'll try that. Can I think of examples of hypocrites and specify how they behave? Immediately, I recall a state university administrator who seemed to me to act out of self-interest while giving lip service to his concerns for the good of the "academic community." He liked to talk about the importance of our sense of community, our commitment to scholarship, the need to sacrifice for the greater good. This talk resulted in little action. He would talk about the need for keeping promising faculty in all departments through various incentives such as salary increments, increased time for research, and so forth; he received research time and salary increments himself, but the promising faculty kept leaving.

I think of the man as slimy, which suggests possible animals, an alligator or snake who grins eagerly as he talks to the other animals about how he might save them all from hunters, or guard their young, out of his interest in the good of the community, for a fee of course.

Generating Gateway Activities for Fables

At about this point, my thinking begins to alternate between my fable idea and the activities that might be useful with students. It seems to me that simple inquiry into what foibles and vices students find loathsome may be a good starting point. Years of working with junior high students tell me that kids have pet peeves about certain character traits that will predictably come up in brainstorming, for example, "back stabbing." Further, talking about how such people act will be fun. A second strategy would be thinking of animals that might represent the trait, followed by talk about what some of these animals might do if they were personified with the particular trait. To whom would my administrative alligator or snake talk? What would he say? How would he behave? Should we consider role playing some of this? (My snake would be pompous. He might be fond of saying to the other animals, as he glittered in his shiny new skin, "My friends, the most important thing we can learn as members of the animal kingdom is that we are engaged in this great project of life together. I count it a sacred duty to watch over the interests of each of you.") The thinking switches between fable and activity, a good sign.

Having the trait and a possible animal and its behavior in hand could lead to the beginnings of a plot. What might the animal do as a result of his trait that might bring about his own downfall? How might other animals react? (My snake might, as snakes will, eat the young of all of his "friends" in the countryside. It could happen that . . . One day, when the animals had come together in the forest to discuss the affairs of the day, a mother mouse, in tears, complained of the disappearance of a young one without a trace. Other animals made similar complaints of silent disappearances without a trace: a young frog, a salamander, a fledgling wren, even eggs from nests. Finally, the snake arose to express his alarm and sympathy. Said he, "The horror of these disappearances is a great shock to us all. Something must be done. Because we are all in this great project of life together, I want to volunteer as a protector of the young. No one is better suited to this than I, for my agility and my reptilian character give me access to even the remotest corner of the forest. I ask for nothing in return other than the good of the community." All the animals except the eagle cheered at this noble offer. The eagle said only, "We'll see," and flapped to his nest high in the cliffs.)

Having the trait, behavior, and reactions of other animals may generate only the basic plot situation. The climax and the denouement will depend in part on the comeuppance we want for the foolish or evil character and in part on the character's trait and behavior. (Perhaps my snake would become smug in his ability to fool everyone and forget about the eagle. The eagle could be the agent of punishment for the snake, catching him red-handed in a nest with an egg in his mouth but, before disembowelling and eating him, saying "I am only doing this for the good of the community." A possibility.)

Once a plot outline is available, the next part of the task is generating a moral. The easiest procedure is to use a statement that makes explicit the moral implications of what has happened in the fable, pedestrian perhaps, but even some of Aesop's morals are pedestrian. (Assuming the snake is caught in my fable, a suitable, but uninteresting, moral might be, "The hypocrite is soon discovered." A moral that extends the implication of the fable is a little better: "Hypocrites foster their own doom.") The clever moral that serves the fable and is funny to boot is more difficult. I'm not sure how to produce them. I can review the language to see if it suggests a word play of some sort. The monkeys in Cam Amos's fable (in Chapter Seven) may have suggested his use of the adult reprimand to a child, "Don't make a monkey of yourself." (The word play I can think of at the moment for my fable might be a play on the snake's glittering skin, the eagle's ripping it open, and the phrase "only skin deep": "The hypocrite's glitter is only skin deep." A little more interesting than the other ideas but still not quite there.)

The task analysis combined with the self-trial suggests the outlines of activities that involve strategies of inquiry: generating a list of despicable foibles or vices; talking about how such people act; generating a list of possible animals to represent a trait; describing how the animals that represent them might behave; predicting what such a person (and the animal surrogate) might do to look foolish or to bring about its own fall; and considering alternative morals, from the direct to the play on words.

Simply asking students to do each of these subtasks independently is not much better than assigning the writing of a fable. Generating the parts, or some of them, and thinking about how they work together as a group is both easier and more fun. Allowing for more interchange, the collaborative group has the advantage of more ideas and shared responsibility. Ideas from one person will stimulate the thinking of others: "What you said reminds me of . . ." or "that makes me think of . . ." However, the set of ideas to be generated is fairly complex. If students work in small groups without any preparation, they are unlikely to understand the process and what it should generate.

The question is how we can prepare students for the small-group work. (This is not an infinite regress, though it may appear to be.) As in the extended definition activity of Chapter Four, it is possible for the teacher to guide students through the initial inquiry into parts and fitting them together. Using an overhead projector, the teacher can write the lists of ideas suggested by the students. After developing lists of ideas, the teacher can guide students in considering how the people and animals might act. Focusing on one foible and one animal to represent, the class can make suggestions for actions as the teacher writes a plot outline on the overhead. The fable so produced will not be a finished product. The focus has been on inquiry into ideas and the invention of a workable plot that illustrates the foible or vice and provides a warning. Work on the style can come later.

Having been through the process once with guidance from the teacher, we can guess from experience that most seventh- or eighth-grade classes could use the processes in small collaborative groups, generating sets of ideas for fables, perhaps using the lists of foibles and vices already generated by the class. During this period the teacher acts as a coach, moving from group to group, making suggestions about procedures (not substance), asking questions that might help prompt ideas, and being supportive. Once the groups have developed ideas and a plot, they may turn to developing a final product as a group or individually. The teacher may wish to have students share the fables. For those of you thinking that this is just too much spoonfeeding, teachers and graduate students participating in various writing projects have not found this process beneath them. They have certainly always enjoyed reading their fables to the group.

PERSONAL NARRATIVE

The preceding chapter outlined significant features and qualities of empathic personal narrative, features that contrast in a number of interesting ways with those of the fable. The details used in the fable, for example, are few and have a purpose entirely different from those used in an empathic narrative. The details of the former are often ironic and are so recognized by anyone familiar with the cultural conventions associated with the genre. That is, the details of the fable seem to assert that the animal is real and to be taken seriously but at the same moment undercut the assertion because they are such that we recognize them as not possible, even preposterous.

To some extent, the effect is built into a genre that uses anthropomorphic details. The skilled fabulist, such as Thurber, adds dimensions that would be ironic even if applied to humans. Thus, when Thurber's Scotty, acting even more preposterously than a thoroughly arrogant, overconfident human being, enters his third fight in the country with one paw covering his eyes and the other his nose (to protect himself from the "knives" of porcupines and the "vitriol" of skunks), we recognize in the details both a kind of truth-to-type and a clear indication of their condemnation.

The details of the empathic personal narrative, on the other hand, fail if they undercut themselves. That is, they must be accepted as indicative of a reality as experienced by another human being. If the writer exaggerates or presents contradictions (the basis of irony), the thread holding the willing suspension of disbelief breaks. The many more details in this kind of writing must be convincing and precise enough to echo with the reader's memories of comparable experience, an echo that appears to be the basis for the imaginative leap into the narrator's experience. The details of the empathic personal narrative present some difficulty for inexperienced writers, for they must be not simply specific, but selected with a view to the affective response the writer hopes to generate in the reader. Thus Ranakea's piece in the last chapter presents details that are not somehow related to the plight of the characters and cannot arouse empathy. The irony of anthropomorphic details, surprisingly, appears to be easier for young writers, in part because they are anthropomorphic.

The plot of the personal narrative, on the other hand, appears to be easier because the experience supplies the plot line. At the same time, however, for younger writers especially, what the writer conceives as "an experience" appears to determine whether the writer produces a chronicle or a story. The problem becomes one of generating or discovering a focus, an idea not easily defined. We know a strong focus when we see one, as in Arne Kildegaard's and Susan Hack's papers, and we recognize a weak focus. We could say, with Edgar Allan Poe (1979), that everything in a well-focused piece contributes to a single impression, what he called in his "The Philosophy of Composition," "the vastly important artistic element, totality, or unity, of effect" (p. 1321). We would qualify that, as Derrida might, by adding that the art of focusing lies in giving the appearance of unity where there is polysemy. In such a view there is a need to decide, at some point, what the "central impression" will be and which details will support it or, perhaps, to do so intuitively. Writing in this genre appears to require a consciousness of detail and the need to employ it effectively in the service of that impression.

Production Strategies

One major generative problem in empathic personal narrative, then, appears to be detail, which I will address first because so many student pieces in my experience have had a potentially strong focus but virtually no detail: a skiing accident, nerves at graduation time, a beating on the night of a race riot, a fight in a bar, a fire in a house, a gang confrontation, and so forth.

Why is it that inexperienced writers typically lack such detail and frequently lack focus? As with so many other mysteries in writing, the answer is not readily available. We can only speculate. One possibility is that they simply do not know the requirements of the genre. However, when teachers present models of the genre, only a few students seem enabled to produce their own specific prose (Hillocks, 1979, 1982, 1986a). Another possibility is that they do not understand the composing process and the necessity for writing to develop over several drafts. Research, however, suggests that even when students do understand the need for feedback and multiple drafts, their writing improves in relatively marginal ways. That is not to say that knowledge of general writing strategies is not important. When we see young writers constantly dipping into their bottles of Whiteout to correct spelling or make writing neater in an effort to get it right the first time, it is clear that general process knowledge is indeed necessary. But it appears to be not sufficient.

A third possibility is that they do not recognize the need that an audience has for specifics. My hunch is that young writers see their general statements about experience ensconced in the penumbra of details held fast in their memories. They expect an audience to interpret their statements aided by a similar penumbra. That, of course, is a problem that even the most experienced writers must struggle to overcome. If young writers were given many opportunities to write for an audience and receive feedback that would indicate the inadequacy of their detail, would that suffice? I think not. Research indicates that students exposed to such feedback in programs focusing on general writing processes show only relatively weak gains in writing quality (Hillocks, 1986a). Many teachers believe that feedback from peer groups can be very useful, but because students are reluctant to criticize the work of their peers, they require considerable guidance from teachers (S. Freedman, 1987).

Still another possibility is simply the difficulty of generating details from memory and translating them into written words. I have only to think of an iris that comes up in my garden every spring or the Venus comb shell with its rows of fragile white spines that sits in my bookcase and I recognize my knowledge of the appearance of those natural objects and my inability to present those appearances in words. Yet I can call up the visual image with no trouble. The act of describing them entails holding the visual image in mind, concentrating on it, and finding the language to do it justice. No easy task. And this task, finally, involves all of those above.

Finding the right language implies the need for multiple trials, for drafting and revision. Finding the *right* language implies an audience for whom it is right and perhaps knowledge of similar discourse to gauge it against. Still, even though the task of writing effective personal narrative involves all of these, the key problem seems to be the difficulty of holding the image in mind while finding the right language, in a sense, a basic problem of inquiry, learning to look and describe.

Generating Gateway Activities for Personal Narrative

Our analysis suggests that a key problem is holding an image in mind and finding effective language to render it on the page, a basic problem for any kind of inquiry. An important part of the gateway activity may be to make the image or some part of it present so that students may concentrate on the language. A second key may be to work orally to eliminate the mechanical difficulties of writing. Immediately, concrete objects or pictures come to mind. They cannot be just any objects but must have an intrinsic interest for students and present a reasonable challenge. I have seen teachers ask students to describe common, everyday objects such as paper clips and staplers. Students do not find such objects very interesting. Besides, they believe that when they have named them, they have described them. The teacher's desk and the classroom ceiling are not much better. Natural objects of various kinds come to mind: interesting rocks, animals, flowers, seed pods, pine cones. They cannot be readily named and have an intrinsic interest.

The first time I tried this kind of activity, I was teaching an advanced composition course made up of juniors and seniors at a state university. When my students remained unmoved by the usual urging to be specific, having made an analysis comparable to that above, I decided to take specific objects to class for then to describe. I settled on pine cones and rocks that I hoped my midwestern students might never have seen before, including the remarkably large cones of the Jeffrey and sugar pine trees and rocks that included schist and mica, iron pyrite, rose quartz, and so forth. The activity plan was very simple. Students were to work in groups, select one rock or pine cone, and develop a detailed description of it. The students produced the most specific writing they had to that point in the class. After three days of such work, we moved on, but the students' writing remained specific.

A year later, I watched my son and daughter looking at the shells they found on the shores of Sanibel Island, which used to be noted as one of the best shelling beaches in the world. They would kneel or crouch in the hot sun looking at shells this way and that, holding them over their heads to the sun, turning them over slowly. The shells seemed to hold interminable fascination. They seemed endlessly varied in color and shape. Different perspectives revealed different shapes that were somehow regular and irregular but not readily named. I decided to use them for writing with a game twist that would provide an audience; namely, I would ask students to write about a shell so that a reader could identify it in a group of 30 or so shells.

The result of this initial idea was a game with two variations first used in a mixed class of 11- to 15-year-olds. In the first variation, which was preparation for the second, groups of four or five students received two shells that had general shape, size, and color in common but were of different species. (This level of commonality is required to discourage generalities I first encountered with the pine cones.) Each group was to write about one shell so that another group might be able to pick it out from the pair or, to make it more challenging, from all shells used in several groups. After the groups had exchanged papers and shells, each was to read the paper it had received, try to identify the shell written about, and provide feedback to the writers. The second variation involved each student's writing about a different shell, later receiving the writing of another student, trying to pick out the shell, and providing feedback.

Planning does not end with the invention of an activity. Like the writing process, the planning process involves feedback and revision. The feedback consists largely of student responses (oral classroom response, behavior, and written work) that must be interpreted by the teacher.

Describing seashells appears to be a far cry from writing about personal experience. However, the activity can provide the impetus for writing specifically and with a clear focus, for the presence of the shell not only relieves the burden on memory but manifests a focus. Experience suggests that focused and specific writing in the shell activity serves as a strong gateway to more specific writing but that the effects vary with the level of students. With a recent evening state university course, with students whose average age was 25, I found that the shell activity followed by a few others in three classroom hours established specificity as an important feature of writing that appeared to generalize easily to narrative as well as to interpretive and argumentative writing. However, with younger students it will not necessarily generalize to different kinds of details for narrative, let alone other complex writing tasks.

In our workshops for Chicago public school seventh and eighth graders, my students and I plan a variety of key gateway activities aimed at helping students develop representations of the impressions that typically appear in empathic personal narrative: sights, sounds, bodily sensations, personal feelings, dialogue, descriptions of people in various emotional states, people in action, and so forth. Each of these has to be a complete, interesting, and challenging "whole-language" task in its own right. Presenting students with lists of words to use in writing about sounds, smells, and the way people walk, as many textbooks do, will not do the trick. Filling in the blanks of preformed sentences to make similes or metaphors results in mechanical language.

Think of the sounds that might appear in narrative, for example. Students tend not to name them, let alone describe them. But note how effective are Arne's closing with the single word, "click," and Susan Hack's phrase "incessant buzzing of wasps and horseflies" with its alliteration of *s* and *z* echoing throughout the sentence. The easiest activity for helping students use the strategies of characterizing the source and qualities of sounds is to play an audio recording of common, everyday sounds that students attempt to characterize. My son and daughter (ages 10 and 14) made my first tape for me: the screeching squeak of our stormdoor, a kitchen match scraping against the side of the box and the little hissing puff of its explosion into flame, the breathy roar of a clothes drier, a tissue softly scraping out of its box, the toilet flushing (naturally, the scatological sound kids cannot resist), and so forth. After guessing names for the sounds, younger students have to be coached to describe them. The teacher will have to question, prod, hint, and model when necessary.

Other more creative activities can follow: Student volunteers can make and present comparable tapes; small groups can work out "sound stories" (no words—the action must be implied through sounds alone), record them, and play them back to the classmates, who try to explain what they think has happened; finally students write the "sound stories," incorporating a description of each sound. Some of these stories become very elaborate, especially if seventh graders go off on a horror kick. While they take considerable class time, they engender great enthusiasm and awareness of sound that shows up in writing.

Or think of the fine-grained actions of people that usually appear in narrative but that only infrequently appear in student writing. Ordinarily, young writers pass over such actions. But note the action in Susan Hack's skeleton and Arne's description of his own reactions. Students can talk about the fine-grained actions of people in drawings or photographs and then write about them. Groups of students can plan a pantomime, present it to the class, and then write about it as though it were a story. We have used stimuli such as the following and, later, asked students to make up their own "people-in-situations" scenarios: a person becoming slowly angrier and angrier after hearing of being cheated by a "best" friend; a person waiting for serious drilling in the dentist's office; an extremely shy person trying to get up the nerve to ask someone for a date; a student who has been in a fight in school waiting to see the principal.

Our Chicago seventh and eighth graders never include dialogue except of the indirect variety in their stories. Dialogue is not a common ingredient in the stories of older students either. Yet it is a key means of eliciting empathic response. One way to get it going is to provide students with scenarios that involve dialogue between people in conflict, have small groups of students plan a dialogue, act it out in front of the class, and then, working individually, write it out along with appropriate details of the setting and action. After this, students can work out their own scenarios. Initially, we have shown students how to write their dialogues in dramatic form. Later, we show how to punctuate for inclusion in personal narrative writing. This means additional gateway activities.

Taken together, such activities are fragmented and not focused. We need something more. I will take that up in the next chapter.

ARGUMENT

Argument is not a genre. It does not have the many specific, salient characteristics that fables have. Rather, if we view argument as Toulmin (1958) does, or in light of some other theory of argument, it has a small number of basic structural features that may appear as a single set, standing alone (which is not to say decontextualized), or that may iterate into a complex of interlocking sets with one set serving as the superstructure. And it may appear as part and parcel of writing eliciting a variety of responses, including propaganda, scholarly discourse, empathic writing of various kinds, and satire.

Probably arguments in these various guises should enter into the curriculum. Earlier in this chapter, I dealt with fable as an opus-oriented narrative. But that narrative is within the structure of an argument, with the moral usually serving as the warrant, the abstract rule that ties the behavior and fate of the animal to the implied claim, usually one of policy about how one should behave.

Types and Features of Argument

For pedagogical purposes, it is useful to discriminate among three types of arguments, generally recognized as those of fact, judgment, and policy. These frequently occur in combination, so that the issues are difficult to separate. For example, the mayor of a large city proposing a new garbage disposal system is likely to develop a minimum of three arguments, although they may not appear separately: an argument about the actual amount of garbage collected at the present (an argument of fact); another asserting that this amount is a problem (an argument of judgment based on a definition of "garbage problem"); and an argument of policy based on some set of principles regarding the duties of a responsible government.

Arguments of fact are frequently ignored in writing programs. Many rhetorics state that such propositions are not proper subjects for argument. For example, in a chapter entitled "Where Rhetoric Starts—and Stops," Hairston (1978) claims that the only legitimate assertion is "a statement of belief or judgment that can be logically supported with reasons" (p. 127). For her, an arguable assertion must imply "the concept of ought or should" (p. 129). We do not argue about facts, she thinks. Hairston holds a different set of epistemological assumptions than I. This book holds that "facts" are constructions and challengeable.

Another reason for ignoring arguments of fact appears to be that they are often thought to be field-dependent and, therefore, beyond the knowledge of even college freshman. Field-dependent arguments are those in which extensive knowledge of the field is necessary to judge the appropriateness of warrants in arguments about the existence of phenomena and their relationships. Not all arguments having to do with the existence of phenomena and their relationships are field-dependent, however. When newspapers report "facts" about some secret government coverup, usually the source is some inside government official. A responsible newspaper will not report a statement from one source without confirmation from another, independent source. Standard practice is to require corroboration by at least one independent source before reporting any claim about a purported event. Thus claims coming from Bosnians about civilian massacres by one side or the other will be reported as claims until the news agency has independent corroboration. That corroboration, in effect, is the warrant connecting the evidence (reports from sources *x* and *y*) and the claim that the massacre has occurred. If the warrant were expressed in full, it would amount to the following: Because there is no reason to suspect collusion between two or more sources that have been reliable in the past, we can accept their reports as fact. This seems hardly specialized to me. It is the kind of reasoning that ought to occur when we investigate matters of fact.

Other types of argument are certainly within the domain of the nonspecialist: those of judgment and policy. When the claim in an argument is a judgment, the warrant will be a definition, which may or may not be explicitly stated. A tenure decision at a "research" university will be based essentially on an argument about the quality of the candidate's scholarship, the warrant for which is a definition of "good scholarship." When such definitions have not been agreed upon, debates about the definition and its criteria ensue. Popular book and movie reviews present judgments about their subjects supported by grounds that are often further judgments. ("This is a great movie. The photography is spectacular.") In these, the warrants are almost always implicit in the grounds used to support the claim.

Many arguments fall into this category, though their proponents might like them to appear otherwise (e.g., "This plan is functional" or "The cafeteria serves nutritious meals"). Claims in special fields use specialized definitions as warrants. For example, the statement "the steel is hard," for a metallurgist, is based on a definition of hardness that includes specific degrees, indicated by the depth of an impression made by a steel ball on the steel in question when the ball is under a certain amount of pressure. Such claims are constructions, warrantable by definition, and may be readily challenged by showing that the phenomenon does not conform to the definition or by attacking the definition.

Claims about policy (e.g., whether something should be done) use moral and ethical principles as warrants. The principles may themselves be subject to argument. In questions about the responsibility of government to alleviate poverty and other social problems, the principles are certainly not agreed upon. Arguments about policy are ubiquitous and rest on other claims about facts and judgments and on warrants and backing for the warrants, any and each of which is challengeable and might become a full argument in itself.

In short, argument is a basic structure that informs a discourse and sets up expectations for it, but does not allow the predictions of specific characteristics in the same way that particular genres do, for example, fable or the academic research article. In teaching argument, our concern will be with the features of argument (including qualifications, counterarguments, the backing of warrants, nested arguments, and so forth), their relationships, and their occurrence, depending upon the nature of the claim, the audience, the situation, and the writer's view of that situation.

Students Writing Arguments

Despite the fact that children engage in arguments from a very early age, inexperienced writers have difficulty in producing fully formed arguments. McCann (1989) found that groups of sixth, ninth, and twelfth graders tended to recognize arguments in about the same way as did expert adults. These same students, however, were not capable of producing their own written arguments, even in response to "hot" school issues. Using a set of categories based on Toulmin's analysis of argument, an examination of 400 arguments written by high school and college students indicates that many students fail to provide grounds in support of claims even though possible grounds are available to them, explicit statement of warrants is extremely rare, and the consideration of counterarguments is virtually nonexistent (Hillocks, in progress c).

The 1988 National Assessment of Educational Progress (NAEP) writing assessment appears to support that finding. In the NAEP assessment, eleventh graders were asked "to adopt a point of view about whether or not funding for the space program should be reduced, and to write a letter to their senator explaining their position" (Applebee, Langer, Mullis, & Jenkins, 1990). The following example was rated adequate.

> Dear Senator:
>
> I feel strongly against cuts in funds for the space program. The space program is an important part of our future. Space is one of our final frontiers. If money is needed for something, make a cut in a defense program. I believe it's more important to explore space than to be able to blow things away. If we fall behind in space exploration, we might miss something vitally important. Lives have been lost in trying to explore space and those lives shouldn't be wasted. Seven

> people died on the space shuttle in an effort to explore space, and if the program ends, their deaths were for nothing. Please avoid the cut in the space program. Thank you.
>
> Sincerely,
> A concerned Citizen

This response was comparable to responses by 27% of the students in grade 11 who wrote to this essay prompt. In 1988, 69% of the responses were judged to be less than adequate. Only 1% were judged to be more than adequate.

The focus on the writer's feelings permits an argument justifying them, rather than one that takes a stance on the issue. The second and third sentences appear to be intended as grounds. Clearly, however, they themselves are abstract claims, the warrants for which the writer assumes are clear, but which are not. Why, for example, is the statement that "Space is one of our final frontiers" adequate grounds for refunding the program? It is not obvious to me.

The fourth and fifth sentences make different claims, suggesting another plan of action that might make possible the continued funding of the space program. But they do not contribute to defense of funding for the space program.

Sentence six picks up the idea that the space program may be important to our future but remains at the same level of generalization as sentence two, without providing any more specific grounds. Sentences seven and eight, concerned with the loss of life in the space program, present an argument that has not been examined carefully. They do not provide a convincing warrant explaining why loss of life in the space program constitutes adequate grounds for continuing it.

Upon examination, this piece turns out to be not so much an argument as a collection of vaguely related general feelings about the space program, more closely related to topical writing than to argument.

Deciding What to Teach

Because argument is a broad, encompassing structure, rather than a discrete, clearly definable genre, it is necessary to decide what dimensions of argument to teach. The specific goals of instruction for argument will vary from one context to another. But we can think about what a good argument is likely to include at various levels of sophistication and in various curricular contexts. At the least, it would include a claim, appropriate grounds, and warrants. In addition, we want students to be aware that statements of grounds and warrants are themselves open to question, with the result that nested arguments will appear throughout any effective argument. Further, conditions under which an argument may be rebutted must be addressed.

Production Strategies

If we believe that the writing of arguments grows from the consideration of problems or issues or from the analysis of data that prompt the formation of problems, then the context for teaching argument must involve what I have called inquiry. Students need to be engaged in analyzing a range of related data, in observing, comparing and contrasting, generalizing, interpreting, hypothesizing, testing, questioning, and imagining, indeed, in using all the strategies of inquiry. In addition, argument calls for laying out the parts of the results of the inquiry in a meaningful way and establishing relationships among them. Students have to begin with the inquiry, or deal with it very early, so that they can see the whole process of how arguments evolve. If we separate inquiry from argument mechanically, asking students to list topic, claim, and reasons without going through the process of inquiry, then we trivialize argument and invite our students to produce shallow, unexamined discourse.

Because of the complexity of argument, what we should reasonably expect of students will vary from group to group and from one instructional context to another. Some students will exhibit very strong performance, arguing closely thought-out positions. Most will not, but they cannot be categorized together simply as weak in writing argument. Differences in background knowledge and experience in writing will demand attention in selecting and planning activities.

In addition to considering the performance of students, planning will vary from one instructional context to another. For example, the argument involved in interpreting a literary work will likely call for an interpretation of a text (a claim), supporting evidence drawn from the text and other sources (grounds), and statements showing how the evidence supports the interpretation (warrants). The sophistication of the argument will vary with the complexity of the interpretation. Feminist theory applied to Fielding's *Tom Jones* will likely result in a very lengthy and complex argument involving many aspects of the novel as well as eighteenth-century thought.

But narrower questions will result in less involved arguments. For example, I recently observed ninth graders discussing what they thought good parenting involved, developing a definition of that idea, and later applying it to Harper Lee's *To Kill a Mockingbird.* (A class discussion of the novel had originally given rise to the question.) Student papers focused on interpreting the behavior of a good parent and a not-so-good parent in the novel, arguing the writer's interpretation, with the definition developed by the class serving as the backing for warrants. Because interpretations of the characters' actions had differed in class discussion, the arguments also included brief rebuttals of alternative positions.

In a different context, say, when students do research on school problems or community history, their writing may be directed at establishing that a certain problem or condition exists or that certain events occurred. Here, the nature of the claim and evidence requires a different kind of warrant. In general, such warrants require explanations of how the data were collected, why those methods are valid, and what their limitations are. In a curriculum developed by Tom McCann of the West Chicago public schools, for a Chapter II program, students collect information about school problems and student attitudes through interviews and questionnaires. After collecting data, they interpret their findings, supporting claims with data, and write up their ideas along with explanations of how they collected the data. The principal visits the class to hear an oral report and to receive a written report.

In a similar context, students may argue recommendations for policy. In this case warrants will involve statements of principles used to guide actions. Such arguments are often quite complex, involving several component arguments nested at various crucial points of the main argument. Arguments about policy almost necessarily involve at least two sets of grounds: one about the existing state of affairs and one about the predicted benefits of the change being recommended. In addition, arguments for changes in policy are likely to involve conflicting warrants, one of which will have to be argued and the other countered.

Gateway Activities for Argument

If these are the abstract features of the activities that engage students in the development of arguments, how can we develop such an activity, one that engages students in both inquiry and learning about the features of argument? To begin with, it is useful to list the features more concretely. The following list has developed over several years as my students and I have groped about constructing such activities.

1. We need a set of data in which a problem lurks, is discoverable by the students, and has the potential to capture interest almost immediately.
   a. The problem must be within their ken. That is, when they look at the data, they must be able to recognize something strange or interesting in it.
   b. It must be such that students are likely to be willing and able to make some conjectures about it. It cannot be so complex or abstract that they are unable to think about it in a reasoned way.

   c. At the same time, it must not be so simple that there is nothing to reason through.
   d. The problem embedded in the data must be open to a variety of solutions and/or interpretations, at least initially. If the data set promotes no controversy, it will not engage students in using argumentative strategies.
2. The problem or issue may be made explicit or may be implicit in the data or both. That is, for example, the teacher may wish to set up the various issues in the controversy. Relevant data upon which students may build are still a necessity.
3. If students discover a problem in the school, campus, or local community that concerns them, so much the better. In fact, the teacher can encourage that. The guidelines above still apply.
4. Usually it is wise to avoid problems for which there are ready-made solutions on one or more sides of the issue. Problems that have received a lot of publicity or about which emotions run high (e.g., abortion) seem to inhibit thinking through the problem independently. Students tend to gravitate toward the ready-made solutions or positions they are familiar with.
5. It is important that particular data be available or collectible by the students themselves. If they are not, the positions that students develop are unlikely to be anchored in grounds. Data also particularize the problem.

Having the features and guidelines is one thing. Inventing or finding the issues and materials is another. I cannot explain how to make that leap. That is something that is certainly not algorithmic. The best I can do is provide examples of activities that students at various levels have found interesting. First some simple sets of materials that have elicited generalizations or interpretations that require support:

- A set of eight drawings of Mickey Mouse from 1922 to the present. Sara Hart Wernz invented this activity for use with a "basic" class in a Chicago high school as an introduction to argument. Students think Mickey has always been the same. He has not. Students talk and write briefly about the changes and what they think of them. Why does he seem to become cuter? This activity elicited a very positive response from students who tend to find nothing about school very interesting.
- A late eighteenth-century etching by John Gilray entitled "A Voluptuary under the Horrors of Digestion," a satire of the Prince of Wales, showing him as an unmitigated "slob," as our seventh graders called him. I first used the drawing with college students to elicit details about the actions, appearance, and expressions of people. Subsequently, my graduate students used it, against my better judgment, with seventh graders in our writing workshop

in a Chicago school for the same purpose. I was wrong. The students loved it and were irrepressible in their response to it. The seventh graders first responded with generalizations which made it clear that we could use it for working on supporting generalizations. The possible generalizations can take many levels of sophistication, even with younger students.

- Profiles of the 18 homicide victims in a single week in Chicago published by *The Chicago Tribune* as part of a story about hand-gun violence. The data in the profiles provided the basis for a number of generalizations and hypotheses about the nature of homicide: All but one victim were males; two-thirds of homicides involved hand guns; in 15 cases the victims knew the assailants; about two-thirds of the victims were between the ages of 18 and 26; most homicides took place between 5:00 p.m. Friday and 3:00 a.m. Monday, over the weekend; most victims were unemployed or had menial jobs; and so forth. It was possible to consider what, taken together, this might indicate about the nature of homicide, recognizing that the sample was from a single week. It evoked very high interest in high school and college students, who discussed ideas in groups and wrote about them individually.

Activities eliciting more complex arguments include role-playing games centered on problems that require consideration of a data set, the perspectives of different individuals or groups on the problem or data, and reaching agreement on a solution. Starting from different positions and reaching a compromise solution demands a willingness to rethink arguments in light of other positions, an important disposition:

- Troyka and Nudelman (1975) developed a set of role-playing situations focused on a variety of problems from purchasing a fleet of taxis to dealing with a serious community pollution problem and a prison uprising. Each of these provide a set of data including information that may be interpreted in various ways, depending on the perspective of the individuals involved. In the pollution problem, for example, a chemical plant, the town's main source of revenue and major employer, is purportedly responsible for the pollution that has been spoiling the beaches and streams that once attracted tourists. The roles include chemical plant officials, tourist industry leaders, unemployed citizens who hope to hired by the chemical plant, conservationists, and so forth.
- I developed a simulation for high school students involving a proposal from a fictitious senator to raise the legal driving age to 25, argued in terms of the actual auto accident and auto death rate statistics by age and sex. Roles include male drivers from 16 to 25, females in the same age group (the death rate is much lower for females), older drivers, insurance representatives, auto

manufacturers, and so forth. Students work toward a plan that helps to alleviate the problem of traffic deaths among young people.

As in the case of fables, such activities must be evaluated before foisting them on students. Similar evaluations apply. Can the inventor imagine people writing about these data? Is the process envisaged reasonable? Can you write an interesting piece about this data? Once the activity has passed through those evaluations, the next step is to try it with students, remembering the constant necessity for revision.

That is about as specific as I can be about the invention of such activities. We can analyze the writing task, its features, and the production strategies. We can examine the abilities and attitudes of the class. And we can be quite specific about how to evaluate the impact of the activity. But I cannot be more specific about the invention of the activity. "Try to find something that will engage students in using the strategies that seem to be demanded by the task," I tell my students.

Not so easy, but curiously, not so difficult either. Once the analysis of the task is solid, and once one is attuned to what is involved, appropriate ideas and materials seem to suggest themselves serendipitously, even when we least expect them. And after inquiry into the effects of using the materials and activities, there is always revision.

Chapter Nine

The Art of Planning III: Sequencing

Having invented strong gateway activities is no guarantee that students will be able to use the knowledge they gain in writing. For one thing, once the ideas have been generated, writers need to know how to think about arranging them. For another, as already indicated, a single gateway activity, especially an introductory activity, may not be enough to consolidate what has been learned for independent use. It is usually wise to develop a series of activities that prepare students for the most difficult tasks. For example, as suggested in the last chapter, a teacher-led whole-class activity developing the character and plot for a fable prepares students for the group activity, which in turn prepares for the independent writing that follows. In working with extended definition, it proved useful to help students become accustomed to the idea of working with multiple criteria already established before asking them to generate several criteria that they might apply in defining. In addition to these preparatory activities that are related to the key generative activities, other kinds of knowledge will be important. As I have argued in Chapters Five and Six, these include general discourse knowledge, general process knowledge, and inquiry. The question is how to put all this together in a meaningful, efficient, and powerful way.

EPISODES IN THE TEACHING/LEARNING PROCESS

In classrooms where teaching is telling, the sequence of teaching/learning activities is quite simple, often developing in four activities: the teacher talking about the writing to be done, the students writing, the teacher grading the results, the students receiving the results as feedback indicating what they should do or avoid next time. This book has been concerned with far more complex sequences, primarily because it recognizes the futility of teaching as telling and, at the same time, the need to provide support for students as they first engage in new writing tasks and then move toward independence in using the procedural knowledge required by those tasks. What governs the sequencing of activities in which students learn procedural knowledge?

Episodes in Teaching

Observations and analysis of more than 300 hours of classroom teaching as part of formal studies (Hillocks, 1971, 1992, in progress a) and several hundred hours in a less formal capacity indicate clearly that teachers think of their classroom teaching in chunks. Ask a college teacher what she intends to do in class, and a typical response will be as follows: "I'll talk about the comparison/contrast theme, the different ways of organizing; then we'll discuss the essay they were supposed to read; and I'm going to return the narratives they did last week and give them a chance to ask questions."

I have called these chunks episodes to emphasize the sense in which teaching constructs an ongoing narrative made up of episodes through which the characters move in pursuit of some goal. (In successful teaching, the characters, including the teacher, share comparable goals.) If we think of the chunks of teaching in this way, we are almost forced to consider not only their content, but also their sequence and coherence.

In one study of college teaching (Hillocks, 1992), my research assistants and I marked a new episode with each change in the material under consideration, in the teacher/student relationship (e.g., a move from lecture to group work), in the instructional focus or goals (e.g., a shift from discussion of the content of an essay to its organizational structure), or a change in materials used. Teachers almost always give some verbal clue to the change in episode, some more obviously than others. Many use a simple phrase such as, "OK, now we're going to . . ." Some will make the shift far more obvious. One, for example, was in the habit of saying, "OK, now we're going to shift gears for a while." Then he would add an explanation of the shift.

Links among Episodes

Each episode has some sort of instructional content, some knowledge to be conveyed that can be examined to determine its relationship to the content of other episodes in the same and contiguous classroom sessions. We may think of these relationships as being very strong, as when one episode prepares or seems to prepare students for work they will be engaged with in the next. On the other hand, the relationship may be very weak, as when one episode follows another with no apparent relationship other than temporal proximity. In the strongest relationships one episode engages students in the development of procedural knowledge that will be used in the next and/or in later episodes.

It is not uncommon to find very weak links in English classes at all levels. In one college freshman English class, for example, the teacher uses five episodes in class with a sixth coming after class in the form of homework: the first, writing in journals, 15 minutes; the second, drill on vocabulary, 13 minutes; the third, discussion of a definition of jazz that students were to have read with a focus on reviewing the content, 31 minutes; the fourth, a loose discussion of what the students thought about jazz, 12 minutes; and the fifth, a listing and brief discussion of topics that students might use in writing their own definitions of some type of music, about 9 minutes; a sixth episode is the writing of the essay.

In this example, the first episodes, writing in journals and vocabulary drill, are related to each other only in the most tenuous way: It is arguable whether either belongs in a composition course. But there is no specific or explicit way in which either contributes to the learning in any of the other episodes. Their presence has to be justified in terms of long-term goals to which the teacher hopes they will contribute. The third, discussing a definition of jazz, provides a model for the kind of writing that the students will do in episode six. However, it offers no procedures to be used in this writing, not even in declarative fashion with the teacher explaining what they are. Students will have to work them out on their own. The link between three and six has to be seen as more than temporal, but still quite weak, little more than a thematic relationship.

Episode four appears to have an even weaker relationship to three, five, and six. Since students talk about jazz, it is at least thematically related to three, if less so to five and six. While giving personal opinions about jazz might have some motivational force, I can see no way in which one might predict that it would prepare students for doing the assignment. The fifth episode, talk about what the students think about jazz, provides a kind of substantive aid on the current assignment and possibly procedural aid for the future when students will have to do their own brainstorming for topics. In this case, however, that relevance will have to be inferred by the students. But the episode does invoke general process knowledge. Taken together, however, the links among these episodes are weak, the coherence low.

Analysis of Episodes and Links

Let us turn to an example in which the links are arguably stronger, that is, in which episodes prepare students to do what is coming. Charlie AuBuchon and her colleagues designed the following sequence for a class of eighth-grade students for whom English is a second language at McFadden Intermediate School in Santa Ana, California. The sequence she has designed amounts to an introduction to argument. Her students are in what is called a transitional class. There are 21 of them, one a native speaker of Chinese, one of Vietnamese, and the remainder of Spanish. (Standard classes have a much larger student-to-teacher ratio. Her preceding class had 34 students.) Fairly recently these students had very limited proficiency in English. In Charlie's class, they are one step from moving to a "standard" class.

When I observe, she and the students are in the second part of a writing unit entitled "Making Connections." At the beginning of class, she asks students to take out a sheet with three columns on which they were to have recorded what was important to the students themselves as well as the results of interviews with an adult "close to them" about things important to the adults now and that were important to the adults when they were the age of the student. Today they are going to examine what is important to them as a group. Mrs. AuBuchon asks students to indicate one of the four things most important to the students themselves. As each idea is named, she makes a count of those who listed it and writes it on the board: life, 14; education, 10; family, 16; health, 7; money, 6; cars, 4; and so forth.

Then she says, "To get a picture of what you think of as the most important values, you're going to graph this." She then explains how the graph will work as she draws a histogram on the board. "Along the *x*-axis put the things you said you value most. Along the *y*-axis indicate the number of students holding each as most important." She tells the students that they will also be making graphs for what the adults they interviewed value "today" and what they say they valued when they were the students' ages. As I watch, students work on graphs, and three are using the computer terminals that are situated near the teacher's desk in one corner of the room.

I learn that in the next writing assignment students will write a "composition comparing and contrasting what is important to you with what was important to the person you interviewed when [that person] was your age." However, before they do that, they make a diagram of overlapping circles (somewhat like a Venn diagram), placing comparable values within the overlap, and so forth. The remainder gives explicit directions about what is to go in each paragraph, setting up one of the standard textbook formats for comparison and contrast: person 1, person 2, comment on similarities and differences.

Clearly, this lesson does not stand alone. In fact, the sequence began with students "clustering" what is important to them as individuals, followed by sharing their ideas and creating a "class cluster." If they wish, students may use the ideas from the class cluster to supplement their own. Next they think through and "identify their ten most important things," followed by a further reduction to "four most important things" and then "do a quickwrite saying what their four things are and why they are important."

In the next activity students, using a teacher-supplied outline of a shield, "design a coat of arms depicting what is important to them." Upon completing the coat of arms they receive the following prompt: "Write about each of the four things that are most important to you. Say why they are important, how they affect your life, and what you do each day to show that these things are important to you." When students are ready, they enter their writing at one of the three computer terminals, where they can draft, revise, and edit.

The next activity in the sequence is conducting the interview with an adult, which brings us back to where I started. Let us review the whole sequence to discover the reasons for including the various activities, some of which might seem, at first glance, somewhat removed from a writing class.

The sequence is rich in engaging students in strategies that they will be using again. Several activities involve students in inquiry, and several involve discourse knowledge and the organization of the content. Still others involve students in general process strategies. The sequence begins with a general strategy of inquiry, gathering what one knows already about a topic. "Clustering" as it is used here is a variation of brainstorming, a technique to relate ideas through association. Sharing with the class provides a kind of constructive feedback on the early stages of thinking. Later, the interview serves to introduce the practice of gathering data from other sources. That is followed with using a strategy (graphing) for comparing the three sets of data collected. Integrating mathematical concepts with English is clearly unusual, but it makes very good sense and is a goal of the school's curriculum.

Several activities engage students in processing information for organization in writing. The shield activity appears, at first, to be unnecessary. But the students clearly enjoy illustrating their shields, and the activity provides a rehearsal for what they are about to write and, once complete, a visual guide to the organization of their writing. In doing so, it reduces one of the burdens of such writing, an important help for these writers.[1] The other two visual activities serve a similar function. Both the overlapping circles and graphing lead to a much more complicated task, a comparison of the three sets of information about values collected by the class, clearly an activity that involves making and supporting claims—argument, in short.

Finally, activities early in the sequence help students establish a focus. It is difficult for anyone to winnow through important values and to decide, in a reasoned fashion, which are the most important. The process of choosing ten, then four provides aid for this piece of writing and, more important, illustrates a strategy for focusing any piece of information-oriented writing.

The links among the activities of this sequence are strong. Each successive activity is based on one or several of the preceding, building on the material foundation provided by those activities. Thus listing ideas about what is important provides the data for choosing the "ten most important things." Choosing the ten is the basis for choosing the "four most important things," and that in turn becomes the basis for inventing the coat of arms. The writing about "the four things that are most important to you" grows out of all these activities and the writing prompt supplied by the teacher. Each activity provides support for the particular writing to which it leads.

In my judgment, this sequence is very rich and unusual, with its integration of art and math. Its implications for work on additional writing tasks, particularly argument, are impressive. The writing prompt for the first piece of writing, "What's Important," for example, engages students in presenting simple arguments. The prompt calls on students to "say why they are important . . . and what you do each day to show that these things are important to you." In other words, students are to suggest two arguments, one of which requires providing evidence that the "things" named are truly important, with evidence to be drawn from the specifics of daily living. The second remains more abstract, requiring that students make a claim about why the things named are important, but allowing them to presume that what is named as important requires no defense and that the warrant (importance) can be accepted without explanation or defense. We can see all this in a composition by Nohemi Chavez, who writes as follows about what is important:

What's Important

> To me, there are a lot of things that are important. Some more than others. The four most important things are health, family, money, and education.
>
> The most important thing to me is health. With good health, I can go to many places, and enjoy life. It affects my life because if I'm sick, I can't do anything, just sit down or lay down. I always try to take care of myself. When I play sports, I don't drink cold water if I'm still hot.
>
> The second thing is my family. My family always listens to me and tries to help me whenever I have a problem or question. My family is also very fun to be with. We go to nice places and do a lot of things together. This affects me because if I didn't have any family, I would be alone, bored and insecure. To show that my family is important, I give them gifts for their birthday, help them with problems or questions, baby-sit, or help with the chores.
>
> Money is very important to me. With money I can buy beautiful things such as jewelry, clothes, cars, etc. I could also travel to many places. If I didn't have any money, I would not be able to do any of these things. To show that money is important to me, I save 75% of my allowance and only buy things that I need.
>
> Education is important to me. A good education can get me a

> good job and money. This affects me because I have to get good grades in school. To show that education is important I try to do all of my work at school and study for tests and quizzes.

Nohemi claims that her family is important to her and gives four pieces of evidence, reports of how she acts toward them, indicating that she really does believe her family is important. In addition she gives three reasons why the family is important. She deals with the other three "important things" in a comparable fashion. This young writer, along with several of her classmates, shows an ability to use the fundamentals of argument in the relatively abstract context of a discussion of values. One clear extension of this sequence is in the direction of more formal argument.

It would be a relatively simple matter to ask students to rank-order the top four values and engage different groups in defending different rank orders. Such arguments would necessitate the interpretation and definition of warrants (How does one decide what is important?) and the interpretation of the values involved (What do we mean by life and under what conditions is it important? Is anything ever more important?). One indication of an activity sequence likely to have reverberations throughout a curriculum is this power to imply new directions.

When I observed this sequence, students were engaged in an important set of specific strategies. In other writing sequences, students will use them again, and finally they will use them independently without the benefit of explicit instruction from teachers about what to do, without peer support in developing ideas, and without the aid of writing prompts that lay out the organizational pattern to be used, the questions to be asked, or the procedures for collecting and analyzing the data. This will take place in a workshop setting that encourages students to test their own ideas and their writing with their peers as their ideas and texts develop.

PRINCIPLES FOR SEQUENCING

Not all sequences develop in the same way, with comparable links among the episodes. In the example from Charlie AuBuchon's class, the links over several days are very tight, with each episode leading to the next. We may conceptualize these as linear in the sense of being causally related. That is, each episode prepares for the next, with the conclusion standing as the result of the foregoing episodes.

In longer sequences, that call for work on different kinds of problems a different structure emerges. Sets of episodes may be conceptualized as parallel to each other, each set moving toward a different dimension of the same goal, while having only abstract intersections with the other sets. For example, in our Chicago workshops with seventh and eighth graders over the last 15 years, we have often included work on inventing dialogue and work on writing specifically about observed phenomena. The two sets of episodes have little in common except that both provide gateway activities preparing for features of personal narrative and both emphasize specificity. But one influences the other in only relatively general ways.

The order of these sets in classrooms appears to be close to interchangeable. In fact, over all those years, no two sequences have ever been the same. They have varied in terms of the design of gateway activities, their arrangement, and their relationship to standard activities. Yet our goals have always been comparable from year to year (to put it bluntly, strong, empathic personal narratives).

This is not to say that sequence does not matter or that one particular activity is just as good as another. Indeed, we argue over what activity to use and what ought to come first, second, and third. The question is, what are the relevant principles for guiding the sequencing and selecting of activities? Before attempting to answer that, let me set out an adumbrated version of a typical four-week sequence focused on personal narrative.

A Sequence for Personal Narrative

The following sequence assumes a 50-minute period for 22 school days. It is typical of sequences developed recently for seventh-grade classes in Chicago city schools. In one school, the classes have been over 90% African American. In another, about 60% of the students are Latino, most having Spanish as their first language, a few still very uneasy with English. About 30% are African American. The remainder are Asian, with a small percentage of Caucasian students of various ethnic groups. In one class, first languages included Polish, Persian, Bengali, and Spanish. Ninety-five percent of the writing samples collected from these students ranked well below the quality of Ranakea's paper in Chapter Seven. Several have been below the quality of Maurice's piece, also in Chapter Seven, largely because they have produced so little. The following sequence, presented in highly abbreviated sets of related episodes, was designed to help students to produce effective personal narratives with the kinds of features discussed in Chapter Seven.

It is important to note that this sequence is designed for students whose writing performances show almost none of the characteristics of effective narrative. The sequence would vary for students whose writing showed those features to a greater degree. We might focus on inner monologue, *in medias res* openings, or developing character through dialogue. If students were highly skilled, there would be little need to devote time to any of these. They would simply work on their own projects in workshop fashion, as at the end of this sequence.

1. *Initial writing sample.* "Write about an experience that is important to you for some reason. . . . Write about it so specifically that someone reading what you have written will be able to see what you saw and feel what you felt."
2. *Examples of personal narrative.* Students read and talk about examples by professionals and other students, for example, Richard Wright's story, from *Black Boy* (1945), about winning the right to the streets of Memphis (When his mother sent him for groceries, other boys hit him and stole his money; she kept sending him out, and he learned to fight back.) and Verita's piece about her first day at a new school, which appears at the end of Chapter 10.
3. *Idea sheets.* After receiving a sample from the teacher, students work individually, writing a few sentences about their own experiences, times when they were sad, happy, angry, determined to accomplish something despite fears or apprehensions, and so forth. Students may continue adding to these over the next few days.
4. *Introduction to using specific detail.* Describing shells in teacher-led session, small groups, and individually with feedback episodes following. Demonstrate revision techniques and revise descriptions.
5. *Details about people and places.* Teacher-led talk about an interesting drawing or photograph of a person in action or in a mood, small-group work with photos, group representatives read work to class, workshop with individuals working on character from one scenario from idea sheets, read to classmates, feedback, revision.
6. *Describing sounds.* Teacher-led talk about recording of various sounds.
7. *Writing about bodily sensations.* Students do various exercises and write briefly about what they feel, for example, pulling up on the bottom of their chairs with as much force as possible for 30 seconds. Talk about some of these, followed by writing about other sensations. Individuals write about a strenuous activity from their own experience, possibly idea sheets.
8. *Writing about the "dumpster scenario."* This activity asks students to make an imaginative leap into the following scenario. "You are walking home alone in Hyde Park. It is late at night and the street lights are out again. You hear footsteps, although you thought you were alone on the street. You begin to walk faster. The footsteps behind you go faster. You look over your shoulder and see that a man is about 50 feet behind you. You begin to run. The man begins to run. You run for a block and dart quickly into an alley, then turn into another and duck behind a dumpster. There

you are crouching behind the dumpster, waiting. Now, write what you see, hear, and feel as the man approaches." Students write, with the teacher coaching as useful. Read pieces in small groups, with group selecting one to be read to class. Feedback, revision.

9. *Pantomime of characters in emotional states.* Teacher-led planning of one pantomime, everyone thinks about doing the pantomime, volunteer acts it out. Similar process in groups of three or four with some group representative presenting pantomime to the class. Class writes details for an audience who did not see the person. Read several aloud to class or groups.
10. *Invention of dialogue.* Examine and talk about two or three examples of dialogue from professional and student pieces. Teacher-led development of dialogue (in play form) based on a scenario followed by small-group work on a different scenario. Students write and present the dialogue. Feedback.
11. *Individual work on dialogue from idea sheet scenario.* Read aloud to groups. Groups select one to be read to class. Feedback and revision.
12. *Punctuation of dialogue.* Teacher demonstrates simplest form on overhead: speaker, verb of saying, quotation. Groups punctuate dialogue that is already written out, simply supplying the punctuation. Feedback. If fairly successful, they convert their previously written dialogue from play form to running prose form. Students edit each other's punctuation. Feedback.
13. *Workshop.* Students select an incident to develop from their idea sheets. Individual work on drafting, periodic reading to small groups, and feedback from student and teacher. Revising as the piece develops. Feedback from groups using a checklist to prompt ideas for revision.
14. *Class publication.* Students choose which pieces to include, with all students represented, if possible.
15. *Final writing sample,* comparable to the first.

Although various formal studies (e.g., Hillocks, 1979, 1982; Hillocks et al., 1983; Sager, 1973; McCleary, 1979; Troyka, 1973) display sequences with features comparable to that above, and although some use comparable content, they were not designed to examine sequence per se. Therefore, the principles outlined below cannot be drawn from research. Nevertheless, some principles of sequencing can be deduced from the kind of experience that allows for informal comparison of many trials of comparable activities with a variety of students, what Schön (1987) might call multiple "frame experiments," when the results of those trials are carefully considered. Therefore, I will use this example of a longer sequence to illustrate what experience, carefully considered, indicates are the principles involved in both the tightly knit sets of episodes and the more loosely structured sequence.

Fun

Bloom's work (1985) on the development of talent indicates that having fun in the early stages of introduction to work in a variety of fields plays an important role in establishing interest in the field. Perhaps the most important principle in designing and sequencing is to ensure that the students enjoy doing the work. We have to ask whether the sequence will prevent appropriate challenge from becoming frustration and drudgery. Describing a seashell could be frustrating and little more than drudgery without any preparation, especially among students who have been categorized as "low ability" by the school system. But with appropriate preparation and the game-like environment of writing so that another student will be able to identify the shell, the set of activities results in eager response, high attention to the task of writing about the individual shell for as much as half an hour, and up to something over 300 words for many students.

Learning to punctuate dialogue can be about as much fun as latrine duty, especially for students who know little or nothing about punctuation. Hence, the decision to use only the simplest form, to invent dialogue using play form, and to sequence the work on punctuation so that students already have a dialogue written to apply it to. From time to time, we misjudge student interest. When a sequence is going well, students are eager to come to class and eager to participate. When eagerness goes, the plans go, and we rethink.

Building

The principle of building is related to ensuring that our students have fun in learning. But the two are not identical. The teacher-led generation of a dialogue with the class from a scenario (as in Chapter Four) requires only a few minutes but is important in modeling what is to take place in the group work. The group work, in turn, provides the groundwork for the individual work. Such a sequence moves from the simple to the more complex. At the beginning students are responding with words and phrases rather than generating a whole piece of writing. It reduces frustration, makes the goals clear, and provides for success. So much in each tightly structured cluster of episodes is obvious.

But building across the clusters is also important. One reason for doing the "shell game" early is that it clarifies the idea of specific detail so well and enables students to produce it. That notion of detail is a basic in the sequence. That activity also provides what at first was an unexpected benefit, impetus for creating metaphor. We noticed that many students used similes or metaphor to describe a shell. Finding language to describe a shell is difficult. Fortunately, students are prompted to ask themselves what it looks like, for example, "the lines on the shell look like sea weed moving back and forth under water" or "like a tiny castle at the top of a mountain with a road twisting up to it." When we noticed that some students did this naturally, we built in the teacher-led discussion of a shell large enough to see around the room to insure the use of figurative language. The main question is, "What else does it look like?"

If we place the shell activity early in the sequence, we can build on the students' use of figurative language from then on. So when we talk about people in pictures, pantomimed actions, sounds, bodily sensations, and so forth, we can push for metaphor. Several of my M.A.T. students have traced seventh graders' use of figurative language across the workshop sequence. They find that, prior to the shell activity, virtually no metaphor appears. The shell activity prompts about 70% to use metaphor, and that level of use is sustained through the final writing sample. The principle of building provides for a coherent set of experiences that students are likely to remember and use.

Integration

Another important principle of sequencing is the integration of learning from multiple sets of episodes, including those that provide declarative discourse knowledge, standard process knowledge, and task-specific procedural knowledge in the gateway activities. The sequence above integrates all three of these. Declarative discourse, which research indicates has little value by itself (Hillocks, 1986a, 1986b; see Appendix), is an important part of the sequence above. Reading and talking about the Richard Wright piece clarifies the goals, by providing concrete examples that may act as guides to thinking about one's own writing, even when one writes about totally different subjects. The use of detail in one piece, for example, can be illustrative for another.

In addition, any writing sequence ought to include what I have called general writing processes, activities that provide opportunities and encouragement for students to generate ideas, draft, give and receive feedback, and revise. Without such experience, seventh and eighth graders we have taught in Chicago have learned that cosmetic correctness is more important than content. They spend considerably more time with bottles of Whiteout correcting spelling, or trying to, than they spend on generating ideas. Researchers have shown that engaging young children in these general processes of writing enables them to write fluently about their own experiences (Atwell, 1987; Calkins, 1981, 1983; Graves, 1983).

In addition, standard activities reinforce the learning of the gateway activities, provide important context, and help to integrate sets of gateway activities. For example, the dumpster assignment in the sequence above provides an opportunity to pull together learning from the previous sets of lessons, specifically incorporating the use of visual detail, sounds, and personal sensations.

Experience strongly suggests that such integration makes preceding episodes more meaningful and forceful.

Independence

A major assumption underlying this book is that teaching should lead to independence from teachers. A major question is what constitutes independence. Many teachers provide a great deal of support for the production of a piece of writing, so that students have help in generating and analyzing ideas in teacher-led discussion and small-group discussion, drafting, revising, and so forth. It is unquestionable that little or no writing is totally independent. Nearly all writers whose work is purposive seek or receive feedback at some point, whether at the stage of generating a research question or at some late stage of drafting. However, there is a difference between fully supported and relatively independent work. If students write a fable individually that has been developed through teacher-led or small-group discussion, their independent work on the task is minimal. When they develop the ideas initially themselves, write a draft, and revise it, though they receive feedback on occasion, their work is relatively independent. When classroom teaching does not allow for relatively independent work in a workshop or test setting, it yields two related problems: There is no way to gauge student growth or the impact of teaching.

Considering only the part of Charlie AuBuchon's sequence observed above, the composition written is the direct product of all the activities and as such is part of them. Its particular content and structure have all along been the focus of the set of activities. The writing, therefore, can only serve to gauge the effect of the activities on the particular piece of writing (and then only if there has been a comparable writing sample at the beginning to determine the extent to which students might have been able to write comparably without such aid).

The question remains whether students have merely used the strategies in the service of the particular piece of writing or learned to use them such that they will be able to use them on some other occasion, at least relatively independently of teacher or peer support. The distinction that I am making is between using a strategy as directed and learning to use it at one's own discretion. The first entails following directions; the second involves using the strategy when and where appropriate without directions.

In a sequence focused on learning strategies for independent use in other writing tasks, we would expect to find sets of two or more activities using similar strategies, opportunities to generalize the strategy from one writing task to another, a movement from support to independence in their use, and opportunities to judge whether the strategy has been learned so that students use it independently. The sequence above provides two opportunities for independent work following structured activities: the workshop and final writing sample.

In the fable sequence (Chapter Eight), the initial teacher-led discussion of foibles, the consideration of possible animals to represent them, the discussion of how these animals might act if possessed of such and such a foible, the generation of a plot and a possible moral provide, at the outset, strong support in the use of the generative strategies. When students work in small groups to generate a fable, they use the same strategies but with less teacher support. At the same time, this second activity provides an opportunity for the teacher to both coach the strategies and assess learning to this point. Finally, when students write a fable independently, they use the whole process or their own version of it. At this point it is possible to judge what they have learned. Without this relatively independent work, there is no way to judge what students are capable of doing without teacher and peer aid and no way of knowing what additional instruction is necessary.

The shell game sequence described earlier also exhibits these features. When students generate details and figurative language to describe a single large shell with the teacher's guidance, they engage in using strategies they will use later in small groups and again as they work individually in describing a shell. Again, the group activity provides a reduced level of support (peer support and teacher coaching) while providing an opportunity to assess learning. The individual shell descriptions require the students to use the same strategies in a new situation, for each shell is so different that it will require the generation of new details and figures.

The two feedback activities, after both the group and individual descriptions, provide experience in identifying effective details and figures, thereby helping to crystallize the abstract idea of effective detail and figures that we hope might be brought to bear in later writing. In addition, they provide experience in the general processes of writing.

Sequencing Argument

Because argument is an overarching structure, as indicated earlier, the problem of sequencing is more complex than identifying specific task strategies, inventing gateway activities, and productively linking them with standard activities in learning sequences. We need to consider carefully where students are and what strategies of argument they can learn most readily with greatest interest in what context.

Let us begin with the students. Arguments by students are typically chains of unsupported claims. Concrete data do not appear even when provided directly to the students. Sometimes the reasons given in support of claims are so abstract as to be nearly tautological. Warrants and backing are typically omitted even when the connection between the claim and its support is not clear. Conditions for rebuttal remain unexplored. We have found this to be true of many students in many environments, from small-town to urban schools and colleges and even elite suburban schools. The following is typical of the strongest responses to a "hot" issue, one that was of immediate concern to students. High school juniors were asked to write a letter to their principal about the recently announced addition to the school dress code.

> Dear Mr. Smith:
>
> I think you should get rid of the new rule about no wearing jackets to class. Class rooms are cold especially in the winter. We need the jackets to keep warm. Another reason is that I don't have time at the end of the day to get from my class to my locker to get my jacket and then to my car so I can get to work on time. Another reason is that if we have our jackets all day nobody will be able to steal them from our locker. This is why I think you should change the rule. I hope you will consider all these reasons and change the rule.

Warriner (1988) would probably approve this paragraph. It makes a claim and provides three reasons. However, the reasons are themselves claims that could be usefully supported, although Warriner would not be able to see them as claims in need of support. Warrants might tie each of the three reasons more closely to the claim, although the first might not need one. The third reason requires additional arguments: that there is a problem with jackets being stolen from lockers and that keeping them all day would prevent additional theft. Finally, the writer does not consider the arguments of the opposition, even though the piece is addressed to the main member of the opposition. Given such performance, what will be our goals for these students?

Goals. In a curriculum that values learning to learn, students and teachers will be engaged in inquiry, in examining data from a variety of sources, developing assertions, judgments, and recommendations on the basis of their interpretations of it, testing them to determine whether or not they are warranted, connecting evidence to claims, formulating and defending warrants, and generally engaging in the processes of argument and inquiry, which are inseparable. If that is the case, the curriculum needs to include the three types of arguments alluded to earlier and their warrants.

The argument above includes several claims involving a variety of warrants. The suggestion that jackets are stolen from lockers demands evidence and a warrant of facticity. The claim about the temperature of rooms demands an argument of both facticity and judgment (How cold is too cold?). The entire position requires one or more warrants dealing with why the principal should care (e.g., better learning environments). In addition, the writer needs to deal with the main counterargument that, in this case, has to do with the administrative effort to keep gang symbols out of the school.

Undoubtedly, with so many dimensions that appear to be so difficult, argument must be a continuing project through the entire course or curriculum. So little is known about teaching argument that very little can be taken for granted. We need to think of every part of every lesson as a frame experiment. For the moment, let us turn to possible approaches.

Many high school and college classes treat argument as part of the literature program. Teachers ask students to take a position on the interpretation of a literary work and argue it. Although this approach to teaching literature is out of favor (e.g., Probst, 1988), the current emphasis of post-structuralism, with its emphasis on teaching the conflicts (Graff, 1992a), is very likely to take English back in that direction.

At their best, in my observation, such efforts have focused on supporting interpretations and have helped students develop definitions that they subsequently use as warrants in their arguments supporting those judgments. In one class students explored the idea of good parenting, developing their definitions as they encountered various examples in their reading. Student papers focused on interpreting the behavior of a "good" parent and a "not-so-good" parent in *To Kill a Mockingbird*, arguing the writer's interpretation, with the definition developed by the class serving as the source of warrants and backing. The ultimate, specific objective implied in this kind of instruction, keeping independence in mind as a major goal, is something very close to the following:

> To develop an interpretive generalization about an important dimension of a literary character encountered in independent reading and to write an argument in support of that generalization, supporting it with evidence taken from the text, and explaining how and why the evidence supports the generalization.

However, we cannot expect this kind of context to help students move much beyond the confines of interpretive generalization.

It seems to me necessary to include arguments of "fact," interpretation, and policy in the curriculum. For example, if students do research on school or community problems, their writing may be directed at establishing that a certain problem or condition exists or that certain events occurred. Here, the nature of the claim and evidence requires warrants that, in effect, explain how data were collected, why those methods are valid, and what their limitations are.

Once the condition has been established, it may be necessary to argue that it is a problem of a certain degree of urgency. For example, an argument leading to change in some school policy would need to demonstrate that current policy creates a serious problem. In Chicago there has been considerable debate over whether schools should distribute contraceptives. Conditions underlying the arguments in favor of distribution are increases in teenage pregnancies, venereal disease, and AIDS. Basic to the argument is the contention that the increases are a problem of significant proportion. What is significant to some is not significant to others, however. This is an argument of interpretation, one that implies or makes explicit some definition of "significant" in this context.

In the same context, students may argue recommendations for policy. In such cases, warrants involve statements of principles used to guide actions. When serious disagreements exist at this level, it is because principles come into conflict. In the case of contraceptives in the schools, the groups in conflict both favor lowering the rate of increase in teenage pregnancies and venereal disease. The conflict arises over the method to be used in attaining reduction in the rates. Groups opposed to the distribution of contraceptives favor abstinence on the principle that sexual intercourse out of wedlock is sinful. Groups in favor base their arguments on a pragmatic principle that accepts indulgence but seeks to halt the consequences.

Such arguments of policy are often quite complex, involving several component arguments nested at various crucial points of the main argument. Arguments about policy almost necessarily involve at least two sets of grounds: one about the existing state of affairs and one about the predicted benefits of the change being recommended. In addition, these arguments usually deal in some fashion with the principles that serve as warrants at the policy level. At the same time, they necessarily involve recognition of opposing positions, the conditions for rebuttal.

The specific goal of instruction in this case might read as follows:

> To write an argument proposing some change in a policy of concern to the writer, addressed to an audience concerned with the problem, and including (1) an argument or arguments establishing the nature of the problem presented by current policy; (2) an argument or arguments supporting the predicted benefits of the proposed change; (3) at least one argument dealing with a major condition for rebuttal; and (4) statements of appropriate warrants and backing along with arguments resolving any conflicts in the warrants involved. All nested arguments should include appropriate claims, grounds, warrants, and backing, as necessary.

There is no reason why a curriculum may not include objectives dealing with policy, literary interpretation, and other types of argument as well. The objectives above will necessarily involve different sequences. The focus on interpretation of literature involves an analysis of the strategies involved in dealing with a literary work and definitions. Any interpretation necessarily involves categorization. Whether it deals with a relatively simple problem of whether a character may be considered courageous or a good parent, or a more complex problem such as whether the work as a whole reflects a set of values, the evidence supporting the claim must be warranted by a definition of courage, good parenting, or whatever values are involved.

The latter objective, however, implies a curriculum involving data collection from a variety of sources and interpretation of that data to establish what conditions apply, arguments supporting the judgments involved, arguments invoking principles as warrants, and opportunities to explore different claims about the same data and the arguments underlying them. To develop a full curriculum would probably involve developing several different problems and contexts, each of which includes inquiry and the various kinds of arguments. I will return to the problem of developing one such sequence in the next chapter.

THE WRITING CURRICULUM

The question of sequence implies attention to the broader question of what the overall writing curriculum should look like, what kinds of writing should be included, and at what levels and how often those should appear. These questions cannot be answered easily and represent matters for argument that go far beyond the scope of this book.

I do not, by any means, wish to imply that there is some idealized curriculum that should be in place for every school system and college. On the contrary, for a variety of reasons, writing curricula must be developed locally. In the first place, there is no way to ensure that teachers will follow some prescribed curriculum guide. That, I think, is as it should be. Teachers who plan their own curricula are more likely to be reflective about them, although, as we have seen in the case of the profile described in Chapter Two, freedom to plan does not in any way entail reflective teaching. In the second place, as any teacher knows, different classes react differently to the same materials, a fact that requires variability in planning. Third, to put some idealized curriculum in place would be to ignore the potentially rich local resources for writing. Finally, to establish a uniform curriculum of some sort would be to make innovation even more difficult. We do not need more obstacles to change.

So much depends on the students that only the most general recommendations are viable. I would argue for inclusion of the basic structures and affective response types at every level and as many different kinds of writing tasks as time permits. How many and how much time each receives will be a matter for the teacher to decide on the basis of some rationale that considers students' interests and needs. Not all writing tasks make sense in most curricula. I have seen college students put through the exercise of copying from dictation every day. Several years ago, Richard Hammer (1983) wrote an article, published in the *English Journal,* describing a "basics" program that confined its mostly African American population to filling out application forms and other simplistic tasks, the rationale being, "They can't do it." Such programs have not disappeared today. Writing formulaic book reports, outlining chapters or whole textbooks, writing a sonnet for which the only characteristics that count are the rhyme scheme and 14 lines of iambic pentameter—all of these I believe to be unjustifiable. The fact that we are willing to include some tasks and exclude others implies a bias of some sort. If our bias is not to be entirely arbitrary, we should be able to defend what we choose to include.

Note

1. There is no research that I know of about the problems that young students have when the organizational demands are other than narrative. My own experience is that abstract organizational patterns are difficult for seventh and eighth graders. Most ninth graders can deal with them with effective teaching. However, I have seen a good deal of college writing in which organization is so mechanical that the piece might have been better had the author not tried to organize. We need research on this problem.

Chapter Ten

Reflection in Planning and Teaching

In teaching and planning, as in writing, not all elements of what we do are under our conscious control all the time. Ideas come to mind, apparently unsolicited. We use procedures without thinking about them, simply because we have used them before and nothing else has presented itself. We respond to situations from the perspective of roles our culture has taught and that we have learned without trying. We respond to sudden classroom events intuitively, without much apparent thought. Although we may not exercise control over the sources of what we do, sooner or later what we do comes under conscious control. That is, to the extent that we are aware of our actions, we have the option to continue or discontinue them.

In that sense, every decision in planning and teaching implies a frame experiment. Since we cannot know, in advance, with certainty or high-level precision how anything will work, every piece of material, grouping arrangement, question, whatever we decide to use in class, everything constitutes a frame experiment. In planning and teaching, we can think of the frame experiment as having four major components: students and our knowledge of their past performance, interests, proclivities, and so forth; the trial event, which may be a single move such as a question or a sequence of events over a day or several weeks; a specific goal for the particular students involved, but understood within the context of an array of educational goals; and the curricular context of the event. The experiment or trial takes place within the frame of these other components. The teacher judges the success of the trial in terms of the specific goal for the particular students both as a group and as individuals; in terms of the array of educational goals for those students; and in terms of the impact of the trial on the movement of those students in the curricular sequence.

By definition, anything assessed must be judged in terms of what is desirable and what is not. Our formulations of specific goals outline what we think is desirable. If teaching takes place without specific goals, as Cain (1989) suggests it should, frame experiments are impossible. Further, it is almost always the case, at least in the kind of teaching recommended here, that a teaching move is heavily interconnected with the array of educational goals and much of the curricular sequence. Its evaluation, then, has to do with many desirabilities.

Take, for example, the lead question from the shell game sequence described in Chapter Eight: What does this shell look like to you? That question sounds fairly silly out of context. Nevertheless, my students and I have come to think of it as an important opening for this sequence of activities with shells that, paradoxically, has to do with narrative. At the most specific level, if the question works, it prepares students for the group work that follows, not only suggesting an instrument through which they may work collaboratively, but also giving them ideas about how to proceed in describing a different shell, which in turn prepares them for the individual work.

But the question is nested not only in the first of the shell activities but also in the entire empathic narrative sequence of several weeks and the writing curriculum as a whole. The use of metaphor is a major goal for the sequence, and this is the juncture at which we hope it begins. If the question works, it prompts models that the students themselves provide, making the products of their thinking an important part of the classroom text. More importantly, in prompting models, it triggers the use of procedures that result in metaphoric thinking, procedures that we cannot teach directly. But if we can prompt students to use this tacit knowledge, in the supported context of describing a shell that seems almost to demand comparison, then we believe that making comparisons will be easier in another context, or more likely at least.

Beyond that, the impact of the question has ramifications for the curricular concerns with inquiry and the processes of thinking. Its emphasis on "what the shell looks like to you" is involved in the larger educational goal that holds writing as a means for the invention and reinvention of the self (see Chapter One). Questions such as these emphasize how the "you" interprets what is perceived.

This question is not an anomaly. Any moment in teaching may be thought of as a trial with similar ramifications. Every question has multiple meanings and implications. Every planning and every teaching decision allows some things and denies others. Each deserves subjection to comparable analysis of relationships and benefits and, whenever possible, the careful evaluation that reflective planning and teaching allow. Given so many possibilities for reflection, how can we possibly subject everything to such scrutiny? Fortunately, our knowledge is not fragmented. The bridges among the theories we work with allow us to move from one perspective to another, bringing different knowledge to bear as appropriate. The evaluative reflection on and questioning of planning and teaching may occur at any time. Let me turn to each of four possibilities for specific examples: during planning, after a trial, during the trial, and at the end of a sequence.

REFLECTION IN PLANNING

During planning the test audience for materials is the planner, who tries to bring knowledge of the student audience to bear on the activities and materials being considered for use, projecting or imagining the kind, range, and pattern of responses as students encounter them. These projections include students' reactions to materials, activities, and the problems they present; the groupings of students and their reactions to one another; and the logistical procedures. As planning proceeds, the teacher needs to project these reactions as they develop over time. The frame experiment exists in the planner's imagination, as the planner asks the extent to which students are likely to reach the goals, given the materials and activities and his or her projection of students' responses to the various dimensions of the plan. However, planning is not linear. Ideas come at strange times (while brushing teeth, at a cocktail party, walking to the store) and not at all in a logically ordered fashion. Generalized goals prompt ideas for activities. On the other hand, specific ideas for activities appear to prompt new goals and often result in the modification of goals.

What follows is an attempt to reconstruct this hodge-podge of what seems to me to be reflective planning. The best I can do is necessarily an approximation, an attempt to represent the actual thinking that went on as I considered developing a context for teaching argument. It is impossible to present all the thinking in the following, if only because some of it unavoidably took place before I began the protocol. Merely anticipating doing it begins the process.

In the previous chapter, I speculated about some of the various possibilities for teaching argument. One of the possible contexts that allows the integration of work on various types of argument is a school or community problem that is researchable by students. Since I had already thought about this idea years ago, reconstructing the planning would be impossible. Yesterday, in thinking about how to develop this chapter, it occurred to me that a focus on advertising might provide a strong context. The idea came to me, I think, because I had also been thinking about using parts of a group discussion about nineteenth-century patent medicine ads in this chapter. In what follows I will try to take this planning a bit further, at least to the point of deciding whether or not the idea has enough merit to continue the work of planning down to the nitty-gritty of finding materials for gateway activities.

I know that students have knowledge about and interest in contemporary ads, down to being able to recall the language of particular TV ads. Recently a discussion of modern patent medicine ads prompted many to recall slogans and melodies, with several chiming in amidst general laughter and giggling. Students at various levels might enjoy this focus.

I remember that Michael W. Smith developed materials using ads to illustrate the structure of arguments. How else might the focus apply to argument? Certainly controversies about advertising abound, I think. Cigarette advertising, liquor, beer, truth in advertising. How about the deluge of direct-mail advertising? The material about conservation presents arguments of various types, maybe all types. I'll have to check, but I am sure that several agencies send material that argues that particular conditions exist, that they are problems, and that my gift will help to alleviate the problem. Every now and then, we receive mail requesting money (a gift) in exchange for blessings and a lucky number. Are those arguments? Parodies. I have had students do parodies of ads before. They loved it. Once groups did some on TV—home TV, that is. I'll bet that would illustrate the structure of arguments. Kids could invent outlandish evidence and warrants for the benefits of smoking or political campaigns. Al Capone, the ultimate law-and-order candidate, the one who cares that the guilty are taken care of with despatch. Decrease judicial logjams.

What else? Are there reports from government committees or commissions about the impact of advertising? Writing could involve three affective response types: detached, information-oriented (analyses of types of ads, ad campaigns, or individual ads); direct involved response (ads for real purposes in the school or community); detached, opus-oriented response (parody).

The unit could begin with inquiry into modern patent medicine ads and writing simple arguments about their characteristics, or maybe begin with nineteenth-century ads. That could serve as introduction to argument, without getting into structure of arguments explicitly. To look at the structure of argument, maybe I could use the nineteenth-century ads where the claims, evidence, and warrants are fairly obvious, if phony. Could parody enter in here as a means of reinforcing the understanding of structure?

How about arguments of policy? Could examine some controversies. Are there local controversies? There are in Chicago over ads aimed at ghettos for the lottery, cigarettes, malt liquor. I wonder what students think about the appropriateness of certain ads aimed at them or younger kids. Does the problem of conflicting principles work in here? I cannot think how at the moment. A problem.

I have taken a break and have lost what I was thinking about during it. Do we have conflicting principles involved in the ad controversies? The conflict about lottery ads says there are more ads in the ghetto than in other areas of the city. No conflict in principle there. That has to do with analysis of evidence. Malt liquor ads. One part is a conflict in principle. Breweries argue rights to advertise and of the consumer to know, I think. Protesters argue that ads take advantage of a highly susceptible audience. That would be true for the lottery ads and some of the cigarette ads as well. Maybe there is a conflict of principle as well as conflicting interpretations of evidence. This could be fairly interesting. I need to do research on the problem. Are there reviews of the controversies in newspapers, magazines?

Perhaps it is time to evaluate. Will this work as a context for teaching argument? It ought to. There seem to be many possibilities. It could include all kinds of arguments and different response types. The material is potentially of high interest in itself. If students develop an ad for some real issue or event and create parodies, those will be of value in themselves and also stimulate interest. The unit could include simulation games focusing on an actual controversy, maybe one that is current, and provide plenty of work on considering opposing points of view and the conditions of rebuttal. If it begins with inquiry into the nature of advertising, students could continue to use the ideas and evidence developed there throughout the unit and could continue inquiry especially in the simulation games and in their developing written arguments about those issues. If the students examine real issues, their arguments could be intended for the real audiences of local and school newspapers. The more I think about the idea, the more possibilities I see, and the more I feel fairly certain it would work.

Continuing with this planning would involve far more space than I have available. Nor, I think, would anyone want to continue to read the kind of back-and-forth rambling that planning necessitates. I think such rambling is an essential part of reflective planning. Without this associative process, planning would result in Warrineresque sequences that have no more power to affect learning than a worm has to escape a lead cell. However, the rambling is not without goals. On the contrary, the goals are clearly stated and the rambling is guided by theories of inquiry, discourse, teaching, and learning. Even at this early stage the planning shows traces of the kinds of group activities that will be included. At the same time, the ideas are not fully warranted. The possibility remains that it will not work. This is an early stage. Nearly everything is still open to question.

DESIGN AND TRIAL OF A GATEWAY ACTIVITY

The following activity was designed for an initial trial with the high school juniors whose group discussion follows. Their written arguments, as a group, shared characteristics with the piece arguing the need to wear jackets to classes in the previous chapter. Their teacher was particularly concerned that they did not cite evidence well and did not "explain it" when they did. In other words, they did not use warrants.

The sequence in which the activity appeared began with the reading and teacher-led discussion of a model argument from *Time* magazine, followed by a teacher-led discussion of modern patent medicine ads. The questions simply prompted students to talk about what ads for patent medicines they were familiar with from TV, print, or radio. After listing ten or so ads the teacher asked students to tell what they are like, what they show, and what they promise to do for whoever takes them. This talk, not really a discussion, went forward with great enthusiasm, as students seamed to enjoy recalling the exact words and even melodies used in certain ads.

The idea for using 100-year-old advertisements came from watching adults comment on antique ads, some for patent medicines, that had been reprinted on wallpaper. (Ideas come from strange places!) Several different ads from newspapers, the Sears Roebuck Catalogue for 1892, and *Harper's Weekly* were assembled. I selected ads that were interesting to me and that I thought might interest students. When I asked teachers and my graduate students what they thought about using them, they were reasonably positive. I selected three ads, one from an edition of the 1882 edition of *The Chicago Tribune* and two from the Sears Roebuck Catalogue. All the ads in the group assembled promised to cure or alleviate a wide range of problems by taking care of some root cause responsible for all the problems. The text of one is shown in Figure 10.1.

Students were asked to work in small groups to compare the three ads they had received and to consider how they were different from and similar to contemporary patent medicine ads. Discussion guidelines asked them to examine the promises made by the ads, the strategies used to convince an audience, and the writers' views of their audiences. The guide then asked students to use what they had learned about the 100-year-old ads to compare them to contemporary ads they were familiar with, a number of which had been discussed earlier in class. During the group work, the guidelines told students, "list as many promises as you can" and "find as many strategies as you can."

The plan assumed that students, at the very least, would see what the old ads were like and make claims comparing them to contemporary ads. The old ads make far more promises about a far greater variety of ailments than do modern ones. The language of the former was far more inflated than the language of modern ads. On the other hand, some of the strategies remain the same: testimonials, explanations of how the drug works, and so forth. After making these comparisons, students would have data at their fingertips and warrants would be simple accounts of how the data were collected. This was the plan in a nutshell.

The major questions in the trial of the activity were whether the students would enjoy it, attend to the data in each ad, and make inferences and interpretations that demand support and explanation. To gain a better understanding of how the groups responded, we made audio recordings of three of six

Figure 10.1 Example of a 100-year-old advertisement.

DR. CLARK JOHNSON'S

TIGER Blood Syrup.

CURES *Dyspepsia, Liver Disease, Fever & Ague, Rheumatism, Dropsy, Heart Disease, Biliousness, Nervous Debility, etc.*

The Best REMEDY KNOWN to Man!

9,000,000 Bottles SOLD SINCE 1870.

This Syrup possesses Varied Properties

It Stimulates the Ptyalin in the Sylvia which converts the starch and sugar of the food into glucose. A deficiency in Ptyalin causes Wind and Souring of food in the stomach. If the medicine was taken immediately after eating the fermentation of food is prevented.

It acts upon the Liver.
It acts upon the Kidneys.
It Purifies the Blood.
It Regulates the Bowels.
It Quiets the Nervous System.
It Promotes Digestion.
It Nourishes, Strengthens, and Invigorates.
It carries off the Old Blood and makes new.
It opens the pores of the skin and induces Healthy Perspiration.

There are no spirits employed in its manufacture, and it can be taken by the most delicate babe or by the aged and feeble, *care only being required in attention to directions.*

TESTIMONIALS.

Disease of the Stomach and Liver.

Cairo, Alexander Co., Ill.

Dear Sir: Suffering for some time with headache and Disease of the Stomach and Liver. I was induced to use your reliable TIGER BLOOD SYRUP which restored me to perfect health and strength.

No. 30 Eighth St. **CHAS SHELLEY**

An Excellent Remedy.

Belvidere, Boone Co., Ill. Feb. 4, 1879.

Dear Sir: I have been using your TIGER BLOOD SYRUP for some time, and am perfectly satisfied with the results. It Purifies the Blood, Restores Lost Appetite, Strengthens the Nerves, Regulates the Stomach and Bowels, and Relieves Rheumatism. I would not be without it.

Mrs. WESTFALL

Kidney Disease.

Fisher, Champaign Co. Ill.

Dear Sir: This is to certify that your TIGER BLOOD SYRUP has done me more good for Kidney Complaint, and Heart Disease than any other medicine I ever used. It also cured one of my children of Chills and Scrofula.

Mrs. Jackson

---

groups. As happens in these efforts, one of the recorders did not record (the pause button was in the ON position). The result was two recordings that allowed us, with observations of all groups, to put forth at least tentative answers to our questions. Let us turn to some portions of the group discussion. The first transcript begins moments after students had begun the discussion. They are examining the ad in Figure 10.1:

ANGELA: It promises it's the best remedy known to man, too.
LISA: We have to do all of them.
DARLENE: Oh. So number one we have to answer for all the things?
LISA: Yeah, but like one individual, make an individual set for each. That would make more sense.
DARLENE: We only have like—
ANGELA: Look at this. It promises also that 9 million bottles have been sold and it's the best remedy known to man. By saying, that, you know . . .
LISA: Where is that at?
ANGELA: Right underneath.
LISA: Best remedy.
ANGELA: Don't you think that's a promise?
LISA: Yeah.
ANGELA: The next sentence, too, right?
LISA: Yeah. Nine million bottles sold?
ANGELA: This is a lot different than Mr. Miller's class.
LISA: Yeah.
DARLENE: Look at all this stuff. It promises it acts upon the liver, it acts upon the kidneys, it regulates the bowels and purifies the blood, it quiets the nervous system, it promotes digestion, it nourishes, all those?
LISA, ANGELA: Mmhm.
LISA: All the—
DARLENE: Right here, too. It stimulates the ptyalin in the saliva.
LISA: Exactly how it works.
ANGELA: I'm not sure. What's the next question? It's too long.
LISA: The next question is, what does the ad do to convince the audience?
ANGELA: Well, we've got the testimonials, so those are going to be easy for that.
DARLENE: I think you probably have to just—everything up here. [laughs]
LISA: That's what I'm thinking too.
DARLENE: Tiger Blood Syrup.
ANGELA: Look at it. It says even right here. It says, tells what it does by, like it says a deficiency—
DARLENE: I'm going to put down, stimulates the, whatever that is.
ANGELA: Yeah, I am too.

In this first segment of the discussion, the three students are concerned with answering the first question, identifying the promises in the ads. Even though Lisa brings up the second question about what the ad does to convince the audience, the girls stay with the first for some time following this excerpt. The excerpt indicates two problems with the design so far, and both lie in the first question.

First, not all students interpret the word *promise* as intended. Angela seems to interpret it as "claim" or "assure." She says, "It promises also that 9 million bottles have been sold and it's the best remedy known to man. By saying, that, you know . . ." Unfortunately, her final comment is cut off, and she never comes back to it. She may have been on the verge of explaining why such a statement is a promise, or implies a promise. Perhaps the earlier teacher-led discussion should have clarified the meaning of the term as intended in the guide. It would have been a simple matter to clarify the term when it came up in reference to contemporary ads that the students referred to. However, this is not a serious problem. Indeed, if Angela is referring to implied promises, it is not a problem at all, but a benefit. Even if she did not have that in mind, the idea can be fruitfully explored in the follow-up full-class discussion.

The second problem is a bit more serious. The first question, with its insistence that students "list as many promises" as they can find, demands that they attend to the texts at a very low level of interpretation and that they take the time to write them down. They examine every statement to decide if it is a promise or not and then take the time to write them. Because the ads list many individual promises, this question not only takes more time than it should, but it does not produce very exciting results. As it stands, the question of what counts as a promise never is raised.

What are the alternatives? One useful function that the question serves is having students attend closely to the text of the ads. For that reason it would be unwise to throw the question out altogether. But we need to abolish the listing activity. One alternative is to change the prompt to make the kind of interpretation more explicit, as in the following: *What kinds of promises does the ad make? Be prepared to explain the sense in which each of your choices is a promise.* This prompt asks students to think about what a promise is and the ways in which each of their selections is a promise. This emphasis should raise the level of interpretation and eliminate the listing problem by allowing students to group promises together.

At the end of the segment of discussion above, students turn to the second question. Angela recognizes the function of the testimonials immediately. Darlene seems to indicate that the whole set of promises is there to convince the audience. She also appears to recognize the name of the medicine as indicating a promise but does not explain it. Angela seems to recognize that the explanation of how the medicine rectifies a deficiency helps to convince an audience, and though the others agree, how that might work remains unexplained. Angela appears to make a claim about a bit of the text (grounds), but allows the warrant to remain unstated.

The girls revert to listing promises for several lines of transcript before returning to question 2.

ANGELA: How does it convince them? I think it might be how it convinces because it's just telling you exactly what it does, how it, how it, why it promises these promises.
DARLENE: It promises that it can be taken by the most delicate babe or by the aged and feeble.
LISA: Mmhm. That's cute.
DARLENE: Put that down?
LISA: Mmmhm.
DARLENE: Just put it can be taken by anyone, probably.
DARLENE: [whispers] My stomach's growling.
ANGELA: But you have to follow directions. So that's like another thing.
DARLENE: What are you writing? If directions are followed?
ANGELA: Mmhm.
LISA: All right. Next one.
DARLENE: What does the ad do to convince the audience?
ANGELA: It shows you how? I think it's just like—
LISA: Testimonials of—
ANGELA: Well, the testimonials.
LISA: Three people.
LISA: It says the ninth—
DARLENE: Three people on three different topics, I mean, three different, like . . .
LISA: Yeah, and three different cures. I know what you mean.
DARLENE: With different examples probably.
LISA: Yeah.
DARLENE: Just put there's three different people with different examples.
LISA: It also says that 9 million bottles have been sold.
ANGELA: I think that was a promise, because—
LISA: Well that's also like 9 million—
ANGELA: Well, that's kind of like a convincing too, though.
LISA: Like a stratagem.
ANGELA: Yeah. Because it has other people bought it.
LISA: Probably said like what we're doing—
ANGELA: Like McDonald's and their hamburgers. That's what I keep thinking of. [laughs]
LISA: Millions sold.

DARLENE: Daily. [laughs]
LISA: Million customers served daily.
DARLENE: Is it million or billion? I thought it was billion. [all talking at once, laughing]
LISA: Oh my gosh, I don't know. Can you imagine?
ANGELA: Number of bottles sold.

In the first turn of this segment, Angela provides a partial explanation of why she thinks the language explaining how the drug works convinces the audience. This comes close to being an articulated warrant. She says, "It convinces because it's just telling you exactly what it does . . . , why it promises these promises." However, her statement does not explain why "telling you exactly what it does" is convincing. After that, the girls once again revert to finding pieces of text that convince the audience, without any explanation of why the text is convincing—with no warrant, in other words.

By the time the girls reach the third of the three ads, Mike has joined them. They have begun to move faster and instead of examining each statement, they make a swift summary, listing the promises about the benefits of "Celery Malt Compound" in rapid order. They turn to the second question:

DARLENE: OK, that's what it cures. Number two. What does the ad do to convince the audience? Well, first it says like if you're, if you have any intelligence, where does it say that? It was in there.
MIKE: If you have any intelligence.
DARLENE: It says something with that—oh. Will show any person of ordinary intelligence why it is such a useful preparation and should be kept in every household. So you would feel stupid if you don't get it.
LISA, ANGELA: Yeah.
MIKE: It's telling you that if you feel really bad, then try it.

Here we have nearly a complete argument. The girls and Mike note the implications, claim that it is an attempt to convince the audience, and explain why. This statement of claims, grounds, and warrant is more complete than anything else so far for this group. A revision of question 2 might prompt this higher level of discussion throughout. One useful revision might be to deemphasize finding "as many strategies as you can" and, instead, emphasize explaining why the various strategies are convincing. This proposed change is similar to that for the previous question.

Revisions such as these come after the teaching has ended and there has been an opportunity to reflect on the effects of the procedures in light of the materials and procedures used. Some revisions come during the process in response to problems that are more readily perceived. At the point we have reached in the classroom discussion above, the teacher had been aware that the timing was far off the original intent. With only a few minutes of class time left, the groups are only half-way through the intended discussion. Students have not discussed the audience of the ads and will clearly not have time to compare the 100-year-old ads to contemporary ads they are familiar with. (The discussion of the model piece of writing took nearly 15 minutes. On another occasion, the teacher will shift it to a point immediately before students write, where it should be more effective.) At this point, as a summary of the days's work, the teacher wants students to make explicit ideas they may have generated while looking at the ads, ideas that can be used to reorient the class discussion the next day.

TEACHER: Have you talked about all three ads?
ANGELA: We're almost done with the last one.
TEACHER: OK. When you finish the third one, don't worry about the contemporary ads question. You know, you can always think about that in your heads. . . . Try to write a sentence that synthesizes your ideas about these ads and what they're doing and how they work. . . . Don't put all the ideas into one sentence, but take one idea that you think is interesting and put it in one sentence that would serve as a thesis statement for a piece of writing. OK? Understand?
LISA: Something about how they said to cure so many aches.
DARLENE: Yeah. And it was impossible for something to cure some things, like cancer.
LISA: Yeah, like cancer. Like cancer and eczema have nothing to do with each other, I mean, how could it cure both of them?
ANGELA: Right. Like this guy who used to go out on like those cars(?), I think they were gypsies or something, or something like that?
LISA: You want to write something about the lack of intelligence of the people to believe that.
DARLENE: Yeah.
LISA: To believe that it cured all those things.
ANGELA: And the lack of medical knowledge really, though.
LISA: What about (inaudible)? Because if we were, then we would be like, yeah, right. If you lived then, you probably would believe it.
DARLENE: I would. [all laugh] Believe everything. OK.
LISA: We could just write the lack of medical knowledge caused people to believe anything they were told.
ANGELA: OK. That's good.
MIKE: So what are we doing now?
DARLENE: [loudly—to get teacher's attention?] What years are these about?
LISA: 1900s. During the early.

MIKE: It says here 1880 to 1902.
LISA: The late—during the late?
MIKE: Late 1800s, early 1900s.
LISA: [slowly, as writing] 1800s and early 1900s people's lack of medical knowledge [voice tapers off] caused them, caused them, caused them to believe?
ANGELA: Yeah. Something like that.
DARLENE: Yeah.
LISA: During the early 1800s and early 1900s the lack of medical knowledge caused people to believe everything they heard.
LISA: We should pick another aspect and do another one.
ANGELA: Well, these people selling it had—what do we say about them?
DARLENE: What does it say?
LISA: During the late 1800s and early 1900s people's lack of medical knowledge caused them to believe impossible things.
DARLENE: Oh, OK.
ANGELA: Caused them to believe the ads.

The group goes on to begin developing another claim about how the "con-artists" were able to take advantage of the people's gullibility to make a lot of money. The teacher will use these the next day to examine what can be claimed and supported from the data available. Angela has already prepared the way for work on qualification, for restricting generalizations appropriately. She has changed the generalization from one about ignorance to the more limited "lack of medical knowledge." Later she qualifies Lisa's overgeneralization about lack of medical knowledge causing people to "believe impossible things" to "caused them to believe the ads."

In rethinking this lesson in light of the trial, the teacher had a new insight into the ads: that many in the sample collected seem to share a certain underlying theory of disease, namely, that all diseases are linked to some central failure in the body's functioning. If the elixir advertised can rectify the central problem, then it seems reasonable to expect all the related ailments to be affected. The teacher decided to add a question at the beginning of the hour on the next day: What similarities do you note among the medicines? She would be more specific if necessary. She believed that if students infer this common conception of ailments, they should also see that what operates is not so much lack of medical knowledge as a conception of disease and illness different from the one we accept today.

This trial of a new activity set out to determine "whether the students would enjoy it, attend to the data in each ad, and make inferences and interpretations that demand support and explanation." The trial suggests affirmative answers to all of these. The students were highly attentive to the ads.

They found them quite interesting, were able to reason about them, and began to make interpretations that required support and explanation, some of which they began to supply, even by the end of the first hour. Because they had used the ads to formulate their claims, they would be able to find the evidence necessary to support them.

However, the trial suggested several revisions that will help students move in the direction of developing better explanations of how their data support claims. Even more useful, the insight into the theory of ailments underlying elixirs' powers provides a second competing explanation of why the ads appealed to people. When students set out to find evidence for one or the other or both, they automatically become involved in a more sophisticated exchange of ideas and more complex arguments. In short, although the first plan did not work as expected, the activity on the day examined above and the following day were beneficial for the students and resulted in their writing arguments supporting different claims about a larger set of ads, with all students citing appropriate evidence for the major claim and with about two-thirds citing warrants for the main arguments. In my opinion, the material or material like it has several advantages. The ads are brief, they are intriguing, and they are complex enough to support interesting inquiry and argument.

REFLECTION IN ACTION

Most of the reflection that occurs in teaching is not available to anyone other than the teacher. A departure from a previously laid-out plan usually indicates that the teacher has reconsidered certain variables and decided to change the plan. However, much of the reflection and resultant decision making is more finely detailed than most of the considerations included in the explicit plan. Reflection-in-action is based on the moment-to-moment observation of student responses to logistical, instructional, and social particulars of learning activities. In effect, the teacher is asking how any particular observation matches the expectation for that activity.

To illustrate, let me take a case from work that I have fairly complete records of, namely, my own teaching of the shell lesson mentioned above. In our fall composition workshops with seventh or eighth graders, only one person teaches at a time, while the others act as observers, each making some sort of observational record. Frequently, when none of my M.A.T. students have had classroom experience, I teach the first day.

Each day our observational data permit us to examine what happened, how particular students respond to activities, what their levels of attention are, and how they have handled particular writing tasks. We consider how lessons might or should have changed and how we might have responded to individual students. When did we begin to lose student attention? When might an activity have been halted? When did signs appear that students had failed to understand? How might the lesson structure have been changed to deal with the problem? Those records along with my own notes permit me to reconstruct the following case.

The class includes 24 African Americans, 3 Asians, and a Tanzanian. Two boys from Cambodia have limited English skills. One speaks pretty well and is eager to talk, but the other is very shy. A Vietnamese girl carries an English/Vietnamese dictionary about two-and-a-half inches thick with the cover ripped off. From time to time she surreptitiously slips it from her desk to check words. The student from Tanzania has been in the United States for only a year. She has very limited English but works very hard and wishes to speak English and be successful.

The M.A.T. students and I have planned the lesson in detail. For example, because the M.A.T. students have never taught, we spend considerable time planning for grouping. How many groups should we set up? We decide on six so that we have no more than five students per group. On the basis of pretests collected the week before we arrive, we decide to assign a stronger writer to each group and to spread the weaker writers among all groups. At the same time, we try to balance boys and girls among all groups. Finally, we plan the directions for the group work, which are quite involved because we expect, on the basis of past experience, that students have not done collaborative group work before.

This lesson will include several different activities. To begin, it will use a model composition that will give the students an idea of the kind of personal narrative we hope they will write by the end of our time with them. This year we have decided to use Verita's final composition because it is by a former student in a comparable class and because it treats a simple subject that our students will recognize (coming to their school as a new student) in a very powerful fashion. We will use other pieces later in the course. We will use a selection from Richard Wright's (1945) *Black Boy* and several selections form *Merlyn's Pen,* a magazine of original writing and artwork by students in grades 7 to 10.[1]

Following the reading of Verita's piece, which appears at the end of this chapter, students will respond to a single large shell in a teacher-led discussion, the goal of which is to indicate the kinds of phrases that might be used to describe a shell and, particularly, to encourage figurative language. Next follows an introduction to the group shell game and then to group work, which includes assignment to groups, an explanation of group responsibilities, an explanation of how to move into groups (these are seventh graders likely to do a lot of furniture banging), and finally a brief comment about the activity. At the end of the hour, I am to give a simple proofreading inventory designed to determine whether students can identify the ends of relatively simple sentences.

Since this is our first day in the class, I introduce all of us and distribute Verita's composition, read it aloud, and ask what details the students liked. One student responds that she liked the way the writer talked about her reactions. I ask for a specific reference in the text. The girl reads a simile, "my heart was pounding like a volcano about to erupt." I ask for another detail that people liked. There is a very long, long pause. I wait. Then I say, in an attempt to be encouraging, "You can look at the piece of writing and see what there is." (A stupid thing to say, I think, after having said it.) Another long pause ensues. "Yes?" say I, hopefully. Another long pause. Out of the corner of my eye I can see the M.A.T. students begin to fidget in their seats. I wait longer. Finally, I decide to go through the piece a few lines at a time, and I begin, "Let's take a look at," when a student raises a hand. This student refers to the details about entering the auditorium and seeing all the strange students present. Then another hand is up. I get five responses in succession, each to a detail the student thinks is effective. Soon, 12 students have responded. My impression is that they have some idea of effective detail.

Noting that we are behind schedule, I pull a large "helmet" seashell out of a paper bag and explain that I'm going to ask them to describe a seashell as specifically as they can. I begin to walk around the room with the large shell, allowing students to touch and hold it momentarily. All of them seem eager to touch the shell and look at it closely.

I ask, "How would you describe it if you had to describe this shell in language, in words, so that somebody else could picture it without seeing it? What would you say about it?" My intent is to get some details about color and texture. There is a long pause again. "Take a look at it," I say. A girl says it is cream colored. "Good," I say. She has reminded me of the key question, and I decide to use it. As I hold it the shell between my hands, I ask, "What does the shell look like to you?" There is silence. But I see that everyone is looking at the shell. I hold it by the narrow end. A boy says, "It looks sort of like a trophy cup." Another boy says very softly that it has different kinds of colors, tan, white, a "pinky color." Another says that it looks like an ear. I am surprised: "All right, if you look at this part, it does look like an ear. That's very good." I shift the shell about. Another student says, "Looks like a mouth with teeth." Eventually there are other similes: a beehive, a little elf's cap with a twisted top, a tepee, "rough and scaly like an old person's skin."

I decide that students have the idea of describing the shell and begin the process of setting up the groups. When that is complete, I explain the first shell game. "Your group will receive two shells. I want you to pick out one and describe it so well that some other group will be able to tell which of the two shells your group described." I note some students looking blank and try again: "You get two shells. Your group writes a description of one. Then we'll pass what you have written and your two shells to another group. We want to see if your group writes clearly enough to help the second group identify which shell you described."

Most seem to understand and several begin to move. I quickly explain the ground rules for movement into groups: find a desk near where your group meets, move it into position quickly and quietly, and so forth. Then I ask them to move. During my initial visit to each group, I ask if someone has been selected to write and if the students have picked a shell. I urge that each student contribute to the description. Observer notes indicate that subsequent visits focus on asking questions, making suggestions, and giving praise. During the first 15 minutes, I make 18 visits to the groups.

Despite these relatively frequent visits, two groups present problems. One observer notes that in group 2 a boy and a girl have a disagreement about the foot space available under the desks and engage in some under-the-desk kicking. Another observer is watching an even more obstreperous group. In that group, LaTonya volunteers to be secretary and asks the students to describe the shell. A boy opens up, saying, "I don't know. It's ugly." LaTonya responds, "You want me to write that down? It's ugly? What makes it ugly?" LaTonya complains that the boy isn't doing what he's supposed to be doing. Jake begins to draw. Kiva, a tall, aggressive girl, snatches Jake's paper from his desk. He snatches it back. The observer notes, "They snatch back and forth." I am aware of the problems in this group and see that LaTonya is doing her best to control the rambunctious Jake and get the work done. Every time I move to that group to listen, they settle down. As soon as I move to another group, Jake gets things going again. Finally, I ask him if he would rather work alone. He says, "No," and slouches in his chair, scowling alternatively at me and his paper. I realize that we are going to have to win Jake over somehow. We learn later that we have six "behavior-disordered" students. Jake and two others have wound up quite by accident in the same group.

After about 18 minutes of group work, four groups are finished. My visits have revealed that every group has written several details and, I think, at least one figure of speech. Three of the groups have three or more. I collect group compositions from those that have finished and distribute the proofreading inventories to those groups that have completed the composition. The students, relatively quiet now, work away on their punctuation inventories. When all groups have completed their writing about a shell, I exchange shells and compositions for pairs of groups.

I ask each group to read over the composition, identify the shell described, and underline the most helpful details. A visit to the first group indicates that students have not understood what to underline. I try again: "Underline the details that were best in telling you which was being described." I continue to circulate among the groups, listening as they read and talk, watching to see what they underline. I point to specific images in three groups, asking if those were helpful in identifying the shell. When the pairs of groups have finished, I make a decision to change the plan. I ask that each of those groups send a representative to the other group to tell what shell they identified and what was good about the other group's description.

I notice that one group is laughing at a representative because her group picked the wrong shell. She is not about to take their ridicule quietly. She goes back to her group, snatches the two shells and marches back to the writers. "Look," she says, scowling at them and holding one shell in each palm for them to see, "They're both kinda brownish. They're both kinda round. And they're both kinda bumpity. So that is stupid to say. And we couldn't tell." Right on, I thought. I couldn't have made the point more clearly. In fact, I wouldn't have dared make it in quite that way at all. As the groups finish, I ask that they complete the punctuation inventories. They do not have time to finish them.

Even though this is a practiced lesson, evaluation must proceed at all times. Those assessments prompt the suggestions and questions to groups and decisions about when to move to another part of the lesson. The only changes I made were based on an intuition that it would be better to let the groups give feedback the same day of the writing because it would be fresher and because I knew we had the time. But throughout there is a fine-tuning necessary for responding to what the students say and do, because there is no way to know in advance how students will respond to Verita's piece, the large shell, the shells used in groups, or to other students. But a teacher with experience has a range of expectations for the possible responses, a range that provides a kind of safety net, so that while one might be knocked off the high wire by an unexpected turn of events, the fall is never fatal.

Some of the reflection that occurs in the midst of teaching is instantaneous, important but fleeting, and difficult to reconstruct, even with stimulated recall methods. In this program some reflection takes place in public, immediately following our teaching. Because it occurs aloud in a group, it is relatively easy to reconstruct. On the day in question above, the "postmortem" begins almost as soon as we reach the stairwell. The first question from the M.A.T. students is, "What did you think when nobody answered?" I admit that I was beginning to think perhaps no one would answer and was just getting ready to be more direct when someone did speak up. I emphasize the necessity of waiting while students collect their ideas or identify things that interest them. We talk about that. The M.A.T. students spend a few minutes commenting excitedly on what they saw.

Out of all their commentary, the main concern obviously is that the groups did not appear to be as productive as the M.A.T. students had expected. We talk about why that might be. The seventh graders are not used to us. They seem not to be used to true collaborative work in groups. I note a colleague's finding that group work in elementary school often means sitting in a small group but working independently. We have asked the students to work together to develop a piece of writing, a difficult task. We consider the possibility of moving students in or out of the obstreperous groups, but decide to wait. We will give students clearer directions about collaboration and encourage them to be responsible for working together. (These discussions continue over the next few days. By the fifth day, we have decided to change group membership, and the groups function well. One observer writes, "The changes work." But there will be relapses.)

We go through the lesson step by step, examining problems along the way. We examine the compositions developed by the groups. Four groups have written the kind of composition we expected, a unified piece incorporating descriptive phrases and comparisons. One group wrote two paragraphs, one about each shell. Clearly, they misunderstood the directions and the teacher's visits did not pick up this problem. Each paragraph, however, contains some strong detail. The weakest effort appears to have come from our most obstreperous group. Rather than write a unified paragraph, LaTonya has recorded separate sentences for each student, such as the following from Jake: "It's ugly, badge [sic] is a ugly color. The brown design is ugly." We decide to move ahead to the activity of the students' independent writing about specific shells.

The next day each student writes about a shell so that another person reading the composition will be able to pick out the shell from the 30 that will be on the table. They work diligently for nearly 30 minutes. In this class 21 use figurative language, and all use specific detail.

EVALUATION OF A SEQUENCE

In reflective teaching, every move may be subject to scrutiny, but no move stands alone. Each is part of a sequence of some sort or another. In this book, I have been advocating sequences in which the episodes are tightly bound, in which each contributes to the next so that student learning is cumulative, at least within particular sequences. Such a position entails that we evaluate the effect of the sequences on student learning. It is clearly not enough to think carefully through curricular designs and activities and daily teaching. All of these have to add up to something. And that ought to be something we can see by the end of the sequence. We need to look at our students' writing and ask to what extent and in what ways it has improved as a result of our teaching. There is no reason that most students should not show improvement. If they do not, the teaching needs to change.

Making the assessment of writing is no mystery anymore. In study after study, effective teaching not only makes a difference, but shows up on posttests (see the Appendix). Teachers who do not like conventional scales may invent and defend their own. If we study the features of the writing we hope to teach, we can devise a scale and use it. We can describe the features that show change. To evaluate a full writing program we need to look at several different kinds of writing tasks across all students. We need the kind of portfolios that my superintendent demanded in Euclid, Ohio, many years ago. We need pieces from early and late in the writing program collected under comparable conditions. In particular, we need to examine the impact of teaching on those who appear to be our weakest students.

Take Maurice, for example, whose initial sample writing was weaker than Verita's. These pieces represent one end of a scale that my students and I have found useful, while Verita's posttest and Arne Kildegaard's "Understanding" represent the other extreme. At about the middle of these is Ranakea's initial sample about a trip to Wisconsin Dells (Chapter Seven). It represented the best performance on the initial sample in that particular class, with only one other student at that level, while Maurice's represented the weakest. By the end of instruction, Ranakea had moved to the high end of the scale. Maurice, who had been in the seventh grade before and for whom no one had expectations, could not move that far.

Nevertheless, Maurice's growth is impressive. On his final sample, written under conditions comparable to those of the first, Maurice writes 605 words (over four times as many as in the pretest) about a trip to Detroit that includes a Pistons' basketball game, a little cousin who broke his leg, and two minor adventures. Maurice includes details about the game and the incident of the broken leg. He uses dialogue and simile, and reveals his feelings in a variety of ways about the game and the broken leg. His personality begins to emerge. He seems to be inventing himself. As an added bonus, he includes periods at 35% of the accepted locations (as opposed to none on the first sample) and doubles the frequency of subordinate clauses. Clearly, Maurice's writing has improved substantially, from the bottom of the class to a point where the best student writing had been before instruction.

Some students make gains like Verita's, from the bottom of the scale to the top, a transformation that shows change in narrative structure, focus, use of detail and imagery, personal response, and dialogue, nearly everything we have dealt with. The following piece is her posttest, written under conditions comparable to her pretest, which appears in Chapter One.

First Day at Ray School

I was half scared and half excited. All night I had practiced my times table chart. I got up and walked to the bathroom and took a nice hot shower. I thought about how I would like my new teachers, or how they would like me. I got out of the shower and started to dry myself. The thing I wanted most was to be in the same class as Tracy. She wasn't one of my best friends, we had gotten in plenty of fights, but still when you're going to a new school, anyone you can pal around with would be great.

Our doorbell rang. It was 8:25 just as I popped the last bit of toast into my mouth. I ran to the front hall and opened the door. There was Tracy. She said, "C'mon, or we'll be late!" Marian, Tracy's mom, had brought her car around. I hopped in and we drove off.

As we got nearer and nearer to school, my heart started pounding like a volcano about to erupt. We got out of the car, and someone told us that if we were new we should go to the auditorium. So we finally found it, and there were already about one hundred people there. The lady on the stage was dressed in black and white. Her hair reminded me of the Gloria Vanderbilt lady. She had spectacles on and was talking about rules and regulations. We sat down near the edge. She went on with her lecture for about forty-five minutes. It was really boring, but I listened. Finally, at the end, she called out names and room numbers. I was in 314 and Tracy was in 315. I felt my heart jump, and I could tell Tracy wasn't the happiest person on earth either. This guy came down to our row and told us to follow him to the room.

By the time I got up to the third floor, my feet felt like a ton each, and the rest of my body was well exhausted. We walked into a room marked 314, and the man left. I was all alone with everyone staring at me. Finally, my teacher broke the silence and said, "Find a seat. I'm your homeroom teacher, Mrs. Lanier. I will tell you what you need for this room."

I sat down in back of a girl. She turned around and said, "Hi. Welcome to Ray School. I'm Clara." That's how I came to Ray.

The next problem for reflection is how to help all of these students journey beyond this point.

Note

1. *Merlyn's Pen: The National Magazines of Student Writing* has two editions now, one for grades 6 through 9 and one for grades 9 through 12. All writing and all major artwork are by students in the grade levels indicated. They are remarkable for their

high quality, and at the same time are of very high interest, both because the material is by authors at the age level of the readers and because the selections have their own intrinsic interest. Writing teachers at these grade levels will find it valuable as a motivator and as a source of models. For information write to *Merlyn's Pen,* P.O. Box 1058, East Greenwich, Rhode Island 02818–0964.

Chapter Eleven

A Summation

We do not need best-selling books to tell us that our world is changing. We are in the midst of a worldwide population explosion. Our neighborhoods are rapidly changing. Crime rates mount at unprecedented rates. New diseases are among us.

Curiously, the only change that receives attention in school is technological change. Certain states have enacted legislation to make all the English curricula serve the purposes of technology. In Indiana the program is called "Tech-Prep" and promises to better prepare all students, but particularly what they call the "forgotten middle" 50%, for an increasingly technological world. What will such programs mean to education?

The word *technology* refers to sets of specific techniques for accomplishing particular results. A review of entries in the *Oxford English Dictionary* indicates that the words *technique, technical,* and *technology* have become more and more applied to the "formal or mechanical part of an art" and particularly to the mechanical and industrial arts and the applied sciences. When one is accomplished in technology, one knows in a very precise manner exactly what has to be done to accomplish certain ends. Technology is algorithmic. If you fail to follow precise rules with your word processor, you will not be able to use it. When you want to save a document, only certain key strokes will do the job.

If education is the process of coming to understand the world around us and how to act in it, and if the world around us is in a constant state of change, then education must endeavor to prepare students to deal with what no one has dealt with before. An emphasis on technology appears to be precisely the wrong move to deal with change. Technology, after all, is one of the primary foci of change. Technologies disappear. Try to find someone who can repair a record turntable, for example.

Only when people become involved in the processes of serious inquiry do they learn how to inquire into new problems and reexamine old interpretations. A central argument of this book is that writing lies at the heart of education when it is connected to inquiry and when inquiry is in the hands of the students, who themselves construct, exchange, test, and revise interpretations in dialectical processes. Writing is a chief means of extending, shaping, and rethinking that inquiry and carrying on the dialectical processes involved.

Further, when these conditions obtain, writing helps to shape the individual as few other school subjects can. As I have suggested in Chapter One, each writing experience, to some extent, provides an opportunity to reinvent the self. With each writing we review our knowledge. In doing so, we have an opportunity to rethink, realign, and reintegrate it, a process that, in effect, changes who we are. To the extent that one's self is one's total collection of memories *and* their relationships to one another, the self that pulls together bits and pieces of experience in ways that they may never have been conjoined before is in the process of becoming a new self.

As I have suggested earlier, this generation of another self is not easily accomplished and may not even be recognized as a need in environments from which the possibility of active dialectical process has been removed. Michael W. Smith has observed, concerning students' writing about literature, that they "have developed sophisticated strategies for . . . writing without genuinely engaging themselves with the text" (1994, p. 96). He quotes, as an example, a student in a study by James Marshall (1987) commenting on how he wrote an essay on *The Great Gatsby:*

> That went all right, I did a five-paragraph essay. The rich were reckless, irresponsible, and out of touch with reality. And then I did an introduction and a conclusion. You see I knew that [my teacher] wanted us to see that about the novel. You really got that from class. And then "out of touch with reality" seemed to describe Daisy sometimes. It should get me an A. It was a kind of report on what I already knew. Now, if anyone ever asks what Fitzgerald's attitude toward the rich was, I won't have to think about it. I'll just say they were reckless, irresponsible, and out of touch with reality. (Marshall, 1987, p. 39)

Marshall comments that "the instructional support [the teacher] provided apparently enabled [this student] to produce an analytical essay without engaging very deeply in the analytical process" (p. 39). In this instance, the teacher has removed the possibility of inquiry and dialectical process by telling students what they should think. In doing that, he has severely reduced the possibilities for personal growth.

The emphasis of this book on inquiry and dialectical process requires an epistemological stance quite different from that of current-traditional rhetoric and the textbooks that use it, one which suggests that truth is unambiguous, monolithic, and transportable by means of language. They agree with Lindley Murray's statement in the 1795 preface to his widely used text on grammar that

> it is evident, that in proportion to our knowledge of the nature and properties of words, of their relation to each other, and of their established connexion with the ideas to which they are applied, will be the certainty and ease with which we transfuse our sentiments into the minds of one another. (1849, p. 5)

Lindley Murray and the textbooks that followed believe that absolute truth could be attained by the careful observation of nature and that the truth so attained could be transferred to others if we used language properly. This book argues that we cannot accept such an assumption for two major reasons.

First, our brains interpret undifferentiated sense perceptions to tell us what it is we perceive. Further, we unavoidably interpret what we see in terms of what we already know. Kuhn (1970) provides a variety of examples indicating how our perceptual categories and our theories determine what we think we see. He cites a study by Bruner and Postman (1949) in which they asked subjects to identify a series of playing cards, many of which were normal but some of which were anomalous, for example, a red queen of spades. The subjects almost always identified the anomalous cards as normal. Kuhn shows also that processes of "discovery" in science are unavoidably influenced by existing theories and perceptual categories, such as oxygen, X-rays, and various aspects of the theories of electricity.

Second, the inherent polysemous character of language and the necessity of interpreting language according to one's personal understandings eliminate the possibility of infusing one's sentiments directly into the mind of another. At the same time, these characteristics of language and its interpretation suggest that no text ought ever be thought complete. We can never manage to complete our ideas, to work out their full implications, to recognize their inadequacies, or to say what "we really meant." Further, since anything we say can be challenged, as Graff (1992b) points out, we can never manage to meet all the possible challenges. Such an idea may seem to be an unbearable problem. But we have always lived with these conditions. We have simply ignored them.

Only the assumptions that knowledge is directly apprehensible through observation and analysis and that it is directly transferable to another through language make the idea of teaching as telling viable. If we reject those assumptions, then we must also reject teaching as telling. Therefore, for all these reasons the dialectical process must be an important part of environments for learning to write. For Socrates, remember, the only environment capable of the "serious treatment" of words is one "which employs the art of dialectic" (Plato, 1973, p. 99, in Derrida, 1981, p. 155), one which ensures the exchange and thoughtful examination of ideas and opinions.

I believe that the thoughtful examination of ideas and opinions, of course, is a part of any good teaching. Here we are concerned with the teaching of not just any subject, but with the direct object of the sentence: composition, about putting words together to create meanings, in the sense that a music composer puts notes together to create new music. Our problem becomes how we can provide the circumstances that promote such learning. *Promote* is the key word. The evidence is that learning to write in the sense of compose does not take place in the absence of appropriate environments to promote such learning.

To create those environments, if they are to be available to all students, regardless of home environments, we need a set of theories that allow us to integrate not only the varieties of knowledge that writers need, but a theory of teaching writing that demands a combination of optimism and constant skepticism about what we do as teachers. Our integration of theories must allow us to act but, at the same time, insure our constant evaluation of each action, whether tried and true or new.

Foremost is our theory of inquiry. If thoughtful inquiry does not lie at the heart of writing, then our students become little more than amanuenses. They cannot be writers unless they are first thinkers. The epistemological theory underlying everything argued throughout this book is that we construct knowledge, or what we take to be knowledge, and make a case for it. That is not to say that we must make a case for everything before we can act on anything. If that were the case, we would be entirely incapacitated. Anything we try or any case we make will necessarily rely on certain assumptions. We assume that, for one reason or another, *x* or *y* is so. On the basis of those assumptions, we try *z*. As Wittgenstein (1972) observes:

> One cannot experiment if there are not some things that one does not doubt. . . . When I experiment, I do not doubt the existence of the apparatus that I have before my eyes. I have many doubts, but not *that.* When I make a calculation, I believe, without doubt, that the figures on the paper do not move themselves about; also I trust my memory during the calculation and trust it without fail. I am certain of these things in the same way as I am certain that I have never been on the moon. (p. 43, my translation)[1]

At the same time, while we may be safely certain that we have never been on the moon, we cannot be quite so certain about the substance of most writing tasks or the impact of the writing. Writing instruction needs to engage students in the construction of that substance and in inquiry into the effects of their own writing. To do so effectively requires a theory that allows us to examine the nature of inquiry from basic epistemological assumptions to particular strategies. I have attempted to outline such a theory in Chapter Six.

Although it is inescapable that inquiry shapes our writing and that almost all writing involves inquiry, it is also clear that the larger purposes of writing, including both the substantive and affective, influence the kinds of inquiry that we engage in. Thus teachers of writing need a theory of discourse that provides a general analysis of structure and affective purposes, one that can provide an adequate map of the territory of writing and that can be used to think about the range of writing tasks that curricula might include. The beginnings of one such theory appears in Chapter Six.

Further, such a theory must extend to the analysis of particular writing tasks, their structures, affect, and processes. For it is clear that particular tasks require particular procedural knowledge for their generation. At this level, the theory must provide an analysis of the features of particular writing tasks and the basic processes involved in generating individual pieces. To assume that these task processes and features are the same, say from argument to narrative or from one kind of narrative to another, is a serious mistake. The features and processes of a satiric narrative will be quite different from those of a personal, empathic narrative. Our teaching must take those differences into consideration. Examples of such analyses appear in Chapters Seven through Ten.

The argument of this book is that while subject-matter knowledge is necessary for teaching, it is not sufficient. In addition, teachers of writing need a special kind of knowledge to which scholars of writing have no necessary claim. Lee Shulman (1986) has called this pedagogical-content knowledge, knowledge that goes "beyond knowledge of subject matter *per se* to the dimension of subject matter *for teaching* . . . ways of representing the subject matter that make it comprehensible to others" (p. 9). The alternative representations that Shulman alludes to include examples, metaphors, explanations, and so forth. McEwan and Bull (1991) contend that such knowledge is not different in kind from the knowledge of any scholar in the particular field. For, they say, every scholar's work has a pedagogic function. That is, when scholars report their findings, they "teach" others what they have learned. However, this parallel holds only if we conceive of teaching as telling.

This book argues that such a conception of teaching is inadequate. Research indicates that if we hold to the notion that teaching is telling, our effect will be slight. (See the Appendix for results of my meta-analysis on presentational teaching, the teaching of grammar, and the use of models.) The special knowledge of writing teachers is far more than what is involved in telling. It is a special combination of content and methods for enabling students to learn it.

In the first place, the knowledge that writing teachers hope to convey is procedural, in the traditional sense, not content at all. It is partly knowledge of how to do things: how to write an effective argument of policy, how to write an empathic narrative. But it also involves how to decide what to do in a new situation and how to think about what to do when the what is new. Such knowledge is not algorithmic. Even at the lowest levels, it is far more complex than that, involving strategies such as how to render convincing dialogue, how to generate effective detail, or how to develop a definition that makes clear distinctions, as in the matter of the right to privacy.

Such strategies are so complex that it may not be possible to specify them in detail. Indeed, much of the knowledge involved is tacit, gained in the processes of engaging in certain writing tasks. Still, the strategies must be identified at least in as much detail as possible if teachers are to be effective in helping all students learn to use them.

Even a thorough understanding of all such strategies does not constitute the writing teacher's special knowledge. It provides only the groundwork. The writing teacher deliberates about the strategies in which to engage students and makes decisions that demand a broad knowledge of writing and the particular students to be taught. That is, the teacher considers which kinds of writing will be most valuable and interesting to students at particular points in their development. Unfortunately, we cannot find a list of "writing tasks" that are appropriate, say, for urban seventh graders or for suburban advanced-placement twelfth graders or for community college freshmen or for any group of learners anywhere. Writing teachers must decide what kinds of tasks and what specific formulations of them will be most appropriate for the particular group of students in terms of their continuing development toward the goals of becoming effective writers.

Most important in differentiating the special knowledge of writing teachers is that kind of knowledge that involves the invention of materials and activities, of environments that bring about and encourage development of strategies for the variety of tasks not already in the student's repertoire. This knowledge, too, is procedural, not concerned with the declarative representation of knowledge, but rather with the invention of sequences of activities that engage students and result in their learning processes that had lain beyond their "zone of proximal development."

This invention depends upon the teacher's integrating a number of factors that intersect in the development of the learning sequence: an understanding of students, their interests, and their performances as writers; a thoughtful analysis of what writing tasks are most appropriately generated in the particular curriculum; an analysis of the writing tasks selected, including their features and their particular generative processes; an analysis of the nature of inquiry and its relationship to various writing tasks; an understanding of general writing processes; a knowledge of activities and sequences that have been used in the past; and an understanding of how to proceed in pulling all these together in the classroom.

All these factors that play a role in the production of the special learning activities are fluid, capable of changing with experience. At the same time, all but the penultimate are theory-based and procedural. A simple declarative knowledge of an underlying theory is of little use. Such knowledge must be dynamic, capable of generating new analyses and understandings. And in the conjunction of these theories for the invention of new learning activities and sequences, their nature remains dynamic, for their very use may result in their change.

There is one more special dimension of teacher knowledge to consider: the nature and operation of reflective practice. Taken together with the strategies of teaching outlined above, we have a theory of teaching writing. Reflective practice requires dimensions of knowledge similar to those outlined above. In addition, it requires processes and understandings for monitoring and evaluating students' affective and cognitive responses as teaching proceeds and for evaluating learning at various points in the sequence.

Such knowledge involves the ability to look across the room and tell at a glance whether or not a group is at work, to listen to a group discussion and determine what kind of guidance to offer, to listen to students and evaluate their progress toward understanding, to examine a set of compositions and determine what the next steps need to be. All but the first of these require the special conjunction of subject-matter understanding and general teaching method and could not exist without the former. But the subject-matter knowledge alone will not insure the reflection-in-action that Schön discusses. That only comes with the experience of trying to teach reflectively.

Active critical reflection is necessary in every aspect of our teaching, not only in front of a class. We must try to reevaluate our own values and experience as they relate to our teaching. Our assumptions and theories about teaching composition must remain open to inspection, evaluation, and revision, a condition that requires an active inquiry paralleling the inquiry in which we engage our students.

All of this means that the teaching of writing is fraught with difficulties. Teaching well, in my experience and that of my students, can be very time-consuming, demanding, frustrating, and, given institutional constraints, sometimes infuriating. It demands the recognition that, in Burns's words, "The best laid plans of mice and men gang aft aglay." At the same time, composition lies at the heart of education. When students make gains as writers, the gains are likely to affect other educational endeavors. And for teachers, the joy of seeing students create some new part of themselves, and do it well, washes the difficulties to insignificance and provides the impetus to try, like the Bruce's unrelenting spider, again, and again, and again.

Note

1. Mann kann nicht experimentieren wenn man nicht manches nicht bezweifelt. . . . Wenn ich experimentiere, so zweifle ich nicht an der Existenz des Apparates den ich vor den Augen habe. Ich habe eine Menge Zweifel, aber nicht *den*. Wenn ich eine Rechnung mache, so glaube ich, ohne Zweifel, dass sich die Ziffern auf dem Papier nicht von selbst vertauschen, auch vertraue ich forwahrend meinem Gedachtnis und vertraue ihm unbedingt. Es ist hier dieselbe Sicherheit wie, dass ich nie auf dem Mond war. (p. 43)

Appendix

A Synthesis of Research on Teaching Writing

The text of this book refers frequently to a meta-analysis or synthesis of research on the teaching of writing that I conducted a few years ago (Hillocks, 1984, 1986a). A meta-analysis, or research synthesis, as the method has more recently been called, permits the comparison of results across studies provided they share certain characteristics.

Traditional reviews use a kind of vote-tabulating method, showing merely how many studies favored one teaching approach over another. The problem is that a simple tabulation does not take into account either the size of the sample or the size of the differences between group gains in the individual studies. The research synthesis deals with both and also allows us to consider variability of results. These become very important when we consider that a very small difference between two groups may be *statistically significant* simply because the sample size is very large, that a large difference may be *not statistically significant* because of a small sample size, and that a high level of variability among results is likely to be misleading.

My assistants and I reviewed close to 500 experimental treatment studies that assessed one or more instructional formats. We used a set of criteria to select well-designed studies for inclusion in the analysis. The review left us with 60 studies for a total of 75 experimental treatments, of which 73 could be included in the analysis.

We coded the salient features of all experimental and control treatments along several dimensions, two of which concern us here, what I call mode of instruction and focus of instruction. Mode of instruction "refers to the role assumed by the classroom teacher, the kind and order of activities present, and the specificity and clarity of objectives and learning tasks" (Hillocks, 1986a, p. 113). In contrast, focus refers to the dominant content of instruction, for example, sentence combining, grammar, or the study of model pieces of writing. The results for these two dimensions appear in Figures A.1 and A.2, respectively.

Figure A.1 Mode of Instruction: Experimental/Control Effects

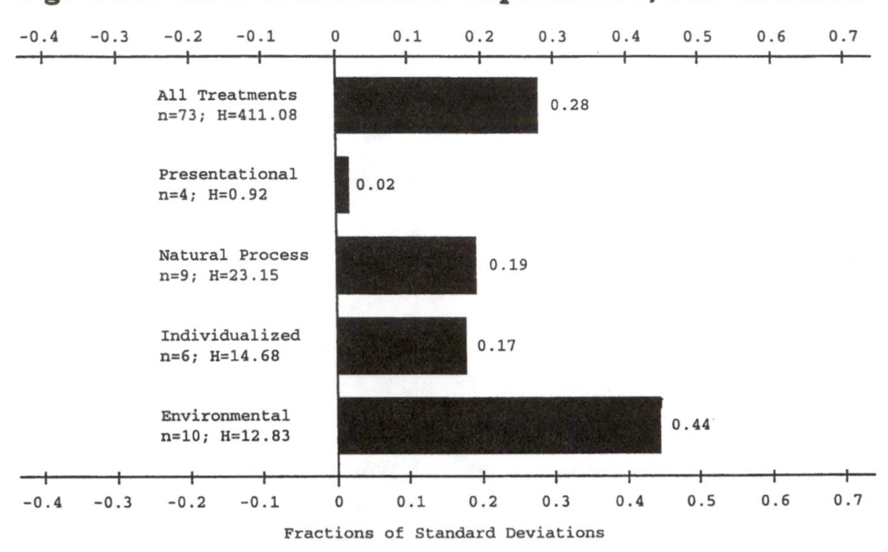

Figure A.2 Focus of Instruction: Experimental/Control Effects

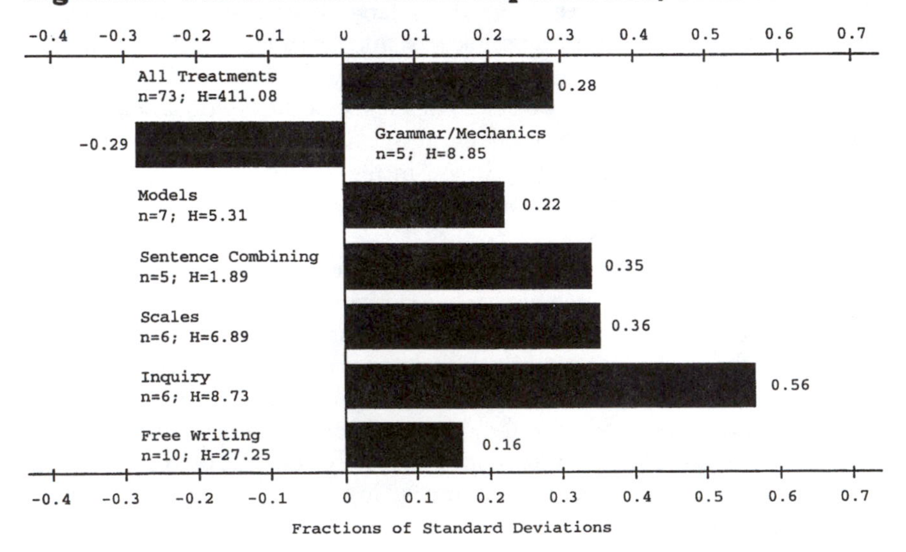

The research synthesis, or meta-analysis, allows the systematic comparison of different methods of teaching on these dimensions. However, because various studies use different scales for judging writing, it is necessary to compute "standard scores" for all control and experimental groups. A standard score tells us where an individual or subsample stands in relation to the mean for the entire group and is reported in terms of standard deviations. (Although statisticians may scream in objection, it is possible to think of standard deviation as a kind of average deviation from the mean, which is not computed as an average.) IQ scores are standard scores with a mean of 100 and a standard deviation of 10, so that a score of 125 is 2.5 standard deviations above the mean.

In the meta-analysis, we computed standard scores for each experimental treatment. These are the difference between the control and the experimental group gains divided by the standard deviation for all groups on the posttest. The results indicate by what proportion of standard deviation the experimental groups outperformed or underperformed their control groups. This is called the effect size.

RESULTS FOR MODE OF INSTRUCTION

Analysis of the studies indicated four clear modes of instruction. In the first of these, the teacher dominates the classroom, presenting information in lecture and from textbooks, setting assignments, explaining objectives to students, outlining criteria for judging writing, and so forth. Professor James's class in Chapter Six is an example of this sort of teaching. Its essential feature is that teaching is telling. For that reason, I have called it presentational.

The second mode of instruction, natural process, is quite different. Rather than presenting rules, criteria, and models to guide writing, teachers in this mode encourage students to write on topics of their own choice, receive feedback from peers, and revise writing as they wish. Most of these make use of small, student-led discussion groups but avoid structured problem solving.

The third mode of instruction is individualized writing conferences between teacher and student. Generally, the nature of the conferences is not explained.

I have called the fourth mode environmental because it places student, materials, activities, teacher, and learning task in balance. To be included in this category, a treatment had to stipulate the use of student-led small-group discussions focused on solving problems that involve specifically stated dimensions, such as judging pieces of writing according to specific criteria and revising some or all of them according to suggestions generated through use of the criteria (Clifford, 1981; Sager, 1973). Examples of environmental teaching appear throughout this book, notably in Chapters One, Four, Eight, Nine, and Ten.

As Figure A.1 indicates, students in the environmental groups outperform those in the natural process groups by a ratio of well over 2 to 1 and those in individualized treatments by nearly 3 to 1. The progress by students in presentational groups is slight. Even when we examine gains from pretest to posttest for all 32 presentational treatments used in both experimental and control conditions, the progress is only one-quarter that for environmental groups examined in the same way.

RESULTS FOR FOCUS OF INSTRUCTION

Focus of instruction refers to the dominant content of instruction. In most experimental studies, it is common to focus on teaching a particular content, such as grammar or model pieces of writing. In this meta-analysis, six foci were the subject of five or more studies each: grammar, study of model pieces of writing, sentence combining, the use of scales for judging and revising writing, inquiry, and free writing. Brief descriptions of each of these categories may be useful.

Studies in the grammar category concentrated on teaching grammatical concepts from traditional school grammar (TSG), except in one case that made use of generative grammar. By grammatical concepts I mean such TSG concepts as parts of speech and parts of sentences, rather than prescriptions on items of usage, for example, the double negative. The goal of such study is to understand how the language works, a goal frequently assumed to be instrumental in learning to write.

The category labeled "models" includes studies that examine finished pieces of writing to help students understand the characteristics of the kind of writing represented. In Chapter Six Professor James's focus is on such characteristics. Accordingly, he uses abstract and concrete models to exemplify them. The abstract descriptions of characteristics amount to theoretical models and predict the features of the particular kind of writing. The concrete models are actual pieces of writing that display the desired features.

Sentence-combining treatments ask students to combine sets of usually prewritten sentences in certain ways. (See Strong, 1986, for a complete description of a variety of approaches to sentence combining.) While sentence combining is related to grammar, it is quite different. It does not deal with naming the parts of speech or sentences. Rather, it focuses on the procedures of putting phrases, clauses, and sentences together.

Studies in the scales category made use of criteria to help students judge and revise pieces of writing by others. In one such study, Sager taught fairly simple writing scales to sixth graders, which they used to rate pieces of writing by others not known to them. Following the ratings, they revised the low-rated pieces to meet higher-level criteria. Thus the focus in this mode is on applying criteria and using them as a guide to revising.

Inquiry appears in several treatments and was operationally defined for this meta-analysis as focusing on sets of data and "activities designed to help students develop skills or strategies for dealing with the data in order to say or write something about it" (Hillocks, 1986a, p. 211). Inquiry is discussed at length or exemplified in Chapters Four, Six, Seven, Eight, Nine, and Ten.

Free writing is a technique that asks students to write whatever they have on their minds in journals, which may remain inviolate, or as preparation for sharing ideas and experiences with others. This approach views free writing as a means of helping students discover what they have to say and their own voices for saying it.

The results for focus of instruction appear in Figure A.2. Although the figure suggests that students studying grammar lost ground, they actually made no change, but they did lose ground to their comparison groups studying no grammar. The study of models results in gains smaller than the average gain for all experimental treatments. Free writing makes even less headway. The most powerful treatments are sentence combining, scales, and inquiry, with the inquiry treatments resulting in gains over and above their controls of nearly six-tenths of a standard deviation, a very large gain.

It is interesting to note that the treatments with the largest gains all focus on teaching procedural knowledge, knowledge of how to do things. While free writing engages students in procedures that they already know, it does not help students learn new, specifiable procedures. Both grammar and models focus on learning what I have called declarative rather than procedural knowledge (Hillocks, 1986b). They teach declarative knowledge that teachers hope may result in procedures, but they do not aim at the procedures themselves.

For more precise information about the conduct of this meta-analysis see *Research on Written Composition: New Directions for Teaching* (Hillocks, 1986a). For more information about research synthesis generally, see *The Handbook of Research Synthesis* (Cooper & Hedges, 1994).

References

Adams, V. A. (1971). *A study of the effects of two methods of teaching composition to twelfth graders.* Unpublished doctoral dissertation, University of Illinois at Champaign–Urbana.

Anderson, E. M., & Hamel, F. L. (1991, November). Teaching argument as a criteria-driven process. *English Journal,* pp. 43–49.

Anderson, P. V. (1985). What survey research tells us about writing at work. In L. Odell & D. Goswami (Eds.), *Writing in nonacademic settings* (pp. 3–83). New York: Guilford.

Anderson, V., Bereiter, C., & Smart, D. (1980, April). *Activation of semantic networks in writing: Teaching students how to do it themselves.* Paper presented at the annual meeting of the American Educational Research Association, Boston.

Applebee, A. N. (1978). *The child's concept of story.* Chicago: University of Chicago Press.

Applebee, A. N. (1981). *Writing in the secondary school: English in the content areas* (NCTE Research Report, No. 21). Urbana, IL: National Council of Teachers of English.

Applebee, A. N. (1986). Problems in process approaches: Toward a reconceptualization of process instruction. In A. R. Petrosky & D. Bartholmae (Eds.), *The teaching of writing* (85th Yearbook of the National Society for the Study of Education) (pp. 95–113). Chicago: National Society for the Study of Education.

Applebee, A. N., Langer, J. A., Mullis, I. V. S., & Jenkins, L. B. (1990). *The writing report card, 1984–1988.* Princeton, NJ: National Assessment of Educational Progress, Educational Testing Service.

Aristotle. (1932). *The rhetoric of Aristotle* (L. Cooper, Ed. and Trans.). New York: Appleton-Century-Crofts.

Aristotle. (1947). Nichomachean ethics (W. Ross, Trans.). In R. McKeon (Ed.), *Introduction to Aristotle* (pp. 308–543). New York: Random House.

Attneave, F. (1974). Multistability in perception. In R. Held (Ed.), *Image, object and illusion: Readings from* Scientific American (pp. 90–99). San Francisco: Freeman.

Atwell, N. (1987). *In the middle: Writing, reading, and learning with adolescents.* Portsmouth, NH: Heinemann.

Bakhtin, M. (1981). *The dialogic imagination: Four essays* (Michael Holquist, Ed.; Caryl Emerson, Trans.). Austin: University of Texas Press.

Ball, A., & Heath, S. B. (1993). Dances of identity: Finding an ethnic self in the arts. In S. B. Heath & M. W. McLaughlin (Eds.), *Identity and inner-city youth: Beyond ethnicity and gender* (pp. 69–93). New York: Teachers College Press.

Bereiter, C. (1980). Development in writing. In L. W. Gregg & E. R. Steinberg (Eds.), *Cognitive processes in writing* (pp. 73–93). Hillsdale, NJ: Erlbaum.

Bereiter, C., Fine, J., & Gartshore, S. (1979, April). *An exploratory study of microplanning in writing.* Paper presented at the annual meeting of the American Educational Research Association, San Francisco.

Bereiter, C., & Scardamalia, M. (1982). From conversation to composition: The role of instruction in a developmental process. In R. Glaser (Ed.), *Advances in instructional psychology* (Vol. 2; pp. 1–64). Hillsdale, NJ: Erlbaum.

Bereiter, C., & Scardamalia, M. (1987). *The psychology of written composition.* Hillsdale, NJ: Erlbaum.

Berkenkotter, C., & Huckin, T. N. (1993, October). Rethinking genre from a sociocognitive perspective. *Written Communication,* pp. 475–509.

Berlin, J. (1984). *Writing instruction in nineteenth-century American colleges.* Carbondale: Southern Illinois University Press.

Blake, W. (1906). *The letters of William Blake together with the life by Frederick Tatham* (A. G. B. Russell, Ed.). London: Methuen & Company.

Bloom, B. S. (1964). *Stability and change in human characteristics.* New York: Wiley.

Bloom, B. S. (1976). *Human characteristics and school learning.* New York: McGraw-Hill.

Bloom, B. S. (Ed.). (1985). *Developing talent in young people.* New York: Ballantine.

Booth, W. C. (1974). *A rhetoric of irony.* Chicago: University of Chicago Press.

Braddock, R. (1974). The frequency and placement of topic sentences in expository prose. *Research in the Teaching of English, 8*(3), 287–302.

Braddock, R., Lloyd-Jones, R., & Schoer, L. (1963). *Research in written composition.* Champaign, IL: National Council of Teachers of English.

Bridwell, L. S. (1980, October). Revising processes in twelfth grade students' transactional writing. *Research in the Teaching of English,* pp. 197–222.

Britton, J., Burgess, T., Martin, N., McLeod, A., & Rosen, H. (1975). *The development of writing abilities (11–18).* London: Macmillan.

Brothwell, D. R. (1987). *The bog man and the archaeology of people.* Cambridge: Harvard University Press.

Bruner, J. (1990). *Acts of meaning.* Cambridge, MA: Harvard University Press.

Bruner, J. S., & Postman, L. (1949). On the perception of incongruity: A paradigm. *Journal of Personality, 18,* 206–223.

Buckley, M. H., & Boyle, O. (1983). Mapping and composing. In M. Myers & J. Gray (Eds.), *Theory and practice in the teaching of composition* (pp. 59–66). Urbana, IL: National Council of Teachers of English.

Butler, C. (1990). Qualifications in science: Model meanings in scientific texts. In W. Nash (Ed.), *The writing scholar: Studies in academic discourse* (pp. 137–170). Newbury Park, CA: Sage.

Cain, B. (1989, February). With worldmaking, planning models matter. *English Education,* pp. 5–29.

Calkins, L. M. (1979, October). Learning to throw away. *Language Arts,* pp. 747–752.

Calkins, L. M. (1981). Case study of a nine year old writer. In D. H. Graves (Ed.), *A case study observing the development of primary children's composing, spelling and motor behaviors during the writing process* (pp. 239–262). Durham, NH: University of New Hampshire.

Calkins, L. M. (1983). *Lessons from a child.* Portsmouth, NH: Heinemann.

Campbell, J. (1972). *The hero with a thousand faces.* Princeton, NJ: Princeton University Press. (Original work published 1949)

Clifford, J. P. (1981). Composing in stages: The effects of a collaborative pedagogy. *Research in the Teaching of English,* pp. 37–53.

Cochran-Smith, M., & Lytle, S. L. (1993). *Inside/outside: Teacher research and knowledge.* New York: Teachers College Press.

Cooper, H., & Hedges, L. V. (1994). *The handbook of research synthesis.* New York: Russell Sage Foundation.

Crichton, M. (1992). *Rising sun.* New York: Ballantine.

Crismore, A., & Farnsworth, R. (1990). Metadiscourse in popular and professional science discourse. In W. Nash (Ed.), *The writing scholar: Studies in academic discourse* (pp. 118–136). Newbury Park, CA: Sage.

Csikszentmihalyi, M. (1990). *Flow: The psychology of optimal experience.* New York: Harper & Row.

Csikszentmihalyi, M., & Larson, R. (1984). *Being adolescent: Conflict and growth in the teenage years.* New York: Basic Books.

Csikszentmihalyi, M., Rathunde, K., & Whalen, S. (1993). *Talented teenagers: The roots of success and failure.* Cambridge, England: Cambridge University Press.

Derrida, J. (1981). *Dissemination* (Barbara Johnson, Trans.). Chicago: University of Chicago Press.

Dewey, J. (1938). *Logic, the theory of inquiry.* New York: Holt.

Elliott, R. C. (1960). *The power of satire.* Princeton, NJ: Princeton University Press.

Ellis, R. (1990). *Instructed language acquisition: Learning in the classroom.* Oxford: Blackwell.

Emig, J. (1971). *The composing process of twelfth graders.* Urbana, IL: National Council of Teachers of English.

Fahnestock, J. (1993, October). Genre and rhetorical craft. *Research in the Teaching of English,* pp. 265–271.

Fichteneau, R. L. (1968). *Teaching rhetorical concepts to elementary children: A research report.* Pontiac, MI: Oakland Schools.

Flower, L., & Hayes, J. (1980). The dynamics of composing: Making plans and juggling constraints. In L. Gregg & E. Steinberg (Eds.), *Cognitive processes in writing: An interdisciplinary approach* (pp. 31–50). Hillsdale, NJ: Erlbaum.

Flower, L., & Hayes, J. (1981, December). A cognitive process theory of writing. *College Composition and Communication,* pp. 365–387.

Freedman, A. (1993, October). Show and tell? The role of explicit teaching in the learning of new genres. *Research in the Teaching of English,* pp. 222–251.

Freedman, S., with M. Sperling and C. Greenleaf. (1987). *Response to student writing* (NCTE Research Report No. 23). Urbana, IL: National Council of Teachers of English.

Friedman, P. (1992). *Inadmissible evidence.* New York: Ballantine.

Frye, H. N. (1957). *Anatomy of criticism: Four essays.* Princeton, NJ: Princeton University Press.

Geertz, C. (1960). *The religion of Java.* Chicago: University of Chicago Press.

Gilbert, S., & Gubar, S. (1979). *The madwoman in the attic.* New Haven, CT: Yale University Press.

Goldenveizer, A. B. (1969). *Talks with Tolstoi* (S. S. Koteliansky, & V. Woolf, Trans.). New York: Horizon.

Goodlad, J. (1984). *A place called school: Prospects for the future.* New York: McGraw-Hill.

Graff, G. (1987). *Professing literature: An institutional history.* Chicago: University of Chicago Press.

Graff, G. (1992a). *Beyond the culture wars: How teaching the conflicts can revitalize American education.* New York: Norton.

Graff, G. (1992b, November). *Deconstruction and the teaching of writing.* Lecture presented at the Workshop on Literacy and Numeracy, University of Chicago.

Graves, D. (1981). *A case study observing the development of primary children's composing, spelling and motor behaviors during the writing process.* Durham, NH: University of New Hampshire.

Graves, D. (1983). *Writing: Teachers and children at work.* Portsmouth, NH: Heineman.

Greene, B. (1987). *Be true to your school: A diary of 1964.* New York: Atheneum.

Gregg, L., & Steinberg, E. (Eds.). (1980). *Cognitive processes in writing.* Hillsdale, NJ: Erlbaum.

Gregory, B. (1988). *Inventing reality: Physics as language.* New York: Wiley.

Guba, E. G. (1990). The alternative paradigm dialog. In E. G. Guba (Ed.), *The paradigm dialog* (pp. 17–27). Newbury Park, CA: Sage.

Hack, S. (1977, 8 May). Digging in the time machine. *The Midwestern Magazine in the Chicago Sun Times,* pp. 20–23.

Hairston, M. (1978). *A contemporary rhetoric.* Boston: Houghton Mifflin.

Halliday, M. A. K., & Hasan, R. (1976). *Cohesion in English.* London: Longman.

Hamel, F. L. (1990). *A comparative study of three teachers teaching exposition* Unpublished master's thesis, University of Chicago.

Hammer, R. (1983, January). The immorality of ability level tracking. *English Journal,* pp. 38–41.

Hartwell, P. (1985, February). Grammar, grammars, and the teaching of grammar. *College English,* pp. 105–127.

Hatch, J. A., Hill, C. A., & Hayes, J. R. (1993, October). When the messenger is the message: Reader's impressions of writers' personalities. *Written Communication,* pp. 569–598.

Hayes, J. R. (1993, October). Taking criticism seriously. *Research in the Teaching of English,* pp. 305–315.

Hayes, J. R., & Flower, L. (1980). Identifying the organization of writing processes. In L. Gregg & E. Steinberg (Eds.), *Cognitive processes in writing: An interdisciplinary approach* (pp. 3–30). Hillsdale, NJ: Erlbaum.

Heap, J. L. (1992). Ethnomethodology and the possibility of a metaperspective on literacy research. In R. Beach, J. Green, M. Kamil, & T. Shanahan (Eds.), *Multidisciplinary perspectives on literacy research* (pp. 35–56). Urbana: National Conference on Research in English/National Council of Teachers of English.

Heath, S. B. (1983). *Ways with words: Language, life, and work in communities and classrooms.* Cambridge, England: Cambridge University Press.

Heath, S. B., & McLaughlin, M. W. (1993). *Identity and inner city youth: Beyond ethnicity and gender.* New York: Teachers College Press.

Hedges, L. V. (1987, May). How hard is hard science, how soft is soft science? The empirical cumulativeness of research. *Journal of the American Psychological Association,* pp. 443–455.

Hillocks, G., Jr. (1971). *An evaluation of Project Apex: A nongraded phase-elective English program.* Trenton, MI: Trenton Public Schools.

Hillocks, G., Jr. (1979, February). The effects of observational activities on student writing. *Research in the Teaching of English,* pp. 23–35.

Hillocks, G., Jr. (1982, October). The interaction of instruction, teacher comment, and revision in teaching the composing process. *Research in the Teaching of English,* pp. 261–278.

Hillocks, G., Jr. (1984, November). What works in teaching composition: A meta-analysis of experimental treatment studies. *American Journal of Education,* pp. 133–170.

Hillocks, G., Jr. (1986a). *Research on written composition: New directions for teaching.* Urbana, IL: National Conference on Research in English/ERIC Clearinghouse on Reading and Communication Skills.

Hillocks, G., Jr. (1986b). The writer's knowledge: Theory, research and implications for practice. In A. Petrosky & D. Bartholomae (Eds.), *The teaching of writing* (85th Yearbook of the National Society for the Study of Education, Part II) (pp. 71–94). Chicago: National Society for the Study of Education.

Hillocks, G., Jr. (1989, March). *Two modes and two foci of instruction: Impact on student writing.* Paper presented at the Annual Meeting of the American Educational Research Association, San Francisco.

Hillocks, G., Jr. (1992). *Developing a prototype program for the professional development of community college teachers of writing* [Report prepared for the Ford Foundation]. Unpublished manuscript.

Hillocks, G., Jr. (in progress a). *Teacher thinking and classroom action: Toward a theoretical model.* University of Chicago.

Hillocks, G., Jr. (in progress b). *Integrating qualitative and quantitative data: Studies of learning to write under three foci of instruction.* University of Chicago.

Hillocks, G., Jr. (in progress c). *Examining the dimensions of student written arguments.* University of Chicago.

Hillocks, G., Jr., Kahn, E., & Johannessen, L. (1983, October). Teaching defining strategies as a mode of inquiry: Some effects on student writing. *Research in the Teaching of English,* pp. 275–284.

Hillocks, G., Jr., & McCampbell, J. F. (1964). *An introduction to a curriculum: Grades 7–9.* Euclid, OH: Project English Demonstration Center/Euclid Central Junior High School and Western Reserve University.

Housman, A. E. (1933). *The name and nature of poetry.* New York: Macmillan.

Jakobson, R. (1960). Linguistics and poetics. In T. Sebeok (Ed.), *Style in language* (pp. 350–377). Cambridge, MA: MIT Press.

Johannessen, L. R. (Chair). (1987). *English for the nineties and beyond* (Final report, secondary strand). Queenstown, MD: English Coalition Conference.

Johannessen, L. R. (1992). *Illumination rounds: Teaching the literature of the Viet Nam War.* Urbana, IL: National Council of Teachers of English.

Johannessen, L. R., Kahn, E. A., & Walter, C. C. (1982). *Designing and sequencing prewriting activities.* Urbana, IL: National Council of Teachers of English and ERIC Clearinghouse on Reading and Communication Skills.

Joos, M. (1967). *The five clocks.* New York: Harcourt, Brace, and World.

Kahn, E. A., Johannessen, L. R., & Walter, C. C. (1984). *Writing about literature.* Urbana, IL: National Council of Teachers of English and ERIC Clearinghouse on Reading and Communication Skills.

Koch, C., & Brazil, J. M. (1978). *Strategies for teaching the composition process.* Urbana, IL: National Council of Teachers of English.

Kohler, W. (1959). *Gestalt psychology.* New York: New American Library.

Kosinski, J. N. (1965). *The painted bird.* Boston: Houghton Mifflin

Kuhn, T. S. (1970). *The structure of scientific revolutions* (2nd ed.). Chicago: University of Chicago Press.

Langer, J. A., & Applebee, A. N. (1987). *How writing shapes thinking: A study of teaching and learning.* Urbana, IL: National Council of Teachers of English.

Lederman, L. (1991, 15 March). *Scientific literacy.* Lecture presented at the Workshop on Dimensions of Literacy and Numeracy, University of Chicago.

Lee, C. D. (1993). *Signifying as a scaffold for literary interpretation: The pedagogical implications of an African American discourse genre* (NCTE Research Report No. 26). Urbana, IL: National Council of Teachers of English.

Lewis, O. (1959). *Five families.* New York: New American Library.

Lewis, O. (1961). *The children of Sanchez.* New York: Random House.

Lincoln, Y. (1990). The making of a constructivist: A remembrance of transformations past. In E. Guba (Ed.), *The paradigm dialog* (pp. 67–87). Newbury Park, CA: Sage.

Lloyd-Jones, R., & Lunsford, A. A. (Eds.). (1989). *The English coalition conference: Democracy through language.* Urbana, IL: National Council of Teachers of English.

Lortie, D. C. (1975). *Schoolteacher: A sociological study.* Chicago: University of Chicago Press.

Lowes, J. L. (1926). *The road to Xanadu: A study in the ways of the imagination.* Boston: Houghton-Mifflin.

Marshall, J. D. (1987, February). The effects of writing on students' understanding of literary texts. *Research in the Teaching of English,* pp. 30–63.

Matsuhashi, A. (1981, May). Pausing and planning: The tempo of written discourse production. *Research in the Teaching of English,* pp. 113–134.

McCabe, B. J. (1971). The composing process: A theory. In G. Hillocks, B. J. McCabe, & J. F. McCampbell, *The dynamics of English instruction: Grades 7–12* (pp. 516–529). New York: Random House.

McCann, T. (1989, February). Student argumentative writing: Knowledge and ability at three grade levels. *Research in the Teaching of English,* pp. 62–76.

McCann, T. (1995). *Student argumentative writing in three grade levels.* Unpublished doctoral dissertation, University of Chicago.

McCleary, W. J. (1979). *Teaching deductive logic: A test of the Toulmin and Aristotelian models for critical thinking and college composition.* Unpublished doctoral dissertation, University of Texas.

McEwan, H., & Bull, B. (1991, Summer). The pedagogic nature of subject matter knowledge. *American Educational Research Journal,* pp. 316–334.

McGhee-Bidlack, B. (1991, June). The development of noun definitions: A metalinguistic analysis. *Journal of Child Language,* pp. 417–434.

Miller, P. (1982). *Amy, Wendy and Beth: Learning language in south Baltimore.* Austin: University of Texas Press.

Miller, P., & Sperry, L. (1988). Early talk about the past: The origins of conversational stories of personal experience. *Journal of Child Language, 15,* 293–315.

Murray, D. (1987). *Write to learn.* New York: Holt, Rinehart & Winston.

Murray, L. (1849). *English grammar.* New York: Raynor.

Newton, I. (1934). *Principia mathematica* (Vol. 1; A. Motte, Trans.). Berkeley: University of California Press. (Original work published 1729)

North, S. (1987). *The making of knowledge in composition: Portrait of an emerging field.* Portsmouth, NH: Heinemann.

Olson, C. B. (1992). *Thinking writing: Fostering critical thinking through writing.* Irvine, CA: HarperCollins.

Palmquist, M., & Young, R. (1992, January). The notion of giftedness and student expectations about writing. *Written Communication,* pp. 137–168.

Parker, R. (1979, September). From Sputnik to Dartmouth: Trends in the teaching of composition. *English Journal,* pp. 32–36.

Perkins, D. (1981). *The mind's best work.* Cambridge, MA: Harvard University Press.

Phillips, D. C. (1990). Postpositivistic science: Myths and realities. In E. Guba (Ed.), *The paradigm dialog* (pp. 31–46). Newbury Park, CA: Sage.

Plato. (1973). *The Phaedrus and letters VII and VIII* (W. Hamilton, Trans.). London: Penguin.

Poe, E. A. (1979). The philosophy of composition. In R. Gottesman, L. B. Holland, D. Kalstone, F. Murphy, H. Parker, & W. H. Pritchard (Eds.), *The Norton Anthology of American Literature* (Vol. 1; pp. 1319–1329). New York: Norton.

Probst, R. E. (1988). *Response and analysis: Teaching literature in junior and senior high school.* Portsmouth, NH: Heinemann.

Rian, D. (1992). Tales from the dark side of the dumpster. Unpublished paper, University of Chicago.

Rose, M. (1990). *Lives on the boundary.* New York : Penguin.

Ross, A., & Robins, D. (1991). *The life and death of a Druid prince.* New York: Simon & Schuster.

Sager, C. (1973). *Improving the quality of written composition through pupil use of rating scale.* Unpublished doctoral dissertation, Boston University.

Scardamalia, M., & Bereiter, C. (1983). The development of evaluative, diagnostic, and remedial capabilities in children's composing. In M. Martlew (Ed.), *The psychology of written language: A developmental approach* (pp. 67–95). London: Wiley.

Scardamalia, M., Bereiter, C., & Goelman, H. (1982). The role of production factors in writing ability. In M. Nystrand (Ed.), *What writers know: The language, process, and structure of written discourse* (pp. 173–210). New York: Academic Press.

Schneider, E. (1953). *Coleridge, opium and Kubla Kahn.* Chicago: University of Chicago Press.

Scholes, R. (1985). *Textual power: Literary theory and the teaching of English.* New Haven, CT: Yale University Press.

Schön, D. A. (1987). *Educating the reflective practitioner: Toward a new design for teaching and learning in the professions.* San Francisco: Jossey-Bass.

Serres, M. (1982). *Hermes: Literature, science, philosophy* (J. V. Harari & D. F. Bell, Eds.). Baltimore: Johns Hopkins University Press.

Shaughnessy, M. (1977). *Errors and expectations.* New York: Oxford University Press.

Shulman, L. S. (1986, March). Those who understand: Knowledge growth in teaching. *Educational Researcher,* pp. 4–14.

Sinclair, U. (1962). *The autobiography of Upton Sinclair.* New York: Harcourt, Brace, and World.

Smagorinsky, P. (1991, October). The writer's knowledge and the writing process: A protocol analysis. *Research in the Teaching of English,* pp. 339–364.

Smagorinsky, P., & Coppock, J. (1994, July). Cultural tools and the classroom context: An exploration of an artistic response to literature. *Written Communication,* pp. 283–310.

Smagorinsky, P., McCann, T., & Kern, S. (1987). *Explorations: Introductory activities for literature and composition, 7–12.* Urbana, IL: National Council of Teachers of English and ERIC Clearinghouse on Reading and Communication Skills.

Smagorinsky, P., & Smith, M. W. (1992, Fall). The nature of knowledge in composition and literary understanding: The question of specificity. *Review of Educational Research,* pp. 279–305.

Smith, J. K. (1983, 3 March). Quantitative vs. qualitative research: An attempt to clarify the issue. *Educational Researcher,* pp. 6–13.

Smith, M. W. (1984). *Reducing writing apprehension.* Urbana, IL: National Council of Teachers of English and ERIC Clearinghouse on Reading and Communication Skills.

Smith, M. W. (1989, October). Teaching the interpretation of irony in poetry. *Research in the Teaching of English,* pp. 254–272.

Smith, M. W. (1991). *Understanding unreliable narrators.* Urbana, IL: National Council of Teachers of English.

Smith, M. W. (1994). Democratic discourse and the discussion of literature. In L. M. Morrow, J. K. Smith, & L. C. Wilkinson (Eds.), *The integrated language arts: Controversy to consensus* (pp. 91–104). Boston: Allyn & Bacon.

Smitherman, G. (1986). *Talkin and testifyin: The language of black America.* Detroit: Wayne State University Press.

Stein, N. L., & Glenn, C. (1979). An analysis of story comprehension in elementary school children. In R. Freedle (Ed.), *New directions in discourse processing* (pp. 53–120). Norwood, NJ: Ablex.

Stein, N., & Trabasso, T. (1982). What's in a story: An approach to comprehension and instruction. In R. Glaser (Ed.), *Advances in instructional psychology* (pp. 213–267). Hillsdale, NJ: Erlbaum.

Stern, D. (1992, October). Structure and spontaneity: Teaching with the student at risk. *English Journal,* pp. 49–55.

Stern, D. (1995). *Teaching English like it matters: Developing curricula for and with high school students.* Newbury Park, CA: Corwin.

Stodolsky, S. S. (1988). *The subject matters: Classroom activity in math and social studies.* Chicago: University of Chicago Press.

Strong, W. (1986). *Creative approaches to sentence combining.* Urbana, IL: National Council of Teachers of English and ERIC Clearinghouse on Reading and Communication Skills.

Tolkien, J. R. R. (1936). Beowulf: The monsters and the critics. *Proceedings of the British Academy, XXII,* 245–295.

Tolkien, J. R. R. (1966). *The hobbit.* Boston: Houghton Mifflin.

Toulmin, S. E. (1958). *The uses of argument.* Cambridge, England: Cambridge University Press.

Toulmin, S., Rieke, R., & Janik, A. (1984). *An introduction to reasoning.* New York: Macmillan.

Troyka, L. Q. (1973). *A study of the effect of simulation-gaming on expository prose competence of remedial English composition students.* Unpublished doctoral dissertation, New York University.

Troyka, L. Q., & Nudelman, J. (1975). *Taking action: Writing, reading, speaking and listening through simulation-games.* Englewood Cliffs, NJ: Prentice-Hall.

Tyler, R. (1949). *Basic principles of curriculum and instruction.* Chicago: University of Chicago Press.

Vygotsky, L. S. (1978). *Mind in society: The development of higher psychological processes* (M. Cole et al., Eds.). Cambridge, MA: Harvard University Press.

Warriner, J. (1988). *English composition and grammar: Complete course.* Orlando, FL: Harcourt Brace Jovanovich.

Widvey, L. (1971). *A study of the use of a problem-solving approach to composition in high school English.* Unpublished doctoral dissertation, University of Nebraska.

Williams, J. D. (1993, October). Rule-governed approaches to language and composition. *Written Communication,* pp. 542–568.

Williams, J. M. (1981). *Style: Ten lessons in clarity and grace.* Glenview, IL: Scott, Foresman.

Williams, J. M., & Colomb, G. G. (1993, October). The case for explicit teaching: Why what you don't know won't help you. *Research in the Teaching of English,* pp. 252–264.

Williams, R. (1983). *Writing in society.* London: Verso.

Witte, S. P. (1992, April). Context, text, intertext: Toward a constructivist semiotic of writing. *Written Communication,* pp. 237–308.

Wittgenstein, L. (1972). *Uber Gewissheit/On certainty.* (G. E. M. Anscombe & G. H. von Wright, Eds; D. Paul & G. E. M. Anscombe, Trans.). New York: Harper & Row.

Wright, R. (1945). *Black boy: A record of childhood and youth.* New York: Harper & Bros.

Young, R., Becker, A., & Pike, K. (1970). *Rhetoric: Discovery and change.* New York: Harcourt Brace Jovanovich.

Index

About the Author

George Hillocks, Jr., received his B.A. in English from The College of Wooster, a Diploma in English Studies from the University of Edinburgh (Scotland), and his M.A. and Ph.D. from Case Western Reserve University. He taught secondary school English in Euclid, Ohio, where he was Director of the Project English Demonstration Center from 1963 to 1965. He taught English at Bowling Green State University, and served there as Director of Freshman English Programs. Since 1971 he has been at the University of Chicago, where he is currently professor in the Department of Education and the Department of English Language and Literature and continues to serve as advisor to the graduate program in English Education. His articles have appeared in the *American Journal of Education, Research in the Teaching of English, American Educational Research Journal, English Journal, English Education, College English,* and other journals. He is author or co-author of several books and monographs, including *Research on Written Composition: New Directions for Teaching,* published by the National Conference on Research in English.